# THE DALAI LAMAS ON TANTRA

THE FIRST DALAI LAMA

# The Dalai Lamas on Tantra

*Translated, edited, and introduced by*

## Glenn H. Mullin

SNOW LION PUBLICATIONS

ITHACA, NEW YORK • BOULDER, COLORADO

Snow Lion Publications
P. O. Box 6483
Ithaca, NY 14851 USA
(607) 273-8519
www.snowlionpub.com

Printed in USA on acid-free recycled paper.

Illustrations on the indicated pages are by the following:
Chris Banigan 22, 158, 254, 290, 318; Brian Beresford 176;
Sidney Piburn 202; Kevin Rigby 84; Saki Takezawa ii, 68, 324, 334

ISBN-10 1-55939-269-X
ISBN-13 978-1-55939-269-3

*Library of Congress Cataloging-in-Publication Data*
The Dalai Lamas on tantra / translated, edited, and introduced by Glenn H. Mullin.
  p. cm.   Includes bibliographical references.
   ISBN-13: 978-1-55939-269-3 (alk. paper)
   ISBN-10: 1-55939-269-X (alk. paper)
  1. Tripiṭaka. Sūtrapiṭaka. Tantra—Criticism, interpretation, etc.
2. Tantric Buddhism—China —Tibet. 3. Dge-lugs-pa (Sect)—
Doctrines. I. Mullin, Glenn H.
BQ2147.D35 2007
294.3'85—dc22
                                        2006019861
Designed and typeset by Gopa & Ted2, Inc.

# Table of Contents

# Preface

OVER THE PAST TWO DECADES I have published almost a dozen books with Snow Lion on the lives and works of the early Dalai Lamas. As most readers will know, the present Dalai Lama, who was born in 1935, is the fourteenth in this line of illustrious reincarnations.

When I first started this project, almost nothing was known in the West about these extraordinary men. Coverage of them had been limited to a paragraph or two, or a page or two at best, in academic books on Tibetan cultural and political history. Even though many of these incarnations had written dozens of works on Buddhist philosophy, meditation, mysticism, and other enlightenment-related topics, and had also written hundreds of songs and poems, no significant text by any of them had ever been translated into English.

With each of these books I usually incorporated a traditional biography and a selection of their most accessible writings. Usually the selection would be on diverse subjects, in an attempt to convey the range and depth of these Buddhist teachers, from mystical poems to works on philosophy and tantric practice.

Most of these titles have been out of print for over a decade now. Sidney Piburn, my editor at Snow Lion, thought that it would be useful to bring out an anthology of some of the tantric works that I had used in that series. Tantric Buddhism is becoming better known in the West these days, but there is still a paucity of authentic translations from classical sources. The great popularity achieved by the early Dalai Lamas was due in part to the clarity and power of their tantric writings, so Sid's suggestion did not seem unreasonable. This volume is the result.

On the technical side, I have tried to keep footnotes to a bare minimum so as to allow the reader to enjoy the mood of the originals, rather than create the distraction of a constant barrage of "whispered asides." Moreover, I have also presented any Sanskrit and Tibetan terms that are used in a simplified "phonetic style" for ease in reading. For example, "Khedrup" looks far more palatable to me than does "mKhas-grub," and "Lobzang" seems more accessible than "bLo-bzang." Scholars should be able to easily reconstruct the more formal spellings if they wish to do so, whereas these formal spellings are irrelevant to the general enthusiast.

With Tibetan text titles, however, a system of easy phonetics would be inadequate. Therefore here I have used the formal system of transliteration.

Most Dalai Lamas wrote extensively on Tantric Buddhism. The material chosen for this anthology is intended as a mere sampling of their contribution, with the intent to give the reader a sense of the authentic tradition.

Glenn H. Mullin
Ulaanbaatar, Mongolia,
March 7, 2006

# Introduction

## THE LEGACY FROM BUDDHA SHAKYAMUNI

BUDDHA TRAVELED and taught widely for some forty-five years after his enlightenment, and his audiences were diverse. Even though India at the time was a highly literate society, nothing of what he said was written down during his lifetime. Instead, various individuals were entrusted with memorizing the gist of each discourse. The work of transcribing his words took place only with the passage of generations.

Tibetans believe that this reluctance on the part of the Buddha and his immediate followers to commit the enlightenment teachings to paper, and instead to preserve them as oral traditions, was a purposeful strategy gauged to maintain the maximum fluidity and living power of the enlightenment experience. It only became necessary to write things down when the darkness of the changing times threatened the very survival of the legacy. An oral tradition becomes lost to history should its holders pass away without first passing on their lineages.

This intended fluidity, and the according safeguard against the establishment of an "enlightenment dogma," is perhaps best demonstrated by a verse that the Buddha himself said shortly before his death:

> Do not accept any of my words on faith,
> Believing them just because I said them.

Be like an analyst buying gold, who cuts, burns,
And critically examines his product for authenticity.
Only accept what passes the test
By proving useful and beneficial in your life.

This simple statement empowered future generations of Buddhist teachers to accept and reject at will anything said by Buddha himself as well by his early disciples. If something that was said by them did not pass the test of personal analysis, one could simply discard it as being limited in application to particular times, people, or situations, and therefore as only contextually valid.

## 1. Buddha's Legacy of Exoteric and Esoteric Transmissions

In his *A Brief Guide to the Buddhist Tantras* (translated in Chapter One of this volume) the Thirteenth Dalai Lama quotes two verses from the writings of the incomparable Lama Tsongkhapa:

There are two Mahayana vehicles
For traveling to complete buddhahood:
The Prajnaparamitayana and the profound Vajrayana.
Of these, the latter greatly surpasses the former.
This is as well known as the sun and moon.

There are many people who know this fact
And pretend to carry the tradition of the sages,
Yet who don't search for the nature of the profound Vajrayana.
If they are wise, who is foolish?
To meet with this rare and peerless legacy
And yet still to ignore it: How absolutely astounding!

As readers familiar with Tibetan spiritual culture will know, Lama Tsongkhapa (1357-1419) was the root guru of the First Dalai Lama (1391-1475). These verses, therefore, are relevant to the approach to Buddhism taken by all subsequent Dalai Lamas. And because the Dalai Lamas became Central Asia's foremost incarnation lineage, ascending in 1642 to the throne of combined spiritual and temporal leadership of Tibet, it could be said that the approach outlined above by Lama Tsongkhapa is now a hallmark of all schools of Tibetan Buddhism.

The term *Prajnaparamitayana* literally means "Perfection of Wisdom Vehicle," and refers to the ordinary, or exoteric, path to enlightenment as taught by the Buddha. *Vajrayana* literally means "Diamond Vehicle," and refers to the esoteric path. The present volume brings together various works by the Dalai Lamas on the latter of these two paths.

The former of the two is sometimes also referred to as the Sutra-yana, or "Way of the Public Discourses," and the latter as the Guhya-mantrayana, or "Way of Secret Mantra Practice." Here the words "mantra" and "tantra" have the same meaning. Thus in a general sense these two aspects of the Buddha's transmissions can also be referred to as "the Sutra Way" and "the Tantra Way."

The Thirteenth Dalai goes on to say, "The Vajrayana is to be practiced in secrecy and is not to be revealed to the spiritually immature. Therefore it is also known as 'the secret path.'"

Thus the Vajrayana lineages are generally taught in secret and only to those disciples who are sufficiently mature. This means that the disciples should have a high spiritual status achieved through trainings in previous lifetimes, or else should have ripened their minds in this lifetime by means of the preliminary trainings, as discussed by the Seventh Dalai Lama in his verse work of instruction in the Heruka Chakrasamvara tantric trainings (translated in Chapter Two of this volume).

The Thirteenth Dalai Lama continues, "There is no difference between the exoteric Prajnaparamitayana and esoteric Vajrayana in terms of the buddhahood that is attained, the bodhisattva attitude used as the basic motivating factor, nor the nature of the view of emptiness that is experienced. In these respects the terms 'superior' and 'inferior' do not apply. Nonetheless, the Vajrayana is superior in four ways."

He then lists the four as follows:

(a) Its manner of generating the experience of emptiness is implemented by the peerless means of inducing the wisdom of semblant mind isolation which arises through working with the coarse and subtle energies of the body and causing them to enter into, abide, and dissolve within the central channel. Thus the Vajrayana method of cultivating insight into emptiness is uncontrived.

(b) It has a more vast reservoir of methods, such as the meditation on a causal form that is in accord with the nature of the Rupakaya to be attained.

(c) Its path is quickly accomplished without hardship. On the Prajnaparamitayana many lifetimes of intense effort are required in order to attain the state of enlightenment, whereas on the Vajrayana full enlightenment can easily be achieved within this one short life.

(d) Finally, it is fashioned especially for those of sharpest capacity, who are able to make quick progress along the path.

We will see later just what he means by these statements.

## 2. THE EXOTERIC SUTRA PATH

As said above, the Buddhist legacy can be spoken of as having two facets: the Sutra Way, which is based on Buddha's public teachings; and the Tantra Way, which is based on his secret or restricted transmissions. This twofold classification was made in India during the early days of the Buddhist experience, and was adopted wholeheartedly by the Tibetans when Buddhism became the national spiritual tradition of the Land of Snows in the mid-seventh century.

Although some Indian masters chose one as opposed to the other of these two, most masters integrated both facets within their own continuum of practice. When this was the case, the Sutra Way was seen as a preliminary to and preparation for the Tantra Way.

In the early days of Buddhism in Tibet, the Tibetans seem to have held a stronger interest in the latter, perhaps because of Tibet's shamanic and somewhat esoterically-inclined past, and the more shamanic and esoteric language of the tantras. By the mid-eleventh century, however, the Indian model of the one being used as a preparation for the other had taken deep root, and during the fourteenth century became the official approach of all Tibetan schools.

Sometimes the Sutra transmissions are divided into three categories, known as the *Tripitaka*, or "Three Baskets," in accordance with the three essential trainings of the spiritual path: the *Vinaya Pitaka*, which has self-discipline as its focus; the *Sutra Pitaka*, which mainly addresses meditation; and the *Abhidharma Pitaka*, which addresses the subject of wisdom and the philosophy of enlightenment. These three trainings are the principal means whereby the practitioner works toward the goal of nirvana, which is freedom from karma and delusion. Their subjects are the three higher trainings: discipline, meditation, and wisdom. These three are the practical essence of all the exoteric teachings. The path comprises study, contemplation, and meditation—a threefold application that is pursued systematically both in terms of a daily regime and occasional lengthy meditation retreats.

In general it can be said that the Sutra Way views the human spiritual situation as being somewhat linear. For this reason the Sutra approach as discussed above is also known in Tibetan literature as *gyu gyi lam,* or "the path of causes." In the Sutra approach one looks at one's shortcomings and inner weaknesses, and works on the methods for systematically eradicating them; and one looks at one's lack of enlightenment, and engages in the spiritual practices that cause the enlightenment experience to arise. In brief, one sees oneself as an unenlightened person afflicted with the inner factors of the three emotional and cognitive distortions or poisons—anger, attachment, and ignorance of the true nature of the self—and regards the spiritual practices such as meditation and so forth as being the medicines for systematically curing these afflictions, until eventually full enlightenment is attained. In the Sutra view, many lifetimes of practice are required to accomplish this state of inner perfection.

## 3. THE TANTRA PATH

The tantras take a radically different approach. Rather than accept the conventional appearance of both one's own imperfections and those of the world, one instead sidesteps the conventional appearances altogether, and replaces them with the practice of *lhayi naljor,* or "deity yoga," with the word "deity" meaning "buddha." In brief, one cultivates the vision of oneself as a deity/buddha, others as tantric deities/buddhas, and the world as a sacred mandala.

The process begins with receiving tantric initiation. The First Dalai Lama puts it as follows in his *Notes* on the Kalachakra yogas (translated in Chapter Six):

One should first refine the mind by means of the ordinary
Sutrayana methods. In specific, cultivate a definite understanding of the pure view of emptiness. Then seek out the
complete initiations that ripen the mind and permit one to
enter into the extraordinary Vajrayana path. Thereafter, as
intensely as one cherishes one's life, one should cherish the
disciplines and commitments of the Tantric path, as elucidated at the time of initiation.

And the Seventh Dalai Lama puts it like this in his poem on the
practice of the Heruka Chakrasamvara Tantra (translated in Chapter Two):

Having first trained in the foundation practices,
Seek out a tantric master, embodiment of Buddha Vajradhara,
Lord of the Sphere Beneath None;
Gain the four ripening initiations
And enter into the mystic mandala.

The body transforms into a great vajra-mandala,
And, in the inconceivable mansion of joyful repose,
The real deity—the subtle mind held between the kiss of the
    male and female drops—
Manifests as the blood-drinking Male/Female in Union.

The dakas and dakinis dance a blissful dance
In the mystic channels and secret drops;
Mundane perception is severed from consciousness
And all emanations become ultimately pure.

For this reason the Tantra Way is sometimes called *trebu gi lam*, or
"The Path of the Result" (in sharp contrast to the Sutra appellation

"The Path of Causes"). Here, rather than think of oneself as needing to generate the causes of enlightenment within oneself, one identifies immediately with resultant buddhahood.

In other words, on the Tantric path one adopts an attitude and lifestyle that borrow the essence of enlightenment, and proceeds accordingly. Deity yoga is the application used in order to make this approach successful. One tells oneself, "I am a buddha, you are a buddha, the world is playful theater, and all activity is enlightened exchange." A bit like the "I'm ok, you're ok" pop psychology of the sixties, albeit with a bit more of a yogic tradition to support it.

As the Thirteenth Dalai Lama puts it in *A Brief Guide to the Buddhist Tantras*:

> It is a special method for protecting the mind from the subtle instincts of the three appearances, in which one meditates in the mode of the resultant stage. This means that in the Vajrayana one conceives of oneself and all others as sharing in the four pure qualities of a fully accomplished buddha: perfect body, perfect speech, perfect mind, and perfect activities. Therefore it is also called "the resultant vehicle."

Another passage in this text by the Thirteenth Dalai Lama reveals another unique facet of tantric practice:

> Its manner of generating the experience of emptiness is implemented by the peerless means of inducing the wisdom of semblant mind isolation which arises through working with the coarse and subtle energies of the body and causing them to enter into, abide, and dissolve within the central channel. Thus the Vajrayana method of cultivating insight into emptiness is uncontrived.

In other words, a unique aspect of the tantric tradition is that it works with the chakras, *nadis*, subtle bodily chemistry, and subtle energies in order to induce extraordinary states of consciousness. Meditation is then performed on the basis of these exalted dimensions of body and mind.

The Seventh Dalai Lama puts it like this in his poem in Chapter Two:

> The outer consort, in nature fire,
> Melts the life-drops that course
> Through the seventy-two thousand channels,
> Bringing them into the central channel,
> Giving rise to the four ineffable joys.
>
> Outside, all sensory movement of mind and energy ceases;
> Inside, mundane views, ignorance, and darkness disperse.
> Thus, by yoga even sleep is transformed
> Into the nature of Dharmakaya's clear light.

And also elsewhere in the same poem:

> By mentally reciting the secret mantras of the vajra dharmas
> Of entering, resting, and dispersing energy at the heart
> While controlling the life-drop made of five clear essences,
> The knots of ignorance are easily untied.
>
> The tip of the vajra is placed firmly in the lotus
> And mind as the syllable *HUM* is brought into the central
>    channel;
> One drinks and drinks the essence of nectars
> And goes mad with innate joy unmoving.

By thus settling the mind in the subtle vajra letter
And bringing the drop to the four chakras and sensory gates,
One directly sees all aesthetic objects
Found throughout the three worlds.

And the First Dalai Lama puts it like this in his *Notes on the Two Yogic Stages of Glorious Kalachakra* (translated in Chapter Six):

First the vital energies passing through the four petals of the four intermediate directions at the heart chakra—the *rupel, tsangpa, lhachin,* and *norlegyal* energies—are successively arrested, beginning with those of the southeast channel and moving around to the northwest "petal." From this one experiences the four signs: those of smoke, a mirage, flickering (like that of) fireflies, and a butterlamp. Then beginning in the east and moving around to the west, the energies flowing through the channels of the cardinal directions are arrested. These are the equally-abiding, upward-flowing, all-pervading, and *lu* energies. One perceives the signs that are like (the appearance in the sky of the planet) *kalagni,* the moon, the sun, and (the planet) *rahu.*

One then cuts off the flow of the life-sustaining and downward-moving energies that course above and below, thus experiencing the signs of lightning and the drop.

This phase of the completion stage yogas, which gives rise to the experience of these signs of controlling the ten energies in the production of the (substitute) empty body, is made possible by the foundations that were laid earlier in the generation stage yoga. This involved the meditation on the eight *shaktis,* who were contemplated as being in the nature of the knots in the channels at the heart and navel, together with the petals of the chakra of bliss at the navel. In the generation stage yogas (these eight become ten by counting them together with) Kalachakra and Consort, (thus symbolizing the control over all ten energies). Here Kalachakra represents the element of space, and the Consort symbolizes primordial awareness. Their sexual union is the joining of the upper and lower apertures, and the union of the two principal energies.

## 4. TANTRA AND MANTRA

The word "tantra" literally means "stream" or "thread." Although different tantras present slightly different epistemologies, a common threefold approach is taken from the perspectives of basis, path, and result. When this is done, "basis" refers to the primordial thread or stream of reality that is present in both mind and matter at every moment of existence. That is to say, the thread of perfect being is always present. "Path" refers to the method for attuning to that primordial thread or stream of reality; and "result" refers to the complete integration or fulfillment that is the utter harmony of the radiance of the mind (*selwa*) and the presence of the experiences that arise within the mind (*nangwa*). Put in terms of Highest Yoga Tantra, enlightenment is the complete and unobstructed flow of awareness of the dance of bliss (*dewa*) and infinity (*tongpa*).

The Tantra Way is sometimes termed the *Guhyamantrayana* in Sanskrit, or "Vehicle of Secret Mantras." When this is done, the word "mantra" has the same referent as "tantra," although it is given a different etymology, with *man* meaning "mind" and *tra* meaning "to protect." The idea is that the tantric method comprises a yogic technology (*tra*) for protecting the mind (*man*) from the distorting influences of ordinary appearances. This allows the practitioner to rest within the natural perfection of uncontrived being in every situation, rather than get twisted into knots with the conventional appearances of things.

In a more simple sense, as anyone familiar with Indian-based traditions will know, a mantra is also a formula of syllables or words that is recited as part of a particular meditation technique. Every tantric deity has his or her own mantras, and the practitioner recites and meditates upon these at length, as a means of establishing a link with the primordial stream of inner being (i.e., "tantra"). Each tantric system has a series of strict retreats associated with it, in which hundreds of thousands or even millions of the various mantras are recited. In the tantric retreat of the female buddha Arya Tara, for example, it is most common to recite four hundred thousand of the main mantra.

This is, however, only the outer meaning of the usage of the term "mantra." In a deeper sense, "mantra" refers to a yogic process that involves bringing together the subtle bodily energies until a state of bodily silence is achieved, a silence almost identical to the stillness of bodily functions at the time of death. This gives rise to an extremely subtle state of consciousness, similar to the moment-of-death consciousness and the experience of the after-death state. This subtle mind is then blended with the primordial stream of being, or tantra in its basis aspect, giving rise to the state of enlightenment, which is tantra in its resultant meaning.

The Second Dalai Lama writes in his *The Two Yogic Stages of the Vajrabhairava Tantra* (translated and with a commentary in Chapter Eight):

> May I untie the knots at the heart,
> The knots in the central channel
> At the chakra called "wheel of truth,"
> By means of the supreme Mantra Yoga
> In conjunction with the vase-breathing
> And vajra-recitation techniques,

Thus experiencing the mystical intoxication
Of the innate great bliss.

May I engage in the sacred *Samaya* Yoga
And the stages of the involution compression process,
To unite skillfully with one of the two mudras
And by absorption be led to ultimate mind isolation.

May I dissolve all vital energies into the heart,
Just like at the time of death the energies
Dissolve into clear light.
And may I perfect the absorption of illusory manifestation
Of a form having the net of signs of perfection.

Then by the Yoga of Pure Wisdom
May that radiant form, immaterial as a rainbow,
Be dissolved like a cloud into space, so that
The actual clear light (which is) reality may be known
And the seeds of grasping
For true existence be extracted.

## 5. TANTRA AND MANDALA

As the Thirteenth Dalai Lama explains in *A Brief Guide to the Buddhist Tantras*, the Buddhist tantras are arranged into four categories. Each of these four categories has numerous tantric systems. Moreover, every tantric system has its own *Mulatantra*, or root tantric text, as well as subsequent and supplementary tantras, and commentaries by later masters. Each also has its manuals for daily practice and recitation, as well as retreat manuals, manuals for various "activities" (such as fire rites, etc.), and manuals for ritual application (such as healing, prosperity, etc.).

Moreover, each tantric system has its own lineage of transmission, descending through the generations through lines of masters who practiced, accomplished, and then transmitted it. In brief, every system represents a complete yogic path, and contains complete methodology for the attainment of enlightenment in one lifetime.

Every tantric system also has its own mandala. These are said to be of two aspects: supported, which refers to the mandala deity (or deities, when the mandala is more complex); and supporting, i.e., the cosmogram or residence that supports the deities. The former is the real nature of living beings, which refers to self and others, whereas the latter is the real nature of the environment or outer world in which self and others live.

Usually a tantric system is known by the name of the central deity of its supporting mandala.

## 6. Tantra and the Doctrine of the Three Kayas

A doctrine central to both the Mahayana sutras and tantras is that of the three kayas: Dharmakaya, Sambhogakaya, and Nirmanakaya. This important idea discusses the mystery of what happens to a person's *santana*, or "stream of being," after he or she attains enlightenment. This aspect of the Buddha's teachings also accounts for the vast numbers of buddhas and bodhisattvas encountered in the literature, art, and iconography of the Tantric and Mahayana Sutra traditions.

Here the term *Dharmakaya* literally means "Reality Body," *Sambhogakaya* literally means "Body of Complete Enjoyment," and *Nirmanakaya* means "Emanation Body." These three are sometimes made into two by combining the second and third into the Rupakaya, or "Form Body." When this is done, the first of the three, or Dharmakaya, is sometimes termed Arupakaya, or "Formless Body."

The concept is that mind and matter remain as separate, albeit cooperative, entities until enlightenment is achieved. At the moment of enlightenment, however, they become of one nature. At that time the stream of the person's being utterly dissolves into the Dharmakaya, or formless sphere of infinity, becoming "of one indistinguishable taste" with all beings who have ever achieved enlightenment.

The metaphor is of a drop of water flowing into the ocean. The individual being dissolves into the universal Dharmakaya like a drop of water into the ocean. Just as the drop of water then becomes indistinguishable from the rest of the ocean's water, the individual here becomes indistinguishable from the ocean of universal buddha mind. Perhaps Christians would call this sphere of pan-cosmic consciousness the Godhead.

However, the being that is resting in the Dharmakaya can only be perceived by other fully enlightened beings. Not even tenth-level saints (Skt. *arya*), let alone ordinary mortals, have direct access to the Dharmakaya. For this reason the Dharmakaya aspect eventually comes around to an awareness of the vow taken long ago to be of maximum benefit to living beings. The impetus of the universal love and compassion of the bodhichitta aspiration comes into play.

Because there are two kinds of living beings—those who have attained the arya status of the ten levels of sainthood and those who have not—and because the degree of the powers of perception in these two is dramatically different, the enlightened being therefore sends out two levels of "emanations," known in Tibetan as *trul-pa*. These two are the Sambhogakaya and Nirmanakaya aspects. The Sambhogakaya emanations reveal themselves to the living beings in the arya states, and inspire them to evolve toward complete enlightenment; the Nirmanakaya emanations reveal themselves to the ordinary living beings, to inspire and guide them.

Sometimes these two are grouped together as the Rupakaya, or Form Body. The Thirteenth Dalai Lama used this term in a passage quoted above at the end of Section 1, in which he speaks of the four ways in which Tantric practice is superior to its Sutra counterpart. As he puts it, "It (i.e., the Tantric path) has a more vast reservoir of methods, such as the meditation on a causal form that is in accord with the nature of the Rupakaya to be attained."

Tantric practice is intimately connected to identification with these three kayas, and we will see repeated use of the terms throughout the translations that follow. For example, in his text on Vajrabhairava practice the Second Dalai Lama writes:

> By meditating in four daily sessions
> Upon the profound generation stage yogas
> That open the net of the hundreds of lights
> And totally dispel the darkness of birth,
> Death, and the in-between state,
> May I ripen my stream of being
> And plant the seeds for the accomplishment
> Of the powerful completion stage yogas.

And Lama Chinpa comments:

> The two main practices in the generation stage yogas are clear visualization and the cultivation of divine pride. By applying these to the various phases of the generation stage meditation, one becomes familiar with the meditations of taking death as a path of Dharmakaya, taking the in-between state as the Sambhogakaya, and taking rebirth as the Nirmanakaya.
>
> Firstly one accomplishes coarse clear visualization by meditating on the entire mandala. Then one visualizes the mandala in the mystic seed, which is drawn into the lotus of the consort. This is subtle clear visualization.

Meditating upon the mandala in this way strengthens the seeds of the three buddha kayas and thus opens a net of light to dispel darkness from death, the bardo, and the rebirth process.

Through meditating in this way upon the generation stage yogas in four daily sessions—predawn, late morning, afternoon, and evening—one quickly lays the foundations upon which the completion stage yogas can be engaged and the state of enlightenment quickly won.

This is the general nature and function of the generation stage methods.

## 7. THE TWO STAGES OF TANTRIC PRACTICE

As stated earlier, there are four classes of tantras, and each class has various individual tantric systems within it. Each of these tantric systems is represented by a tantric deity, and also by its own mandala. In fact, each of the individual systems is a complete recipe for enlightenment, a complete Way in and of itself.

All these Buddhist tantric systems hold a number of features in common with one another. They all have *rimpa nyigi naljor*, or "two stages of yogic application." The first of these two stages mostly concerns itself with establishing two inner qualities, known in Tibetan as *lhayi ngagyal* and *selnang*. These translate respectively as "divine pride" and "vision of radiance." The practitioner of any tantric system has to make these two qualities firm within himself or herself. The first quality, as explained above, refers to training oneself in the habit of always seeing oneself as a buddha, in the aspect of the principal deity of the mandala into which one has received initiation; the latter quality refers to training oneself in the habit of always seeing other people and things as being radiant manifestations of the primordial, playful wisdom of the mandala of enlightenment energy. As for the second stage of tantric application, the various systems here provide their own individual techniques.

The Second Dalai Lama explains it as follows:[1]

> One must learn to relinquish the habit of grasping
> At the mundane way in which people and things are perceived,
> And to place all that appears within the vision
> Of supported and supporting mandalas.
> This is the essence of the generation stage yogas.

In the so-called lower tantras (i.e., the first three classes of tantras: Kriya, Charya, and Yoga), the first stage of application is called "the stage of symbols" and the second is called "the stage beyond symbols." This first stage mostly involves the cultivation of meditative powers that are then engaged in the two practices mentioned above, divine pride and vision of radiance. The second stage mostly deals with turning the powers of highly attuned concentration, now infused with a constant spiritual joy, to observation of the various levels of the radiant mind.

With the fourth class of tantras, the first stage is called "the stage of creative imagination" and the second called "the completion stage." Here the first stage utilizes the practices of divine pride and the vision of radiance, in conjunction with highly attuned meditative concentration, for blending the three essential moments—sleeping, dreaming, and waking—to eliminate the ordinary appearance of the three occasions of death, in-between, and rebirth. Spiritual powers such as clairvoyance, supramundane physical abilities, and so forth, are here generated as side effects. The basis of the meditation process is, of course, the supported and supporting mandalas, with the practice of mantra recitation.

The second stage mostly involves yogic application involving manipulation of the bodily energy centers (*chakras*), energy pathways (*nadis*), and subtle bodily chemistry (*bindus*) in order to arouse paranormal states that allow access to the most subtle and primordial mind states, the most primitive of which is simply known as "the clear light consciousness."

The Second Dalai Lama describes this in verse:[2]

> Next one stimulates the vajra body
> And directs the energies flowing in the side channels
> Into *dhuti*, the mystic channel at the center,
> Thus gaining sight of the clear light nature of the mind,
> And giving rise to wisdom born together with bliss.
> Cherish meditation on these completion stage yogas.

As said earlier by the Thirteenth Dalai Lama, one of the four superior features of the Tantra over the Sutra Way is that the former has a richer array of methods. This includes practices for every experience in life, including sleep and dream yogas, eating yoga, death yoga, sex yoga, and so forth.

There is even a killing yoga, so that policemen and soldiers can stay spiritually centered while performing the difficult duties occasionally demanded of their vocations.

## 8. Tantric Activities

An initiate who has achieved some degree of maturity in the above two stages of tantra can then engage in the *trinley chopa*, or "enlightenment activities." This refers to the shamanic aspect of Tantric Buddhism, and to the rituals that are used for purposes such as healing, increasing prosperity, exorcism of negative energies, purifying sites of ghosts, and so forth.

The lion's share of the income of most Tibetan monasteries comes through performance of rituals of this nature. In general it can be said that monk children should study, monks in their early twenties should do meditation retreats, and mature monks should either teach or perform rituals. Most monasteries live and die by this formula. The offerings that a monastery receives from sponsors of tantric rituals are its primary source of support. Almost all other activities are sponsored by it.

Many monasteries maintain a body of monks solely dedicated to the performance of these rituals. Some monasteries establish this body by drafting adult monks into it on a rotating basis, the period of the draft often being two or three years. Of course monks showing a special talent for tantric ritual will dedicate more time to it, and many of the best will become professional ritualists for much of their lifetime.

In this book I have only included one work dealing with this subject. This is the work found in Chapter Seven: the *Hayagriva-Sealed-in-Secrecy Methods for Healing*. It is a method for empowering medicines and healing by means of a technique born from the visions of the Fifth Dalai Lama.

Most Tibetans rely upon Dharmapalas, "Truth Protectors," for many aspects of their secular lives. These are a class of deity invoked for accomplishing tantric activities. The various Dalai Lamas have written extensively on these Dharmapala practices, and these writings certainly make for fascinating reading. However, because this topic can be somewhat controversial, I have decided not to include any in this work.

CHAPTER ONE:

## The Thirteenth Dalai Lama's
### *A Brief Guide to the Buddhist Tantras*[3]

GYALWA TUBTEN GYATSO (1876-1933)

MANDALA OF THE FIVE BUDDHA FAMILIES

# Translator's Preamble

READERS UNFAMILIAR with the structure, literature, and terminology of the Tibetan tantric tradition are perhaps best off to skip over this chapter for the moment, and come back to it after reading the remainder of the book. For although the Thirteenth Dalai Lama's text is not long—roughly ten thousand words in length—it contains summaries of all the principal Tibetan Buddhist tantric systems found in all four categories of tantras: Kriya, Charya, Yoga, and Anuttarayoga. Thus it is both technically dense and content intensive.

Moreover, in addition to outlining the essence of each of the tantric transmissions, he gives the names of the original tantras spoken by the Buddha that serve as the foundation of each system, and also gives the names of the principal Indian commentators in the early lineages of transmission.

These lists may render the text somewhat obscure to the casual armchair traveller in the world of Tibetan Buddhism, but they are very useful to those with some exposure to the tradition and who want a perspective on how the various tantric systems fit together within the overall tantric schema. In this sense the Thirteenth Dalai Lama's treatise is a true jewel of tantric knowledge, and reveals the depth and breadth of his mastery of tantric knowledge. Those well versed in Tibetan Buddhism will find it to be a most amazing guide to the esoteric legacy, a well-cut diamond for the delight of the wise.

Somewhat surprisingly, it is not listed separately in the Thirteenth's *Sungbum,* or *Collected Works,* and I chanced upon it some-what serendipitously. The year was 1985, and I was working on the study of the Thirteenth's life and teachings that was published a few years later as *Path of the Bodhisattva Warrior.*

My approach to all my books in that series on the lives and teach-ings of the early Dalai Lamas was to first present a summary of the subject's life, and then follow this with a selection of translations of his writings in order to illustrate the quintessential character of his teachings. With the Great Thirteenth I chose the transcriptions of his annual sermons at the *Monlam Chenmo,* or "Great Prayer Festival." The Thirteenth frequently delivered a public discourse at the full moon celebration on the first full moon of the new year, which was the highlight of this festival. In that anthology I also included the Thirteenth's collection of spiritual poems and a number of his man-uals on meditation.

Nothing else in the catalog of his works seemed appropriate to my purposes there, being either too long, too esoteric, or too technical for a collection, and thus requiring a separate book in and of itself. Yet his *Collected Works* was seven thick volumes in length and con-tained several hundred titles. I had a feeling that something from within this vast corpus was calling out to be included.

I pored over the seven volumes for several days, but could not find anything that seemed to fill the gap. Then I decided to use an extraor-dinary strategy. First I recited several rosaries of the name mantra of the Great Thirteenth for awhile, as well as the mantras of the princi-pal mandala deities of Tantric Buddhism. After this I recited some rosaries of mantras associated with Palden Lhamo, the Oracle God-dess. That done, I closed my eyes and picked up and put down the various volumes of the *Collected Works* one at a time, until the vol-ume in my hands seemed to hold promise. At that point I randomly opened it at a page somewhere toward the center, and began reading.

The volume I had chosen by means of this method contained the

Thirteenth's biographical account of one of his most revered teachers, Kyabjey Purchokpa by name. I had opened the book to side b of page 179, where the Thirteenth is just about to describe how Purchokpa had received and mastered all the various lineages of the *Sarmai Gyu,* or "New Tantras." Here he first explains that he will elucidate in general the tantric trainings that his teacher had received; he then goes on to provide an account of everything that is included under the category of "New Tantras." It is this section from the Thirteenth's biography of Purchokpa that I have extracted and translated here, giving it the name *A Brief Guide to the Buddhist Tantras.*

It might be useful to point out that the term "New Tantras" (used above) does not refer to a group of tantras that were taught by Buddha at a later period in his life, as opposed to a group called the "Old Tantras" that he had taught earlier. Rather, the expression refers to the period that the transmissions came from India into Tibet, and also to the style of the translations of the canonical literature that were made from Sanskrit into Tibetan.

Tibetan sects are generally divided into two classes: Old and New. This division is made on the basis of the time of the transmission and the language used in the translations. The Old Schools refer to those sects that emerged in Tibet between AD 650 and 1000. They all used the Tibetan technical terminology established by the Tibetan translators of King Songtsen Gampo (mid-seventh century), King Trisong Deutsen (mid-eighth century), and King Tri Ralpachen (mid-ninth century). The "Old Tantras" is said in reference to tantras translated during that period and using the linguistics and terminology in vogue at that time.

However, several movements began in Central and Western Tibet in the early eleventh century, with many Tibetans going back to India and retranslating everything anew, or bringing great scholars from India to Tibet in order to revise the old translations. Here these lama scholars mainly followed the linguistic approach of the emerging great translators of Ngari, Western Tibet, of whom Lotsawa Chenpo Rinchen Zangpo was the most revered. The versions of the tantras that appeared in Tibetan during this period are what is referred to as the "New Tantras."

Numerous schools of Buddhism emerged in the eleventh and twelfth centuries from this work. They became known as the "New Schools," because they were based on these new transmissions of lineages from India, as well as upon the revised system of Buddhist terminology. The seven most important of these New Schools were the Sakya, the Kadam, the Kagyu, the Shangpa, the Zhalu, the Rva Luk, and the Zhichey.

All seven existed as independent entities for several hundred years. However, in the fourteenth century the great Tibetan master Lama Tsongkhapa (1357-1419) appeared on the scene. He gathered the essence of all seven traditions, as well as numerous other minor lineages, absorbing them by means of study and practice. Afterwards he made retreat for five years and achieved realization. Then toward the end of his life he created Ganden Monastery as an institute where the contents of all could be studied and practiced.

Lama Tsongkhapa's eclectic approach eventually evolved into what has become known to history as the Geluk, or "Creative Way," School of Tibetan Buddhism, the order in which all Dalai Lamas traditionally receive their monastic ordination. The first Dalai Lama was a direct disciple of Lama Tsongkhapa. Within a century the Gelukpa had become the largest school of Buddhism in Tibet, and by the sixteenth century was as large as all the other schools combined.

In *A Brief Guide to the Buddhist Tantras*, the Thirteenth Dalai Lama draws from an autobiographical poem written by Lama Tsongkhapa himself, in which Tsongkhapa outlines the source of the many lineages he had gathered together.[4] By quoting this poem the Thirteenth is indicating that his great guru Purchokpa fully accomplished and embodied the Tsongkhapa legacy, coming to equal that venerable master himself.

On a somewhat different note, even though here the Great Thirteenth limits his discourse to the New Tantras, it should be noted that all Dalai Lamas from the time of the First have combined Old and New Schools within their trainings. We will see more on this issue in a later chapter of this book (Chapter Seven).

I originally studied the Thirteenth Dalai Lama's text with Ven. Amchok Tulku of Ganden Shartsey Monastery. At the time, Rinpochey had just completed a tenure as abbot of Tashi Khyil Monastery, and had come to Dharamsala at the request of the Dalai Lama to evaluate the large collection of uncataloged Buddhist scriptures at the Library of Tibetan Works and Archives, where I was studying. Rinpochey's deep learning and years of practice made him an ideal tutor for the reading of this terse yet panoramic text.

# The Thirteenth Dalai Lama's Text

## General Introduction to the Buddhist Path

The incomparable Lama Jey Tsongkhapa wrote,

> There are two Mahayana vehicles
> For traveling to complete buddhahood:
> The Prajnaparamitayana and the profound Vajrayana.
> Of these, the latter greatly surpasses the former.
> This is as well known as the sun and moon.
>
> There are many people who know this fact
> And pretend to carry the tradition of the sages,
> Yet who don't search for the nature of the profound Vajrayana.
> If they are wise, who is foolish?
> To meet with this rare and peerless legacy
> And yet still to ignore it: How absolutely astounding!

The Vajrayana is to be practiced in secrecy and is not to be revealed to the spiritually immature. Therefore it is also known as "the secret path."

It is a special method for protecting the mind from the subtle instincts of the three appearances, in which one meditates in the mode of the resultant stage. This means that in the Vajrayana one conceives of oneself and all others as sharing in the four pure qualities of a fully accomplished buddha: perfect body, perfect speech, perfect mind, and perfect activities. Therefore it is also called "the resultant vehicle."

On this path one applies the yogas of nondual method and wisdom in order to achieve the transcendental results of the secret mantra. Thus it is known as "the path of secret mantra."

This is the nature of the esoteric Vajrayana, the Diamond Vehicle that brings quick and easy enlightenment.

There is no difference between the exoteric Prajnaparamitayana and the esoteric Vajrayana in terms of the buddhahood that is attained, the bodhisattva attitude used as the basic motivating factor, nor the nature of the view of emptiness that is experienced. In these respects the terms "superior" and "inferior" do not apply.

Nonetheless, the Vajrayana is superior in four ways:

(a) Its manner of generating the experience of emptiness is implemented by the peerless means of inducing the wisdom of semblant mind isolation which arises through working with the coarse and subtle energies of the body and causing them to enter into, abide, and dissolve within the central channel. Thus the Vajrayana method of cultivating insight into emptiness is uncontrived.

(b) It has a more vast reservoir of methods, such as the meditation on a causal form that is in accord with the nature of the Rupakaya to be attained.

(c) Its path is quickly accomplished without hardship. On the Prajnaparamitayana many lifetimes of intense effort are required in order to attain the state of enlightenment, whereas on the Vajrayana full enlightenment can easily be achieved within this one short life.

(d) Finally, it is fashioned especially for those of sharpest capacity, who are able to make quick progress along the path.

The Vajrayana teachings appear only very rarely in this world. They are more rare than even the buddhas themselves.

The nature of the Vajrayana path is fourfold, the division being made according to the four classes of the tantras. This fourfold classification is symbolized by the four levels of engaging in passionate communication with the mystical Knowledge Consort as methods of achieving the path to enlightenment.

The four Tantra classes are named as follows: Kriya, Charya, Yoga, and Anuttarayoga.

In the first of these, great emphasis is placed on external rituals, such as washing and physical purification. In the second tantra division there is an equal balance of external activity and inner yoga. In the third division the inner yogas take precedence over the outer activities. Finally, in the fourth tantra division, the emphasis is always on the inner yogas.

## THE KRIYA TANTRAS

Concerning the Kriya tantras, Lama Tsongkhapa wrote,

> One may say that the Anuttarayoga tantras
> Are supreme amongst the four tantra classes;
> But if when saying this one does not understand
> The paths of the three lower tantra divisions,
> One's words fade into meaninglessness.
>
> Understanding this to be the case,
> I first familiarized myself with the Kriya tantras,
> Both general and specific, of the three Kriya families.
> These included *The General Tantra of Secret Knowledge*,
> *The Tantra of Susiddhi*,
> *The Tantra of Questions by Subabu*,
> And *The Subsequent Absorption Tantra*.

The three families of tantras in the Kriya division are: the supreme family of Vairochana, also called the Tathagata family (which includes mandala deities such as Manjushri, Ushnisha Vijaya, and Sitatapatra, etc.); the intermediate Padma family (which includes Avalokiteshvara, Tara, etc.); and the fundamental Vajra family (e.g., Vajrapani, Vajravidarana, etc.).

One should enter into whichever of these is suitable to one's personal karmic predispositions, receiving initiation into either a powder (i.e., sand), cloth, or meditation mandala.

The initiation begins with the claiming of the place of the rite. The mandala deities are invoked, the initiation vase is empowered, the disciples are enhanced, and so forth. Then follows the flower garland, water, and crown initiations, together with the concluding procedures.

The disciples are thus ripened and matured by these processes, and are authorized to enter into practice of the Kriya yogas.

Concerning the actual yogas, firstly there is the *dhyana* of four branches of recitation:

(a) The self-basis, or generation of oneself as a mandala deity. This involves meditation upon the six deities (or stages of arisal as a deity): suchness, mantric sound, mantric letters, emanated forms, mudras, and symbol (i.e., the actual deity).

(b) The other-basis, which means generating the supporting and supported mandala and deities in front, sending forth praises and offerings, etc.

(c) The mental basis, in which one meditates that one's mind rests on a moon disc at one's heart.

(d) The audial basis, wherein one concentrates upon the seed syllable and mantra rosary on that moon disc, and then does the mantra recitation.

Next there is the *dhyana* of abiding within fire. Here one visualizes oneself as the chief mandala divinity, and envisions that at one's heart is a radiant, blazing fire in the nature of the wisdom of emptiness. One fixes the mind upon this fire.

The sound of the mantra emanates from within the fire. Focusing the mind upon this is the *dhyana* of sound.

These are the practices known as "the yoga with symbols," the first stage of the Kriya Tantra yogas.

These methods are complemented by "the yoga without symbols," in which one engages in the shamatha (inner stillness) and vipashyana (higher insight) meditations propelled by physical and mental ecstasy. This is the *dhyana* bestowing liberation at the end of sound.

By relying on these various *dhyanas* in conjunction with the yoga with symbols and the yoga without symbols, one gains highest, intermediate, or basic *siddhis*, and by becoming a knowledge holder of life achieves supreme accomplishment.

The tantric systems in the lower division are of two types: general and specific. In total there are said to be thirty-four thousand of them in number. Of these, Lama Tsongkhapa and his immediate disciples accepted the following as being the most significant.

The most important of the specific Kriya Tantra treatises include: *The Tantra Establishing the Three Pledges*[5] in nineteen chapters; *The Healing Discourse in Eight Hundred Themes;*[6] *The Inconceivable Mansion of Vast Jewels;*[7] *A Hundred Thousand Enlightenment Ornaments;*[8] *The Secret Relics;*[9] and so forth.

As for general Kriya Tantra treatises, the most important of these are: *Fundamentals of the Empowerments of the Three Families;*[10] *The General Tantra of Secret Knowledge,*[11] which explains in detail the mandala constructions in the four tantra classes; *The Tantra of Susiddhi,*[12] which mainly deals with retreat procedures, rituals, and commitments of the Kriya Tantra mandala of Susiddhi; *The Tantra of Questions by Subahu,*[13] which deals with topics left unclear in the above two treatises, and teaches in detail the knowledge mantras and especially the retreat procedures of the Kriya system; the final section of *The Vajra Ushnisha Tantra*,[14] which elucidates the four *dhyanas* common to both Kriya and Charya Tantra divisions; and *The Subsequent Absorption Tantra*,[15] of which there are four fundamental versions.

The two great Indian elucidators of the tantric treatises in the Kriya and Charya divisions were Acharya Buddhaguhya and Acharya Vajrabodhi. They are as well known as the sun and moon. From amongst their writings, *The Commentary to the Subsequent Absorption Tantra*,[16] *A Summary of the Tantra of Questions by Subahu*,[17] and so forth are superb.

## THE CHARYA TANTRAS

Concerning the Charya Tantra division, Lama Tsongkhapa writes,

> The second tantra class is called *Charya*.
> The principal Charya Tantra system
> Is the Vairochana Abhisambodhi Tantra.
> By training in that system I gained definite experience
> In the supreme points of the Charya tantras.

The Buddha, manifesting in the Akanishta Pure Land, took the form of Tathagata Vairochana Abhisambodhi and expounded this supreme Charya tantra.

The path of the Charya tantras begins with receiving initiation. Here one enters into the mandala from the western gate, which is the direction in which the main mandala divinity is facing. There are various names for the four vase initiations and the bases of purification associated with this process. In brief, one partakes of the water, headdress, vajra, bell, and name initiations, together with the concluding procedures, and thus is authorized to take up practice of the Charya Tantra yogas.

As in the Kriya division, the actual practice of the Charya tantras is twofold, consisting of the yoga with symbols and the yoga without symbols.

The body of the Charya path, together with the results attained, is much the same as in the Kriya systems. However, here in the practice of the generation of the mandala of oneself as the divinity it is not necessary to have the complete six deity stages (as was the case in the Kriya yogas explained above). Also, here the *dhyana* of four branches of recitation is applied in both inner and two outer aspects (which was not the case in the Kriya tantras).

The two principal texts in the Charya tantra tradition are *The Vairochana Abhisambodhi Tantra*,[18] which is in twenty-six chapters, and *The Subsequent Tantra of Vairochana Abhisambodhi*[19] in seven chapters.

The text entitled *Tantra of the Vajrapani Empowerment*,[20] which belongs to the Vajra family, is also said to be of great significance, but unfortunately it was never translated into Tibetan. We only know of it through the many references to and quotations from it that appear in the treatises of the later commentators.

Buddhaguhya's *Abbreviated Commentary to the Vairochana Abhi-sambodhi Tantra*[21] is perhaps the most important of the commentaries by later Indian masters.


## THE YOGA TANTRAS

The third division of the tantras is that known as "the Yoga Tantra class." Lama Tsongkhapa refers to this division as follows:

> Foremost amongst the principal traditions of
> The third tantric division, known as the Yoga tantras,

Are the Glorious Compendium of Principles
And the Vajra Highest Peak Explanatory Tantra.
By training in systems such as these,
I experienced a Yoga Tantra feast.

In the Yoga tantras it is said that the four elements arise with the strength of the four basic delusions—the three root delusions of attachment, aversion, and ignorance, together with self-centeredness. These are transformed into the resultant four pristine wisdoms— distinguishing wisdom, the wisdom of equanimity, the accomplishing wisdom, and the mirrorlike wisdom. The principal means is reliance upon the yoga of combined nondual profundity and radiance, which integrates with the Mahayana bodhi-mind and the perfections of generosity, discriminating awareness, and joyous energy.

These four pristine wisdoms manifest in the four buddha family aspects: Tathagata "Diamond Sphere" (*vajradhatu*); Vajra "Victory over the Three Worlds" (*trilokavijaya*); Padma "Tamer of the Living Beings" (*sakalajagadvinaya*); and the Amoghasiddhi nature of "Accomplishing Feats" (*sarvarthasiddhi*), which unites both Ratna and Karma families.

One gains initiation into whichever of these five buddha families is appropriate to one's individual character.

The basis of the initiation ceremony can be a chalk, cloth, or meditation mandala.

The preparatory stages are much the same as in the two lower tantra classes. As for the actual initiation itself, here one takes the bodhisattva vow, the pledges of the five buddha families, the pledge of secrecy, and the five knowledge initiations together with also the acharya initiation. One concludes with the verses of appreciation, etc.

When the disciple is thus ripened and matured by means of receiving initiation, he/she is authorized to enter into the yogas of the two stages—those with symbols and those without symbols.

By means of the mandala and the supremely victorious activities being performed in either extensive, medium, or abbreviated forms, one cultivates the coarse yoga with symbols. Firstly one visualizes oneself as the mandala divinity and then generates the divinity in front, incorporating both supporting and supported mandalas in the meditation.

After this has been accomplished, the subtle mandala is generated at the tip of the nose of oneself envisioned as the divinity. The signs and symbols of the family with which the mandala is linked are similarly visualized. The mind is then held on this subtle image, and by forcefully engaging the methods common to all three lower tantra classes one accomplishes the subtle yoga with symbols.

Next one engages in the yoga without symbols by absorbing the mind in the sphere of purification in emptiness. The objects purified include the self-generation and frontal generation mandalas, the mandala deities, the mantras, and so forth.

In this way the ordinary aspects of body, speech, mind, and activities gradually acquire the visible and tangible characteristics of the supported and supporting divinity forms. This is "the body *mahamudra.*"

The sound of the mantra is spontaneously heard. This is "the speech *dharmamudra.*"

The wisdom of nondual profundity and radiance is maintained by shamatha and vipashyana combined. This is "the mind *samayamudra.*"

The appearance of impure activities automatically ceases, and the four tantric activities of pacification, increase, power, and wrath are accomplished merely by means of *dhyana.* This is "the activity *karmamudra.*"

In our tradition it is said that when the seal of these four mudras is applied by a bodhisattva holding the form of a buddha and who is a knowledge holder on the tenth level abiding near the end of cyclic existence, the all-pervading buddhas are inspired to arise from their samadhi. They then reveal the empowerments and knowledge mantras, by means of which the bodhisattva experiences the five actual purifications and achieves final enlightenment.

As for the precepts that are taken by the trainee who enters into practice of the Yoga tantras, generally these are much the same as those taken in the Anuttara Tantra division (to be explained later), wherein there are fourteen root and eight secondary (branch) downfalls to be guarded against. However, there are some differences. For example, here the thirteenth root downfall is incurred by not relying upon tantric dance and hand mudras. Also, the fourteenth root downfall is incurred by underestimating the importance of the practice of the four mudras.

As for the textual traditions of the Yoga Tantra class, the most important of these are as follows.

Firstly there is *The Glorious Compendium of Principles*,[22] which is in four sections and reveals the purpose of maintaining the *samaya* of the Yoga tantras. Then there is *The Very Nature*[23] in five chapters. To this latter work there is *A Subsequent Tantra*[24] and also *A Later Subsequent Tantra*.[25]

Other important texts include *The Vajra Highest Peak Explanatory Tantra*;[26] *The First Supreme Glory*;[27] *Victory over the Three Worlds*;[28] and *The Tantra Which Purifies the Realms of Misery*[29] in both the original form[30] and the reorganized form.[31]

The three greatest Indian elucidators of the Yoga Tantra systems were Acharya Buddhaguhya, Acharya Anandagarbha, and Acharya Shakyamitra.

Buddhaguhya's main treatise in this area was his *The Extensive Avatarana Commentary*,[32] which unpacks the meaning of *The Root Tantra*, known as *The Glorious Compendium of Principles*. Anandagarbha's *An Extensive Treatise*[33] elucidates the meaning of *The First Supreme Glory*. Finally, Shakyamitra's most significant text here is his *A Silken Ornament*.[34]

## THE ANUTTARAYOGA TANTRAS

### A GENERAL SURVEY

Lama Tsongkhapa then describes the Anuttarayoga tantras as follows:

> Amongst the sages of holy India,
> The two Anuttarayoga Tantra systems
> Famous as the sun and moon
> Were the male tantra of Guhyasamaja and
> The female yogini tantra of Heruka Chakrasamvara,
> Both of which have root tantras, explanatory tantras,
>     and so forth.

The causes which accordswith the nature of a buddha's form body, or Rupakaya, are the impure and pure illusory bodies. The principal sources explaining the methods for realizing this illusory body are the male tantras, foremost of which is the Guhyasamaja tantric tradition.

The causes which accord with the nature of a buddha's reality body, or Dharmakaya, are the semblant and actual clear light consciousnesses. The principal sources explaining the methods for realizing this clear light are the female tantras, foremost of which is the Heruka Chakrasamvara tantric tradition.

The trainees who wish to engage in these profound paths must first complete the according generation stage yogas. After these have been accomplished they must gain the common paranormal attainments such as the eight *siddhis* (i.e., the ability to levitate, walk through walls, etc). For this they should rely upon one of the four types of ordinary sexual consort—red lotus, white lotus, *utpala*, and sandal. Otherwise, in order to achieve supreme *siddhi* in this very lifetime they must rely upon the supreme jewel-like consort.

## INITIATION

The door to Anuttarayoga Tantra practice is the receiving of complete initiation from a qualified vajra master. To be more specific, to enter into the path of the Anuttarayoga tantras one must receive initiation using one of four types of mandala as the basis: chalk, cloth, *dhyana*, or body mandala.

The initiating master should be endowed with the ten inner qualities, and should have a mindstream that has been purified by accomplishing the retreat and maintaining the *samaya* of the system being transmitted.

The disciples receiving the initiation should have completed the preliminary trainings of the Sutrayana and thus have prepared their mindstreams by laying a firm spiritual basis. Only then can the tantric yogas be successfully approached.

All of the Anuttarayoga Tantra initiations begin with the master analyzing, claiming, and purifying the place of the rite. He then establishes protection and consecration. This is followed by the rite for the earth divinity, the mandala divinities, consecration of the initiation vase, enhancement of the disciple's stream of being, and so forth.

As for this last phase (i.e., enhancement of the disciple), this includes the instruction on establishing correct motivation, taking the inner initiation, the disciple's act of making requests and asking to be cared for until enlightenment is attained, establishing the pledges, blessing the three doors (body, speech, and mind), tossing the divination stick, drinking of the vase waters, being given the *kusha* grass and mystical armband, giving birth to appreciative joy, and being instructed on how to observe one's dreams.

Concerning the methods for entering into the mandala, there are three basic forms of doing this: performing self-generation and frontal generation separately but entering in one movement; performing self-generation and frontal generation nonseparately but entering separately; and, lastly, performing the self-generation and frontal generation separately and entering separately.

Following whichever system is appropriate to the specific tradition, one enters into the mandala and takes the initiations.

The disciple here makes the request to be granted initiation. One is given a blindfold, the deity costumes, and a flower garland. Next one is asked about his character and purpose, takes the bodhisattva vow and the precepts of the five buddha families, is instructed to generate the all-encompassing yoga mind, and is given the oath of secrecy.

This all occurs outside the mandala curtain. One then enters inside the curtain. To establish external merit one circumambulates the mandala, offers prostrations, and is placed in the *samaya*. For inner merit one meditates on receiving a rainfall of wisdom nectars. The master pronounces the words of truth, and the disciple throws the prophetic flower into the mandala. One is then given the flower garland initiation.

This is the stage of entering the mandala while still blindfolded.

Next the disciple is instructed to remove the blindfold. One has now acquired the spiritual maturity necessary in order to be allowed to see the supporting and supported mandalas.

One now proceeds to receive the four initiations: vase, secret, wisdom, and sacred word.

The first of these is the vase initiation. This includes the five common initiations of the (five) buddha families, and also the exclusive vajra acharya initiation. As each of these stages are completed with the sprinkling of water from the initiation vase, they are all called "vase empowerments."

Almost all the Anuttarayoga Tantra systems contain these six fundamental stages of the vase initiation (i.e., the initiations of the five buddha families and of the vajra acharya). However, some Anuttara initiation manuals further subdivide these processes, and in these alternative traditions the vase initiation sometimes includes as many as nine, and even eleven, phases.

By receiving these six, nine, or eleven vase initiations, the disciple experiences purification of all coarse and subtle bodily obscurations, such as grasping at mundane appearances. One is empowered to meditate upon the generation stage yogas and to perform the various mandala activities, etc. The potency for accomplishing the Nirmanakaya of a buddha is established.

Then follows the secret initiation. Here the disciple relies upon the use of the special secret substance, and experiences purification of all coarse and subtle speech obscurations, such as grasping at energy and mantra as being separate. One is authorized to cultivate the illusory body, the conventional reality, and to meditate upon the yogas that accomplish this body, namely the yogas of isolation of body, speech, and mind. The potency for accomplishing the Sambhogakaya of a buddha is established.

The third of the four Anuttarayoga Tantra initiations is called "the wisdom initiation." By means of it the mind is purified of all coarse and subtle obscurations, especially the obscuration hindering the perception of all appearance (i.e., all reality) as arising as the sportive play of bliss and emptiness. One is authorized to meditate on the semblant and actual clear light yogas, the highest reality. The potency of the Dharmakaya of a buddha is established.

Fourthly is the sacred word initiation. Here the wisdom of the third initiation is used as a tool to point out the nature of the state of *yuganaddha,* or Great Union. All coarse and subtle stains of the body, speech, and mind are simultaneously purified. Especially, the instincts of the distortion caused by grasping at duality are removed. One is authorized to meditate upon the completion stage yogas of the inseparable two levels of truth, i.e., the inseparable nature of the illusory body and clear light. The potency is established to actualize the state of Buddha Vajradhara, wherein one becomes a revealer of the festival of great bliss.

Once one's continuum has been matured by these four initiations, one should carefully protect the root and branch precepts of the

Tantric path and should enter into the generation and completion stage yogas that mature and liberate the mind.

This is the general picture of the overall structure of the Anuttarayoga Tantra systems. However, here it would also be useful to say something about each of the principal individual Anuttara traditions.

## GUHYASAMAJA: A MALE ANUTTARAYOGA TANTRA SYSTEM

Concerning the Guhyasamaja system Lama Tsongkhapa wrote,

> The Anuttarayoga tantras are
> The highest teachings given by the Buddha.
> From amongst these the most profound is
> That of glorious Guhyasamaja, the king of all tantras.

And also elsewhere,

> Understanding the sublime path of Guhyasamaja
> Bestows fearless, confident understanding
> Of all the teachings of the Buddha.

As said above, once one understands the Guhyasamaja Tantra, this comprehension can be used as an infrastructure for the understanding of all other tantric systems.

### THE GUHYASAMAJA GENERATION STAGE YOGAS

Here, by relying upon a mind mandala, a most wondrous field of merit, one is empowered to enter into the practices that purify the mind by means of engaging in the activities that accumulate vast stores of merit.

The mandala meditations, or generation stage yogas, proceed as follows.

To symbolize the time when the universe previously was destroyed and became nothing, one meditates with wisdom on the emptiness of the three doors of liberation.

Later the universe again began to reform, and the elements once more began to reappear. This process is symbolized by the arisal of the protection wheel, the *dharmodaya* "source of phenomena," the four elemental mandalas, the crossed vajra, the inconceivable mansion, and so forth.

After our universe had once again become developed, the sentient beings began to reappear in it. This was a golden age on earth, and the sentient beings at that time took birth miraculously. To symbolize this, the thirty-two deities of the mandala are visualized as suddenly manifesting simultaneously in a single moment.

Then there are the activities of emanating out from and withdrawing back into the mandala, and the invoking of the Wisdom and Commitment Beings.

There is the entering from above the mandala: the Wisdom Vajra Being enters; the entering from below: Vajra Strength enters; the unhindered simultaneous Vajra Being entrance from above, below, and both the cardinal and intermediate directions; and the entering of the Vajra Disciple from the eastern gateway. These are the four manners of entering.

Next follows the invocation beginning with Vairochana and culminating in Sumbharaja. These tantric divinities are arranged on the body of the principal figure in the mandala. One meditates that they become inseparable in nature from the skandhas, elements, and so forth.

This establishes the basis of the deity visualization.

The sentient beings with the karma to experience birth from a womb on this planet and whose bodies are composed of the six impermanent substances must eventually meet with death. At the time of death they experience the dissolution of the twenty-five coarse substances: the five skandhas, such as form and so forth; the five basic wisdoms, such as the mirrorlike wisdom, etc.; the four elements; the six gates of perception; and the five sensory objects.

At each phase of this dissolution there is the external sign of the respective sensory power losing its capacity of apprehension, and also the according element failing in strength. Simultaneously there occur inner signs, such as the miragelike vision, smoke, fireflies, and the flickering of light like that of a butterlamp.

When the elements have thus dissolved there is the threefold phase of absorption of the vital energies. These three are "appearance," "increase," and "near attainment." The signs of these occur, and the "near attainment" experience melts into the clear light. A sense of luminosity arises, like the vibrant radiance of a clear dawn free from the three obstructions just before sunrise.

With this clear light level of consciousness acting as a simultaneously-present condition, and the flowing energy which is the vehicle of this consciousness acting as the substantial cause, the dying person emerges from the clear light experience and prepares to enter into the bardo, or "in-between" state.

The three phases (mentioned above) of appearance, increase, and near attainment, as well as the visions of mirage, smoke, and so forth now once again arise. However, this time their order of appearance is reversed. In this way the dying person leaves the clear light and enters into the bardo, acquiring a bardo body.

To symbolize the above process, the sadhana now presents five phases of unfoldment. These are known as "the five clear enlightenments": suchness, seat, symbol, syllable, and complete deity body. By means of these five unfoldments one arises as a Sambhogakaya deity.

The bardo being then enters into a womb and eventually takes rebirth. To symbolize this the Sambhogakaya deity transforms into the Nirmanakaya deity Vajrasattva.

The meditations on the processes of formation, disintegration, birth, death, bardo, and so forth of the world and its inhabitants as described above and symbolized by the various phases beginning with purification in suchness until the offering of suchness are known as "the perfect accomplishment of one's own purpose." It is the samadhi of the first application.

To symbolize the physical deeds of the resultant stage of buddhahood, the deities of the space mandala, together with the consorts of their individual families, are summoned to the heart. Clouds of emanations are sent forth and withdrawn in order to purify the world and its inhabitants.

The stage from emanating via the seven doors until the emergence of the wrathful deities is known as "the perfect accomplishment of the purpose of others." It is also called "the supremely victorious mandala."

The mental deeds of the resultant stage of buddhahood are symbolized as follows. To arrest mental wandering and torpor one visualizes mystical hand implements, tiny in size, at the tip of the nose. Alternatively, one generates a coarse single-pointed recollection of a drop the size of a mustard seed, within which is envisioned the complete deity mandala. This is performed together with the processes of emanation and absorption, and is known as "the yoga of subtle realization supported by shamatha."

The buddahood deeds of speech are symbolized by mental and also verbal mantric recitation. This latter has six aspects: pledge, cyclical, flowing, forceful, wrathful, and diamond.

The main steps in the process are as follows.

The principal mandala deity melts into clear light. The four indescribable goddesses offer songs of inspiration, and the deity reappears from the light. Then there is the offering, the praise, the experience of blissful ambrosia, and so forth.

In brief, from the phase of meditating on the mystical hand implements at the upper door until the phase of establishing *siddhi* there are forty-nine steps to be cultivated.

There are the three samadhis, such as that called "the first application"; the four branches, known as "propitiation," "proximate attainment," "attainment," and "great attainment"; four yogas to be cultivated, called "yoga," "beyond yoga," "intense yoga," and "great yoga"; four vajra stages, known as "emptiness enlightenment," "seed absorption," "form completion," and "mantric syllable placement"; and so forth.

These are the processes of the Guhyasamaja generation stage to be cultivated as a preliminary to entering into the completion stage yogas.

### THE GUHYASAMAJA COMPLETION STAGE YOGAS

The subjects taken as the focal points in practice of the completion stage yogas are the general and individual natures of the body and mind on coarse, subtle, and extremely subtle levels.

Here the three topics of energy channels, vital energies, and mystic drops become very important.

By understanding these topics well, one can successfully enter into practice of the various completion stage yogas: body isolation, speech isolation, mind isolation, illusory body, the clear light, and great union.

The yoga of body isolation is explained as follows.

The basis of this isolation comprises the aggregates, elements, entrances, and sensory objects. Each of these is fivefold, making a total of twenty factors. The five buddha families are then applied to each of these twenty, making a total of one hundred supreme natures to be explored.

Here the four elements, together with consciousness, constitute the "five thatness natures" to be meditated upon. Body, speech, and mind, envisioned as being deities of the three vajras, are the three secret natures. Finally, the practitioner possessing the three doors is envisioned as being Buddha Vajradhara, which is "the great secret solitary nature" to be meditated upon.

One seals these various factors with the mark of bliss and void, and isolates them in the nature of a *devarupa*, or "deity body."

Moreover, when one meditates on the yoga of the subtle drop at the tip of the jewel—an element possessing the four factors of substance, time, energy, and object—mind and energy flow together into the central channel. Signs arise to indicate that the vital energies enter, abide, and dissolve at the heart. The yogi achieves absorption in the sphere of bliss and void, and attains the samadhi of the vajra body isolation in which the hundred natures and so forth (as described above) appear as *devakaya*.

The basis of the second isolation, or that of speech, involves the root and branch energies in coarse and subtle aspects, and especially the life-sustaining energy at the heart, together with the undying mystic drop.

This, the basis of all expression, abides as a short syllable *AH*, symbol of the ultimate profundity. The yogi engages the vajra recitation while appreciating the inseparability of energy and mantra, and experiences yogic isolation in the nature of the illusory body. He moves the undying drop to the various places of the body, such as heart, head, secret place, and so forth. Also, one engages in the vase breathing yoga, taking as objects of concentration the undying drop, together with the mantra wheels, the energies in the nature of five radiances, the substances of white and red (i.e., male and female) sexual fluids brought to mystical union and formed into a drop the size of a mustard seed, and so forth.

In this manner all the root energies, with the exception of the all-pervading energy, are brought under control.

The yogi then applies the vajra recitation methods and ignites the mystic heat. The vital energies are absorbed into the undying drop, and the knots in the channels at the center of the heart are released.

This is the process of the yoga of speech isolation, the samadhi of vajra speech.

The basis of the third isolation comprises the three appearances and the eighty conceptual minds. By relying upon the two *dhyanas* as well as upon conducive inner and outer conditions, the yogi isolates (i.e., withdraws) into the sphere of semblant clear light that sees all as emptiness. He relies upon the external condition of a *karmamudra* and/or a *jnanamudra* (i.e., actual or visualized sexual consort) to induce the four joys of downward-showering and upward-rising energies. As an inner condition one focuses the vajra recitation method upon the all-pervading energy.

One then dissolves his body from above and below into the clear light at the heart. The entire world and its inhabitants are in the same manner gradually dissolved into the vision of clear light.

In this way the yogi performs the absorption by means of the two *dhyanas*. The dissolution of the eighty natural conceptual minds is experienced: thirty-three in the nature of appearance; forty in the nature of increase; and seven in the nature of near attainment.

These eighty natural conceptual minds that are carried by the coarse and subtle contaminated energies thus dissolve just as at the moment of death. The wisdoms of the three appearances arise, leading the mind to the experience of the semblant clear light.

This is the process of the yoga of mind isolation, the samadhi of vajra mind.

When these three isolations have been taken to fulfillment, the yogi is given the actual precept on how to generate the illusory body, and also the oral instructions of the nine points in blending and transference.

The basis for producing the illusory body is explained as follows.

The semblant clear light acts as a simultaneously-present condition, and the vital energy of five radiances which is the vehicle of that clear light acts as the substantial cause. It is this (vital energy) that produces the illusory body described by the twelve similes and having the fifteen qualities, the form which substitutes for the merit generated in the exoteric Sutrayana by means of three aeons of practice.

Such is the completion stage yoga of the illusory body, which in the Vajrayana represents the conventional level of truth.

The clear light yoga is explained as follows.

The external time for the experience of clear light is dawn, when neither sun nor moon is in the sky and yet darkness has passed. The internal time is after the subsiding of the three appearances (i.e., appearance, increase, and near attainment), just as at the moment of death. These are the two moments for the manifestation of clear light consciousness.

At a time when these two are possible, the yogi relies upon inner (i.e., energy control) and outer (i.e., a sexual consort) conditions to manifest the clear light, which in the Vajrayana represents the ultimate level of truth and is the remedy that eliminates at once the nine circles of obscurations to knowledge.

The final completion stage yoga is that of great union. It is described as follows.

The yogi reverses the processes whereby he entered into clear light consciousness, pulling back into the consciousness of near attainment and so forth. Simultaneously he experiences the path of freedom, the "great union of transcendence" which is produced from noncontaminated mind and energy.

Arising from that absorption one realizes the inseparable nature of the body and mind. This is the "great union of a trainee."

That practitioner then intensifies his experience by engaging in the three methods known simply as "contrived," "uncontrived," and "utterly uncontrived." Training in this way he experiences the clear light at the fulfillment of training, thus eliminating all obscurations to omniscience and attaining the "great union of no-more-training" which is enriched by the seven mystical qualities.

### THE GUHYASAMAJA FIVE STAGES
### OF THE ENLIGHTENMENT PATH

How are these various Anuttarayoga Tantra practices linked to the categories of the five stages of the path to enlightenment: accumulation, application, vision, meditation, and no-more-training?

"The path of accumulation" comprises the period beginning with the time when one acquires the four complete initiations until by the power of meditation one achieves a glimpse of emptiness through dissolving the vital energies into the central channel.

"The path of application" is experienced from then until the attainment of the impure level of the illusory body yoga that directly perceives emptiness by means of the wisdom of great bliss.

From the first experience of the actual clear light until the attainment of the great union of a trainee is "the path of vision," the first bodhisattva *bhumi.*

"The path of meditation" comprises the period beginning with the moment after that until the first moment of the attainment of the stage of the ultimate clear light of the great union at the end of training.

The yogi then crosses the tenth bodhisattva *bhumi,* and in the second moment of that experience achieves complete enlightenment, "the path of no-more-training."

Everything that has been said above about the Guhyasamaja system can be abbreviated into the mystical syllable *E-VAM,* which is spoken of in terms of path, fruit, and signs.

It can also be abbreviated into the threefold category of the tantras of basis, path, and fruit.

### THE THREE TYPES OF MALE ANUTTARAYOGA TANTRAS

The Anuttarayoga tantras are of two main types: male and female. Of the male Anuttarayoga tantras there are three basic types: those that work with lust, those that work with anger, and those that work with ignorance.

The principal male Anuttarayoga tantra working with lust as the basis of the path is that of Guhyasamaja, the yogas of which have been described above.

The Indian textual traditions of the Guhyasamaja system are as follows.

Firstly there is *The Root Tantra*[35] in seventeen chapters.

Then there are The Six Great Explanatory Tantras.[36]

The first of these is *The Subsequent Tantra*[37] in eighteen chapters, which explains the six facets of *The Root Tantra* by means of the four modes. These six facets are direct, indirect, obvious, nonobvious, literal, and alternative. The four modes are meaning of the words, the general ideas, the hidden meanings, and the ultimate significance.

The remaining five explanatory tantras include *The Vajra Rosary Tantra*,[38] *Revealing the Intent of the Buddhas*,[39] *A Synopsis of Vajra Wisdom*,[40] *Questions of the King of Celestials*,[41] and *Questions of the Four Goddesses*.[42]

Numerous commentarial traditions appeared later in India, including those of the Aryas (i.e., Nagarjuna and Aryadeva), Jnanapada, Anandagarbha, Shantipada, and so forth. Of these, the first two are the most complete (i.e., that of the Aryas and that of Jnanapada).

The Indian commentary most clearly elucidating the generation stage yogas of the thirty-two-deity Guhyasamaja mandala of Akshobhya is Nagarjuna's *The Summary*[43] and also his *A Brief Synopsis*.[44]

Some of the more important Indian commentaries elucidating the completion stage yogas are: Nagarjuna's *The Five Stages*[45] and also his *A Commentary to the Bodhi-mind*;[46] Aryadeva's *Stages of the Self-Blessed Illusory Body*[47] and also his *A Compendium of Practices*,[48] which is a commentary to Nagarjuna's *The Five Stages*; Nagabodhi's *Steps in the Generation Stage*,[49] his *Twenty Mandala Rites*,[50] and also his *Explanation of the Completion Stage Activities*;[51] Shakyamitra's *Supplement to the Two Stages*;[52] and Shrichandra's *Generation Stage*

*Vajrasattva Method*,[53] his *Six Applications on the Completion Stage*,[54] and also his *A Lamp to Illuminate the Tantric Scriptures*.[55]

As for how these lineages came to Tibet, it is said that Manjushrimitra, an incarnation of the bodhisattva Manjushri, once appeared to Acharya Simhabhadra's disciple Buddhajnana. He manifested in the form of the lord of the Manjushrivajra mandala, initiating Buddhajnana into the *dhyana* mandala and also bestowing upon him the complete instructions. Eventually the venerable Atisha received this secret lineage, brought it to Tibet, and in turn passed it on to his chief Tibetan disciple, Lama Dromtonpa.

Another important lineage of instruction is that of the translator Go Lotsawa, who collected the various Indian traditions listed above and brought them to Tibet, passing them on to the Sakya and Zhalu lineages.

A third important lineage was brought to Tibet by Marpa the Translator and passed on through the order of Kagyu gurus.

Lama Tsongkhapa collected together these various lines of transmission and united them into one stream. Later he went into retreat at the Olkha Mountains for a number of years, where he achieved realization. Here he received numerous direct visions of Manjushrivajra and was given special oral instructions. These included the instruction of the three samadhis of the generation stage practice of the nineteen-deity mandala. They also included the completion stage precepts such as the instruction on the body isolation yoga involving the undying drop at the heart, the speech isolation yoga involving the secret drop at the jewel, the mind isolation yoga involving the mantric drop, and also the three higher yogic stages of illusory body, clear light, and great union, which are linked to the drop of suchness.

The yogic stages of these four drops—undying, secret, mantric, and suchness—are the subject of numerous treatises by Buddhajnanapada. Included here are his *The Four Hundred Points Concern-*

ing the Mandala Rite;[56] The Always Sublime Generation Stage Method;[57] The Liberating Drops in the Completion Stage Yogas;[58] and The Sacred Instructions of Manjushri,[59] which explains both generation and completion stage yogas.

Lama Tsongkhapa collected and united all of these oral and scriptural lineages, thus preserving them for future generations. It is due to his kindness that the Guhyasamaja tradition still exists today in such completeness.

## THE VAJRABHAIRAVA TANTRA

The principal male Anuttarayoga tantra using anger as the basis of the path is that of Vajrabhairava, also known as Yamantaka.

The complete root tantra of this system, or the Vajrabhairava Root Tantra,[60] is known as The Three Hundred Topics.[61] However, it was never translated into Tibetan. Only those sections dealing with the methods of accomplishing enlightenment and those dealing with the activities of the wheel of emanation were translated.

The sections dealing with the methods for accomplishing enlightenment were translated in two different forms: The Seven Topics[62] and The Four Topics.[63] As for the sections dealing with the methods of engaging in the activities of the wheel of emanation, these were compiled into The Three Topics.[64]

Other important Indian classics in the Vajrabhairava tradition include Vision of the Practitioner Teulopa,[65] Tantra of the Black Warrior[66] in eighteen chapters, and The Tantra of the Red Opponent[67] in nineteen chapters.

Three basic forms of the mandala are presented in these various texts: red, black, and extremely fierce. Of these, the last is the most important in general practice.

The Vajrabhairava generation stage yogas usually consist of cultivating the three samadhis on one of the mandalas associated with this last form of Bhairava: the forty-nine-deity mandala, the seventeen-deity mandala, the thirteen-deity mandala, the mandala of eight *vitali* deities, and the mandala of the Solitary Hero.

As for the completion stage yogas, the Vajrabhairava system arranges these into four categories. Here the phases of body isolation and speech isolation combine as Mantra Yoga. Mind isolation becomes Commitment Yoga. Both impure and pure phases of the illusory body trainings combine as Form Yoga. Finally, semblant and actual clear light phases become the Wisdom Yoga.

The principal Indian commentators on these four completion stage yogas were the mahasiddhas Lalitavajra, Shridhara, Amoghavajra the First, and Amoghavajra the Second.

The various Indian lineages of the Vajrabhairava system were brought to Tibet by yogis such as Rva Lotsawa, Nyo Lotsawa, Kyo Od-jung, and so forth.

The most authoritative early Tibetan commentaries are those by Rva Lotsawa and the Drikung Kagyu master Paldzin.

## THE TANTRA OF VAJRA ARALI

The third type of male Anuttarayoga tantra—that working with ignorance as the basis of the path—is known as Vajra Arali.

The root tantric scripture of this system is known simply as *The Tantra of Vajra Arali*.[68] Other important related texts are *The Peerless Miracle Net*[69] and *The Vajra Essence Ornament*.[70]

## HERUKA CHAKRASAMVARA: A FEMALE ANUTTARAYOGA TANTRA

As for the Anuttarayoga tantras that belong to the female category, Lama Tsongkhapa writes,

> It is said that the female Anuttarayoga tantras
> Are inconceivably numerous;
> But of all of these the central and supreme

Is that of Heruka Chakrasamvara,
A tantra like the ornament
On the very tip of a victory banner.

The essence of all the female Anuttarayoga tantras is that of Heruka Chakrasamvara, "the Blood-Drinking Lord of the Wheel of Supreme Bliss."

The canonical sources of this tradition are *The Concise Samvara Tantra*[71] in fifty-one chapters, *The Peerless Expression,*[72] *Source of the Mystic Bond,*[73] *Tantra of the Vajra Space Warrior,*[74] and so forth.

Three principal Indian lineages of transmission of the Heruka Chakrasamvara system developed, namely those of the mahasiddhas Luipada, Krishnacharya, and Ghantapada.

In the first of these three systems (i.e., that of Luipada), the generation and completion stage practices are applied by means of the four daily sessions of yogas.

Here the generation stage of practice consists of the five purifications, which are associated with the threefold process of yoga, beyond yoga, and intense yoga (as listed earlier).

As for the completion stage practices, here the yogi fixes his mind at the sound cluster (i.e., seed syllables) at the navel. The karmic energies are brought into the central energy channel and the four downward-showering and upward-rising joys are induced. One then relies upon the meditations of the *dhyanas* of vajra recitation and systematic absorption. In this way, on the emptiness side he gains an inconceivable experience of semblant and actual clear light; and on the appearance side he achieves the impure and pure levels of the wondrous illusory body. He then manifests the inconceivable state of great union, both that of a trainee and that beyond training.

As for the lineage of Ghantapada, in the generation stage practices the outer and inner mandalas are cultivated by means of the three yogas.

In the completion stage practices (of the Ghantapada tradition), the yogas of the three isolations, the illusory body, the clear light, and great union are collected into five stages of yogic application. These five are called "self-consecration," "crossed vajra," "the filled jewel," "*jalandhara*," and "the inconceivable."

The fundamental commentaries in these various Heruka lineages are the two generation stage manuals by Luipada, known as *The Great* and *The Small*. Then there are The Seven Treatises by Ghantapada, and the six texts of Krishnacharya.

## THE HEVAJRA TANTRA

Another very important tradition in the Heruka cycle of mandalas is that known as Hevajra.

Here there is *The Root Tantra*,[75] also known as *The Tantra in Two Forms*;[76] *The Explanatory Tantra*,[77] which is also known as *The Vajra Tent*;[78] *The Subsequent Tantra*,[79] which is also known as *The Drop of Mahamudra*;[80] and *The Later Subsequent Tantra*,[81] also known as *The Essence of Wisdom*.[82]

All of these principal lineages of root, explanatory, and subsequent tantras in the Hevajra cycle, as well as the commentarial traditions, were transmitted in the form of the "Path and Fruit" (Lam Drey) line of transmission (coming into Tibet through the early Sakya masters). Lama Jey Tsongkhapa praised this transmission as being supreme.

## KALACHAKRA:
## A CLARIFIED ANUTTARAYOGA TANTRA

Another important Anuttarayoga Tantra system is that known as the Kalachakra, a tradition that presents the Anuttara path in a manner markedly different than the presentation found in all the other Anuttarayoga systems.

Concerning the Kalachakra system Lama Tsongkhapa wrote,

Another important Anuttarayoga Tantra system
With a quite unique manner of presenting the path
Is that of Kalachakra, "The Wheel of Time,"
Which is based upon *The Abbreviated Tantra*
Together with its commentary, *The Stainless Light.*

The clarified tantra of the Kalachakra tradition is usually mentioned separately from the other Anuttarayoga systems, for its infrastructure is considerably different than those of the mainstream traditions such as Guhyasamaja, Vajrabhairava, Heruka Chakrasamvara, and so forth.

Kalachakra, or "The Wheel of Time," is spoken of in three aspects: Outer, Inner, and Alternative.

"Outer Kalachakra" comprises the six elements of earth, water, fire, air, space, and wisdom; the world of Mt. Meru, the four continents, and the eight subcontinents and so forth, together with everything above, below, and in all the directions; and also all objects of smell, sight, taste, touch, sound, and dharma.

"Inner Kalachakra" includes the topics of the three realms of living beings, the sixteen worlds, the ten planets, the twenty-eight principal heavenly bodies, the five places of rebirth, the six types of living beings, the time cycles of years, months, and days, the six energy centers of the body, the ten vital energies, the eight drops that carry the instincts of the two obscurations, and so forth.

In other words, included here (i.e., in both Outer and Inner) are the living beings and the world as understood in an astrological context.

"Alternative Kalachakra" is the actual practice of the yogas of the Kalachakra system whereby the world and its beings are purified.

The actual basis of the purification is the person possessing the six elements with the karma to be born from a human womb here in this world.

The process begins by taking initiation into a mandala made from colored powders.

This initiation begins with the nine preliminary steps of invoking the earth *deva*, consecrating the vase, the conch of great victory, the action lines, vajra, bell, enhancing the disciple, establishing the seat, and the analysis of the divinity.

The seventh of these preliminary steps above involves placing the disciple within the six families, invoking Vajrasattva, and so forth.

The actual initiation process is constituted of three phases: the seven called "entering like a child," the four higher initiations, and the four higher-than-higher initiations.

When a child is born into this world he undergoes seven experiences: being washed, having his hair cut, having his ears pierced, learning to laugh and speak, using the sensory objects, being given a name, and learning to read and write.

Accordingly, the Kalachakra initiation begins with seven processes that are likened to these seven steps in childhood.

To receive these the disciple in turn stands before each of the four faces of Kalachakra—white, red, black, and yellow in color—and is given the seven initiations: water, headdress, silk ribbon, vajra and bell, activity, name, and permission.

By means of these initiations the disciple experiences purification of the five aggregates, ten energies, right and left energy channels, ten sensory powers and their objects, the activities of the five bodily functions, the three doors, and the element of wisdom.

As for the *samaya* taken during this process, there are seven root vows in common (with other Anuttarayoga Tantra systems), together with seven further root vows exclusive to Kalachakra.

In addition, there are the twenty-five special precepts of the Kalachakra system, relating to the five abandonments, the five misdeeds, the five murders, the five types of anger, and the five attachments.

During this phase of the initiation ceremony these are introduced and one is advised to guard against them.

Next one receives the four conventional higher initiations, also known as "the four worldly initiations." Here the disciple is established in the path of the four joys by means of the vase waters, tasting the secret substances, experiencing melting and bliss, and being introduced to the innate bliss and void.

Finally there are the four higher-than-higher initiations, also known as "the four beyond-worldly initiations." Here the disciple is introduced to the consciousness which directly perceives emptiness while abiding in supreme unchanging great bliss, a consciousness that is of one taste with the empty body arising in the form of Kalachakra and consort in sexual union.

By gaining these initiations the disciple is introduced to the real meaning of being a layman, a novice, a fully ordained monk, a Sangha elder, and a leader of living beings.

Also, during the rite the significance of each of the steps in initiation is pointed out.

Thus, by receiving the empowerments of the three vajras, being shown the commitments, and gaining the initiation of a great vajra acharya, the mindstream of the disciple is ripened and is prepared for entrance into the actual yogic practices of the Kalachakra tradition.

As for the various mandalas that can be used as the basis of the generation stage yogas, *The Root Tantra*[83] speaks of the mandala of glorious moving stars containing 1,620 divinities.

*The Abbreviated Tantra*[84] speaks of 722 divinities in the mandalas of body, speech, and mind.

Other alternatives are the mind mandala of thirty-six divinities and the mind mandala of thirty-two divinities. Then there are the smaller mandalas of twenty-five, twenty-three, nineteen, thirteen, and nine divinities. Finally, there is the mandala with only Kalachakra and Consort, and also the mandala of Solitary Kalachakra.

In the generation stage the yogi contemplates one of these various mandalas by means of the three samadhis, engaging in the four-branched propitiation, maintaining the four vajra points, and cultivating the four enlightenments.

In the completion stage the meditator engages in the six yogas: sense withdrawal, meditative stabilization, energy concentration, retention, postrecollection, and samadhi.

These six abbreviate into the four branches: the branch producing form, the branch producing energy, the branch producing bliss, and the branch of great accomplishment. The first branch is linked to the first two yogas, and the second branch to the third and fourth yogas. Finally, the third and fourth branches are linked to the fifth and sixth yogas.

By means of these six yogas the disciple achieves the *mahamudra* of the empty body. The energies enter the central channel, and the drops of red and white sexual forces flow down from the crown chakra above and flow up from the chakra at the secret place below. 21,600 of each of the two sexual drops (male and female) are gathered together in this way, giving rise to an experience of great bliss understanding emptiness. Each occasion of experience of this great bliss dissolves an according amount of karmic wind and atomic bodily matter. The obscurations of the four occasions, such as the waking state and so forth, are thus destroyed, and one travels to the twelfth stage of attainment, the enlightened state of Kalachakra's great bliss.

This is the system of the Kalachakra initiations, generation stage yogas, and completion stage yogas that produce the four kayas of a fully enlightened being.

Buddha Shakyamuni originally taught this tradition at the Great Rice-Heap Stupa in Southern Jambudvipa. The teaching had been requested by King Suchandra of Shambhala, who was an actual ema-

nation of the bodhisattva Vajrapani. Emissaries from six different kingdoms were also present.

On that occasion Buddha transmitted *The Root Tantra* in twelve thousand lines, and shortly thereafter King Suchandra composed his great commentary in sixty thousand lines.

However, the only section of *The Root Tantra* to survive is that known as *The Treatise on the Initiations.*[85]

Later Manjushrikirti, who was the first of the twenty-five knowledge-holder kings of Shambhala, wrote a summary of *The Root Tantra* that came to be known by the title *The Abbreviated Tantra,*[86] which is in five chapters. Two different translations of the commentary to this, *Essence of the Abbreviated Tantra,*[87] exist in the Tibetan canon.

Another important text is *The Great Commentary to the Abbreviated Tantra*[88] by the second of Shambhala's knowledge holders, Acharya Pundarika. This is perhaps better known in association with the Three Commentaries on the Mind.[89]

Also of significance is the bodhisattva Vajragarbha's *Commentary to the Vajra Essence.*[90] This work unpacks the themes of *The Tantra of Two Forms,*[91] which is regarded as the root tantra of the Hevajra system. However, Vajragarbha's *Commentary to the Vajra Essence* speaks in a manner consistent with the Kalachakra presentation, so often it is read in conjunction with a study of the Kalachakra tradition.

Acharya Vajrapani's *Commentary to the Song of Vajrapani,*[92] which explains the essential points of *The Root Tantra of Heruka Chakrasamvara*[93] in terms compatible with the Kalachakra system, is also important.

Then there is *The Subsequent Tantra of Guhyasamaja,*[94] which presents the path in a manner consistent with the Kalachakra structure and therefore is often read in conjunction with the Kalachakra literature.

Kalachakrapada's extensive and abbreviated commentaries to the

Kalachakra generation stage yogas are also fundamental reading, as are the writings of the two Dro brothers.

Also of relevance to the Kalachakra are works such as The Three Rosaries[95] by Acharya Abhayakara: *The Vajra Rosary*,[96] which contains forty-two mandala rites from all four classes of tantras; *The Rosary of Complete Yoga*,[97] which is a sadhana collection; and *A Rosary of Sunbeams*,[98] which is a collection of fire-rite practices.

Finally, there is *A Compendium of Purification Practices*[99] by Acharya Jagaddarpana.

## THE TANTRIC PRECEPTS

In the Resultant Vajrayana—even more so than in the Causal Sutrayana—it is said to be extremely important to train under the guidance of a qualified tantric master, to avoid wrong attitudes toward him/her, to cultivate positive attitudes, and to remain within the framework of the vows and commitments of the Tantric path.

In order to be able to do this it is useful to know the beneficial effects of conducive attitudes and the shortcomings of faulty attitudes, how to regard the guru's entourage and possessions, the nature of correct and incorrect practice, and so forth.

All of these topics are discussed in detail in *The Root Tantra of Guhyasamaja, The Peerless Miracle Net, The Tantra of Two Forms, The First Supreme Glory*,[100] and other such texts.

The general themes on how to correctly rely upon the vajra guru were gleaned from these early source works and collected into fifty quintessential verses entitled *Fifty Verses on the Guru*[101] by Acharya Vira, who was also known by the names Aryasura and Ashvaghosha.

Although all four classes of tantras involve some type of *samaya*, the two lower tantra classes do not require the taking of the nineteen *samayas* of the five buddha families.

The method for acquiring these *samayas* is expounded in *The Vajra Space Warrior, The Perfect Union*,[102] and so forth.

The general *samaya* of the Anuttarayoga tantras includes topics like the commitment of consumption, such as the vow to rely upon consumption of the five meats and five drinks; the commitment to uphold the sacred materials, such as vajra, bell, the six tantric ornaments, and so forth; the commitment of protection, meaning the *samaya* to protect the root and branch vows; and so forth.

The root vows are fourteen in number, and transgressing them is known as "the root downfalls." By understanding their individual natures, what constitutes each, and being apprehensive of the shortcomings of transgression, one guards against the stains of a root downfall.

Should a root downfall occur, there are numerous methods of restoring the strength of one's disciplines. These are expounded in *The Tantra of the Red Opponent, The Tantra of the Black Warrior, The Vajra Essence Ornament*, and so forth.

In brief, based on these numerous canonical works Acharya Ashvaghosha compiled the list of fourteen root tantric downfalls, and Acharya Nagarjuna compiled the list of the eight secondary precepts.

The tradition of Lakshmikara emphasizes a number of alternative precepts. Here it is said that engaging in the various mandala activities without first completing the formal retreat is a root downfall. Also, included in the secondary precepts are the three commitments to cut off self-interest, arrest attraction to mundane appearances, and abide within the three vows (pratimoksha, bodhisattva, and Vajrayana).

This tradition also lists as a secondary tantric precept the commitment to respect holy images, tantric implements such as vajra and bell, tantric substances such as even old and discarded ritual materials, and so forth. As well, it mentions the commitments to engage six times a day in the practice of recollecting the mind of spiritual determination, to meditate four times daily upon the yogas of the tantric system into which one is initiated, to make a food offering (*torma*) during the last daily session of meditation, and to strive between meditation sessions to maintain the special tantric attitudes (such as seeing oneself as a mandala divinity, the world as a mandala, all sounds as mantra, all thoughts as the interplay of bliss and void, etc).

Practitioners of the female Anuttarayoga tantras are instructed to observe a number of additional precepts, such as beginning all activities with the left side of the body, performing a tantric feast (*tsok*) on the tenth day of each lunar cycle, and so forth.

Should either the root or secondary tantric precepts be transgressed, the strength of the disciplines can be restored by means of taking the initiation again, or else by means of performing the self-initiation practice.

To prevent negative effects arising from any downfalls that have been created it is useful to practice the meditations and mantric recitations associated with the tantric systems of Vajrasattva or Samayavajra, and also to engage in the Vajradaka fire rite.

These methods of purifying transgressions of the tantric precepts are taught in the various scriptures listed earlier.

## CONCLUSION

The omniscient (Zhalu) master Buton Rinpochey, who understood and elucidated all the teachings of Buddha, greatly contributed to the preservation and dissemination of the vast range of the Buddhist tantras here in Tibet. Lama Tsongkhapa and his immediate disciples continued his legacy.

My own root guru Purchokpa received the complete tradition coming from them, analyzed it with pure reason, and internalized its meaning through intense meditation. He thus crossed the vast ocean of study, contemplation, and meditation in the tantric tradition.

It was under his kind guidance that I myself ventured into the Vajrayana. And although I cannot boast of spectacular personal accomplishments, I must say that I feel very honored to have trained in this vast and profound system under the guidance of such an accomplished master.

> Thus is complete my brief presentation
> Of the main points in the Vajrayana system
> Of four classes of tantras,
> The essence of Buddha's teachings,
> As collected by the omniscient Buton Rinpochey,
> Elucidated by the incomparable Lama Tsongkhapa,
> And (given to me by) my kind root guru Purchokpa.

> May any small merits that it possesses
> Be dedicated toward the cause of enlightenment;
> May the Vajrayana teachings last for long,
> And may living beings continually abide
> Within the golden rays of peace and joy.

## Chapter Two:

### The Seventh Dalai Lama's

*Instructional Poem on the Stages in Practice of the Heruka Chakrasamvara Tantra*[103]

Gyalwa Kalzang Gyatso (1708-1757)

HERUKA CHAKRASAMVARA

# Translator's Preamble

THE FOLLOWING mystical poem by the great Seventh Dalai Lama
(1708-1757) puts forth in verse form the quintessential points in
the practice of the Heruka Chakrasamvara Tantra.

We saw a reference to this tantric system in the previous chapter,
wherein the Thirteenth Dalai Lama quotes Lama Tsongkhapa as saying,

> Amongst the sages of holy India,
> The two Anuttarayoga Tantra systems
> Famous as the sun and moon
> Were the male tantra of Guhyasamaja and
> The female yogini tantra of Heruka Chakrasamvara,
> Both of which have root tantras, explanatory tantras,
> and so forth.

Thus, Lama Tsongkhapa identifies the Chakrasamvara system as
being the chief of all the yogini, or "female energy," tantras.

Later in the same text the Thirteenth again quotes Tsongkhapa to
reinforce this same idea:

> It is said that the female Anuttarayoga tantras
> Are inconceivably numerous;
> But of all of these the central and supreme

Is that of Heruka Chakrasamvara,
A tantra like the ornament
On the very tip of a victory banner.

The Thirteenth then goes on to explain, "Three principal Indian
lineages of transmission of the Heruka Chakrasamvara system developed, namely those of the mahasiddhas Luipada, Krishnacharya, and
Ghantapada."

In other words, three different lineages of the Chakrasamvara
Tantra had come to Tibet, each of which had unique Indian sources.
Of note, all three still exist within the Tibetan refugee community in
India, as well as with the great lamas who remained in Tibet. The
main difference in the three, for practical purposes, is the complexity of the mandala used as the basis of meditation in the first stage
of practice, known as "the generation stage." The completion stage
yogas are largely the same, albeit with different experiential commentaries descending from the lineage masters.

The name of this tantric system reveals its approach to the spiritual path: "Chakrasamvara" literally means "wheel of bliss." The Seventh elucidates the meaning as follows in his opening verse: ". . .
Heruka Chakrasamvara, Male/Female in sexual union, / The wheel
composed of all objects of knowledge, / Whose essence is great bliss
clear as the autumn sky." The idea is that the meditations and yogas
of the Chakrasamvara system take all objects of knowledge, and all
the various facets of experience, and cause them to arise within the
sphere of bliss conjoined with the radiant wisdom of emptiness. In
the above verse, "clear as the autumn sky" refers to the *shunyata* clear
light nature of mind, within which the great bliss of experience flows.

The above etymological comment on the meaning of the name
"Chakrasamvara" applies to all three lineages or forms of the tantra
listed above.

The following poem by the Seventh Dalai Lama, however, is

inspired by the last of the three, i.e., that of the Indian mahasiddha Ghantapada, who is known in Tibetan as Tilbupa, "the Bell Master." This lineage is still important today with all the new schools of Tibetan Buddhism, but particularly within the Kagyu and Geluk. Of the three lineages, that of Luipada is mostly used by monasteries and communities, whereas that of Ghantapada is mostly used by individual practitioners and people in meditation retreat.

Ghantapada is celebrated in Tibet not only in literature and history, but also in art. He has been the source of inspiration of hundreds of paintings over the centuries. One of the most famous images of him depicts him flying blissfully through the sky while copulating with his tantric consort. It is based on a famous story that perhaps best captures the mood of Chakrasamvara practice.

According to the tale, Ghantapada began his spiritual career as a monk. He was living in meditation deep in the forest of a small kingdom when the local king requested him to come and live in the town, offering to build him an elegant temple and comfortable residence. Ghantapada declined the offer on the grounds that city life would not agree with his meditations, and replied that the forest had all the elegance and comfort he needed.

This infuriated the king, who decided to disgrace him. To this end the king sent a beautiful courtesan to visit Ghantapada in his forest hermitage and seduce him, thus causing him to break his monastic vow of celibacy. The woman failed, but Ghantapada fell in love with the prostitute's daughter. The two eventually became tantric partners, and the young lady took up residence with him in the forest.

Rumors of the two lovers drinking wine (another no-no for a fully ordained Buddhist monk) and engaging in intense sexual encounters became the talk of the town and further infuriated the king. He decided to go with his chief minister and a body of soldiers to the hermitage and personally punish the two lovers for disgracing his kingdom.

However, after the king had chided Ghantapada and the soldiers were about to seize him, Ghantapada kicked over his jug of wine, took his tantric partner in his arms, and sat in sexual union with her. The two then levitated off into the sky, from where they sang tantric songs down to the amazed royal contingent. The overturned jug of wine, meanwhile, turned out to be bottomless, and so much wine flowed forth from it that a great river formed, threatening to sweep away and drown the king and his men.

Perhaps needless to say, the king offered his humble apologies, asked to become a disciple, and all turned out well.

Such is the legend associated with the Ghantapada lineage of Chakrasamvara, famed in Tibet as *Demchok Tilbu Lha Nga,* or "Ghantapada's Five-Deity Mandala." It is somewhat paradoxical that Tibetan monks, who put so much emphasis upon monasticism and the celibate life, find such profound and long-lasting inspiration from the sexy life of Ghantapada. It has remained a top ten favorite with Tibetans for a thousand years, and its star is not showing any sign of diminishing. Indeed, I received the Ghantapada initiation from the Dalai Lama in the Kulu Valley some two decades ago, on a site where Ghanta himself was once said to have lived. Thousands of people attended the ceremony, an indication of its continuing popularity.

The Seventh wrote the poem for his principal disciple and Dharma heir, the Mongolian master Changkya Rolpai Dorjey, who is regarded as the third incarnation of the Changkya tulkus. The second had been the chief guru to the Manchu emperor and his family, and thus was one of the most powerful monks of Central Asia. Under the patronage of Emperor Chenlung, Changkya Rolpai Dorjey put together several enormous translation committees composed of hundreds of great lama scholars from the various regions of Central Asia, where Tibetan Buddhism prevailed, and oversaw the translation of many of the central Tibetan texts of the Gelukpa School into Manchu, Mongolian, and Chinese. Some ten thousand texts were translated into these three languages under his supervision during this period.

The Seventh Dalai Lama's poem is a classic in structure and tone. He begins it with verses dedicated to the general meditations that should be used to mature the mind prior to taking up the tantric trainings, and then goes on to the actual tantric methods. The preliminaries include subjects like the tremendous spiritual opportunities afforded by human rebirth; death and impermanence; the nature of karmic law; the shortcomings of attachment and importance of inner freedom; the three higher trainings of discipline, meditation, and wisdom; the transformative powers of universal love and compassion; and so forth.

Only when he has made clear the importance of the Sutrayana trainings does he address the actual subject of his poem, i.e., the stages of tantric experience on the Heruka Chakrasamvara path.

Readers will find the work to be an excellent introduction to the Second Dalai Lama's treatise on the Six Yogas of Niguma that follows in Chapter Three, for the *tummo,* or "inner fire" technology, from the Chakrasamvara is the source of the *tummo* teaching in the Six Yogas. Moreover, the generation stage yogas, with the mandala meditations and mantra recitations, that are to be accomplished as a prelude to engaging in the Six Yogas, which are all completion stage practices, are usually drawn from one of the three Chakrasamvara traditions, with the Ghantapada lineage being the most popular.

I originally read this work by the Seventh Dalai Lama back in 1978 with the very learned Geshey Tenpai Gyaltsen of Ganden Shartsey Monastery. Geshey-la was in the Tibetan hospital in Dharamsala at the time, recuperating from an illness, and kindly accepted my request that I visit him for a few hours every afternoon and read the Seventh Dalai Lama's collection of mystical songs and poems; I came to his bedside almost daily over the months to follow. My very dear friend Lobsang N. Tsonawa of the Tibetan Institute in Sarnath, who had just arrived in Dharamsala to work at the Tibetan Library, assisted me in the preparation of the English translation.

# The Seventh Dalai Lama's Text

Homage to Jey Rinpochey, a second Buddha,
Manifestation of Vajradhara, lord of all buddhas,
In whose body reside the awakened ones, past, present, and future,
As well as their retinues and buddhafields.

Homage to the feet of my own root guru,
Who is in real nature inseparably one
With Heruka Chakrasamvara, Male/Female in sexual union,
The wheel composed of all objects of knowledge,
Whose essence is great bliss clear as the autumn sky.

In the hands of one's spiritual masters
Lie the roots of every mystical experience.
All happiness and suffering from now until enlightenment
Come solely from relying upon them.

See the physical world as the guru's body;
Take sounds as the guru's teachings;
Mix thoughts and memories with his bliss and insight;
Rely on this practice, king of all paths.

Fortunate are they who meet with the doctrine
Of all-kind incomparable Tsongkhapa,

Who showed as precepts all sutras and tantras.
Fortunate indeed; an opportunity obtained but once.

Yet breath, like mist, is delicate;
And life, seemingly strong, is ever near to passing.
Quickly pluck the essence of Dharma,
For definite it is you will die at the hands of the great enemy Death.

Have not the three doors stood open to negativity?
Then the inconceivable misery of the lower realms
Certainly will fall upon you;
And, if still weak, you will not be able to bear them.

Some look, and see; in the innermost way they turn
To a *guru-deva*, an embodiment of Buddha, Dharma, and Sangha.
With attentive concentration they focus
On cultivating the white and dispersing the black.

Reveling in objects of greed and attachment
Is drinking poison mistaken for nectar.
The luxuries, securities, and comforts of the world
Are like dramas enjoyed in a dream.

No lasting happiness can be found
In any samsaric position,
And how foolish to sit complacent
In a hole filled with misery.

Turn the horse of the mind upward,
Rein him with the three higher trainings,
Strike him with the iron whip of fierce effort,
And cut unto the open road of liberation.

All beings, mothers who lovingly have nurtured us,
Are floundering in the seas of confusion.
The son who cares not for their anguish,
Are the waters of his heart not bitter?

Wholly discarding selfish thoughts,
Hold close the ways which better the world
And strive to live the six perfections,
Which yield buddhahood, ultimate benefit for all.

Sever the mind from chaotic wandering;
Fix it firmly on its object with mindfulness,
Without falling prey to agitation or dullness:
Train in meditation blissful and clear.

The manifold things we perceive
Are deceptive projections of deluded thought.
When we search for their ultimate essence,
Emptiness free of an essence appears.

The things that manifest also fade
And only footprints of names remain;
The other side of this is called dependent arising.
What else need be known?

Having first trained in these foundation practices,
Seek out a tantric master, embodiment of Buddha Vajradhara,
Lord of the Sphere Beneath None;
Gain the four ripening initiations
And enter into the mystic mandala.

The body transforms into a great vajra-mandala
And, in the inconceivable mansion of joyful repose,
The real deity—the subtle mind held between the kiss of the male
    and female drops—
Manifests as the blood-drinking Male/Female in Union.

The dakas and dakinis dance a blissful dance
In the mystic channels and secret drops;
Mundane perception is severed from consciousness
And all emanations become ultimately pure.

Visualize yourself as Heruka with Consort,
Luminous yet void, body empty,
Energy channels of three qualities vibrating within;
At your heart a Dharma wheel with eight petals

Bears the indestructible drop in the form of *HUM*
Between the sun of method and the moon of wisdom:
Mind firm on this, tremulous misconceptions are cut,
And the clear light, sheer as the autumn sky, arises.

The outer consort, in nature fire,
Melts the life-drops that course
Through the seventy-two thousand channels,
Bringing them into the central channel,
Giving rise to the four ineffable joys.

Outside, all sensory movement of mind and energy ceases;
Inside, mundane views, ignorance, and darkness disperse.
Thus, by yoga even sleep is transformed
Into the nature of Dharmakaya's clear light.

By cultivating these yogic methods,
We can in general see through all distorted appearances
And in particular know the body as dreamlike,
Thus building the dancing form of an endowed deity
And maintaining the according emanations.

By mentally reciting the secret mantras of the vajra dharmas
Of entering, resting, and dispersing energy at the heart
While controlling the life-drop made of five clear essences,
The knots of ignorance are easily untied.

The tip of the vajra is placed firmly in the lotus
And mind as the syllable *HUM* is brought into the
central channel;
One drinks and drinks the essence of nectars
And goes mad with innate joy unmoving.

By thus settling the mind in the subtle vajra letter
And bringing the drop to the four chakras and sensory gates,
One directly sees all aesthetic objects
Found throughout the three worlds.

Thus one opens the windows of the six miraculous powers,
Sees the faces of innumerable deities,
Masters the meanings of the words of the teachings,
And gains the delightful company of an immortal lover.

In the tip of the vajra between the eyebrows
The light of the sun, moon, and stars swirls in the drop.
By bringing mind and energy to that point,
The white bodhi-mind is forever increased.

Then with the fine brush of samadhi paint
A masterpiece incorporating all beauties of life;
One gains the aid of a fully qualified consort
And one's experience of the blisses blazes higher and higher.

Mind fixed on the bliss and mudra of the consort,
A rain of innate joy pours down.
Again and again seducing the beautiful one,
Symbol of the mind embracing reality itself,
One melts into the sphere of spontaneous bliss.

From the center of the navel chakra where meet the three
    energy channels
Shine lights from white and red pyramids.
Looking through the nucleus of five drops therein,
The mind's nature is seen as five buddhas.

White and yellow energies shape into a vase
And the all-destroying fire rages.
The letters *AH* and *HAM* flare, fall, and vibrate,
Transporting one to the end of the primordial path of great bliss
    and wisdom combined.

Lights from the mystic fire flash into the hundred directions,
Summoning the blessings of buddhas boundless as space.
Once again the five natures of mind arise as sounds,
Releasing a rain of ambrosial knowledge.

The apparitions of people and things
Dissolve into light, and the waves
Of misconception are stilled.
No longer is the radiance of clear light obscured.
Even postmeditation mind maintains immaculate view.

In the sphere of semblant and innate *mahamudra*
Empty images appear as rainbows.
Flawless method emanates phantom circles,
Erecting the perfect mandala of deities and abodes.

The illusory body merges with clear light
Like clouds dissolving into space.
The fires of innate wisdom arise
And consume the seed of grasping for self.

This great union of the radiant vajra body
With the vast clear light of mind
Is called "the samadhi moving magnificently,"
A stage not touched by the ordinary intellect.

This consciousness, purified of all transient stains,
Gazes clearly and directly at the sphere of truth.
Like a magic gem it manifests the Beatific Body
Of Heruka Chakrasamvara for the sake of others
And sends out countless emanations,
Each in accord with the needs of the world.

Thus, in this age of short lifespan
Buddhahood is swiftly and easily attained
By turning lust for sensual objects
Towards the friend who instills great bliss.

Think, "By studying, contemplating, and meditating
Upon the flawless Vajrayana teachings,
The highest path, the esoteric way of all tantric adepts of the past,
May I in this very lifetime attain with ease
That point most peerless and supreme.

And if in this life ultimate power is not found,
At my death may the dakas and dakinis protect me
And lead me to the rainbow palace of Vajrayogini
In the Pure Land Kajou Shing, there to enjoy clouds of
    transcendent offerings.

May I and all practitioners of this tantra
Soon complete the esoteric path of secrets
And, within ourselves ever perfecting the practices
Of the sutras and tantras taught by the Buddha,
May we master this mysterious way.

Until then, may the mighty dakas and dakinis
Who dwell in the twenty-four Heruka grounds
Care for us in every time and situation
As a mother watches over her only child."

The (Seventh Dalai Lama's) Colophon: The great Changkya Rinpochey, a supreme illuminator of the Dharma, a master of unsurpassed knowledge and wisdom, wrote to me with the request that I compose a spiritual song, easy to comprehend and that would express the essence of the two stages of Tantric practice in accordance with the dakini visions of the Indian mahasiddha Ghantapada and the five completion stage yogas lineage of his (Ghantapada's) Heruka Chakrasamvara lineage. In response I, the Buddhist monk Kalzang Gyatso, wrote this song entitled "The Essence of All-Beneficial Dakini Nectars."

## CHAPTER THREE:

# The Second Dalai Lama's
### *Treatise on the Six Yogas of Niguma*[104]

GYALWA GENDUN GYATSO (1475-1542)

NIGUMA

# Translator's Preamble

As we saw in Chapter One, Buddha taught a large number of tantric systems, each of which is a complete system of meditation and practice in and of itself. In general these are divided into four classes, with Anuttarayoga Tantra being regarded as the highest class.

In the early centuries of the Indian Buddhist experience these various tantric systems were transmitted individually and were kept as completely unique and separate traditions. By the eighth and ninth centuries, however, a number of "cross-fertilized" systems emerged. These systems took yogic elements from a number of different tantric transmissions and put them together in revised structures intended for easy practice.

Perhaps the two most famous of these "cross-fertilized" systems in Tibet were the Six Yogas of Naropa and the Six Yogas of Niguma. Both of these lineages came through Naropa, although the latter was further developed and refined by Naropa's female disciple Niguma. Today Tibetan sects like the Karma Kagyu often use a blend of these two as the basis of the three-year three-month meditation retreat.

The names of the actual six yogas in the two systems is similar, with one major difference. The Naropa system lists the six as follows: (1) inner fire yoga, (2) illusory body yoga, (3) clear light yoga, (4) bardo yoga, (5) consciousness transference yoga, and (6) forceful entry yoga. Interested readers can learn more about these from my two books on the Naropa system: *The Six Yogas of Naropa* (Ithaca, N.Y.:

Snow Lion Publications, 2005) and *The Practice of the Six Yogas of Naropa* (Ithaca, N.Y.: Snow Lion Publications, 2006). The former of the two discusses in some depth the particular sources of each of the six yogas, and how they function as a cohesive whole.

The sixth yoga in the Naropa system, known as "forceful entry," is a highly esoteric method for projecting consciousness out of the body and directing it into the body of a recently deceased person, as a method of reviving and rejuvenating him/her. The Niguma system does not incorporate this yoga, and instead replaces it with dream yoga. Thus the list of the six becomes: (1) inner fire yoga, (2) illusory body yoga, (3) clear light yoga, (4) dream yoga, (5) bardo yoga, and (6) consciousness transference yoga. The meaning of each of these terms, as well as the meditations and yogic applications associated with them, is made clear in the Second Dalai Lama's treatise.

Thus "dream yoga" appears in Niguma's list, but not in Naropa's. That said, in fact the Naropa system also has dream yoga, but not in as elaborate a manner as the Niguma transmission. In the Naropa system it is instead classified as one of the "illusory body" yogas. The idea is that one accomplishes the power of conscious or lucid dreaming by first becoming aware of the illusory nature of all experience during the waking state, and then maintaining this "awareness of objects as being illusory" into the dream state. This is the logic for teaching it under the "illusory body" category.

Although both of these "Six Yogas" traditions shared or passed through some of the same gurus in ninth- and tenth-century India, and also have much the same language and structure, they came to Tibet in separate lines. Moreover, their essential teachings were translated from Sanskrit into Tibetan by different masters, giving each of them something of a unique flavor. The transmission of the Six Yogas of Naropa was imported and translated into Tibetan by Marpa Lotsawa, who received them directly from Naropa, while the transmission of the Six Yogas of Niguma was imported and translated by

Khyungpo Naljor a generation later, who received them directly from the Indian female mystic Niguma. The Marpa lineages eventually evolved into the the Dakpo Kagyu School, because of the monastery that Milarepa's disciple built at Dakpo in order to house them; the Khyungpo Naljor lineages evolved into the Shangpa Kagyu School.

Here it should be noted that the Dakpo Kagyu and Shangpa Kagyu Schools share the same word "Kagyu," or "Instruction Lineage," in their names, but in fact were separate and completely independent sects, at least in the early days of their history. Later the Dakpo Kagyu split into the famed "four older" and "eight younger" sub-sects because of the great distances between the monasteries and retreat hermitages established by the generations of lineage masters.

As for the Shangpa Kagyu, which held the Six Yogas of Niguma as its principal doctrine, its lack of administrative infrastructure caused it to slowly become absorbed by the other schools. It no longer exists as a separate entity, and instead today its lineages are transmitted mainly preserved within the Gelukpa and also the Dakpo Kagyu Schools.

As was said earlier, these "Six Yogas" systems are fusions of various elements extracted from various Buddhist tantras. The Second Dalai Lama gives the source of the six in the Niguma system as follows:

> The body practice is Hevajra,
> Speech is Mahamaya,
> Mind is Heruka Chakrasamvara,
> Activity is Vajrabhairava (Yamantaka),
> And the essential nature is Guhyasamaja.
> These are the methods taught
> For the sake of future generations. . . .
>
> The yogi who expresses respect in this system
> Should be taught these five tantric methods.

In other words, the Niguma system blends elements from five Buddhist tantras: Hevajra, Mahamaya, Heruka Chakrasamvara, Yamantaka, and Guhyasamaja. As the Second Dalai Lama then goes on to explain, it is good to get initiation into all five tantric systems as a preliminary to engaging in the Six Yogas.

As said earlier, every Buddhist tantra is symbolized by a mandala, as well as a principal mandala deity, or buddha form. These five Buddhist tantras therefore each has its own mandala and principal deity. Often the Niguma system is artistically symbolized by a thangka in which these five Buddha forms appear. Recently when teaching in Ulaanbaatar I discovered one such representation. Made as a silk applique thangka, it depicts the five tantric systems from which the Niguma yogas are drawn. (Of note to art fans, Tibetans and Mongolians alike consider applique thangkas as being higher art forms than their painted counterparts.)

Of note, the Second Dalai Lama also wrote a brief commentary to the Six Yogas of Naropa. However, it is not as passionate or exciting as his Niguma commentary, largely because of his background. He had been born into a Shangpa Kagyu family, and thus received training in the Niguma yogas from a young age. His autobiography states that he first received the five Niguma initiations when only six years old, and began the practice at the age of eight. Moreover, his father was the head of the Shangpa Kagyu School in Tsang, as much as this school was sufficiently organized to have a head. One of the main duties of his father in this regard was to oversee the three- and six-year meditation retreats of yogis engaged in the Niguma trainings, and he spent much of his time wandering around to the remote mountain caves and hermitages where the retreatants under his supervision lived. He usually took his young son with him, and the two frequently stopped in these retreat hermitages for prolonged periods of time. Thus from childhood the Second Dalai Lama became deeply involved with the Niguma practice.

As readers familiar with Tibetan culture will know, the boy was not at that time regarded as a reincarnate lama, nor was the name "Dalai Lama" in use.

Lama Tsongkhapa had not included the Tibetan secular tradition of reincarnate lamas in his newly established Gelukpa School, probably because the tradition contradicts the pure *vinaya*, or Buddhist monastic code. According to this code, a monk should only possess a very small and very particular number of possessions, such as robes, sleeping roll, eating bowl, water filter, walking staff, and so forth. Any material wealth above and beyond those on this list of allowed possessions that were offered to him on a given day should be distributed, and thus disposed of, by the end of the day. On his death his possessions should all without exception be distributed among his monastic community.

However, in Tsongkhapa's time several of the older schools had developed a tradition in which a famous monk could establish a *labrang*, or "lama estate," for himself, thus accumulating and retaining for himself whatever wealth he accrued. On the monk's passing, part of the accumulated liquid assets would be distributed among his related monastic community, with the request for prayers for the lama's quick return, i.e., reincarnation. The remaining part of the liquid assets would then be used to establish a committee to search for a child to be identified as the official reincarnation, and then later also used to support the boy in his education until he became mature.

At the time of the Second Dalai Lama's birth this *tulku*, or "reincarnate lama," tradition had not yet been accepted among the Gelukpa. However, as a young child the Second clearly remembered his previous life as the First Dalai Lama, and frequently spoke of these memories when only two and three years old. Later when his father took him to Tashilhunpo, the monastery that had been established by the First, the boy addressed all the old monks by their correct names, even though he had not met any of them in his young life.

His behavior was so convincing that the Tashilhunpo elders decided to break the taboo on *tulkus*, and asked his father for permission to enthrone him as the officially recognized reincarnation. Later, after the boy moved to Lhasa for higher training in Drepung Loseling, and also completed his studies and retreats, the king of the Lhasa region had a *labrang*, or "lama estate," built for him in Drepung. This became known as the Ganden Potrang, or "Palace of Pure Joy," and is still in Drepung today.

At the time the Second Dalai Lama was known by the name Jey Tamchey Khyenpa, or "All-Knowing Master." This name had been given to the First Dalai Lama by his Jonangpa guru, Bodong Chokley Namgyal, after a series of initiations and teachings in which the young First Dalai Lama deeply impressed the elderly Bodong with his great intelligence and wisdom. "Jey" simply means "master" or "chief," "Tamchey Khyenpa" literally means "all-knowing," and Bodong gave the name as a prophecy that the First Dalai Lama would fully accomplish the Buddhist path. The First became known by this name for the remainder of his life. References to him in historical and biographical writings of the period generally use it, rather than his ordination name, Gendun Drubpa.

Thus when the Second Dalai Lama became enthroned as the First's official reincarnation, the name Jey Tamchey Khyenpa immediately came into popular usage.

As for the story of how "Jey Tamchey Khyenpa" became "the Dalai Lama," we will leave that for the chapter in which I include a text by the Third Dalai Lama, for it was during his lifetime that the epithet "Dalai Lama" came into usage.

I originally studied the Second Dalai Lama's Niguma text with my teachers Doboom Tulku and Khamtrul Yeshe Dorjey Tulku, and prepared the translation in accordance with their commentaries.

# The Second Dalai Lama's Text

Homage always to the lotus feet of the holy guru.

Homage to the holy Guru Heruka Chakrasamvara,
The wheel of all objects of knowledge bound in the nature
    of great bliss
Emanating as the ecstatic dance of a tantric hero
Skilled in the act of union with the beautiful dakini.

Homage to the teachers of the lineage:
Niguma, Queen of the dakinis, whose nature is illusory integration;
The yogi Khyungpo Naljor, he possessed of eight powers;
And all those upholding the Dakini's transmission.

And homage from the depths of my heart
To Lama Tsongkhapa, he famed as Lobzang Drakpa,
Incarnation of Manjushri, the Bodhisattva of Wisdom
Manifest as a human upholding the robes of a monk.
And homage also to his great disciples.

O dakas and dakinis of the three worlds
Who abide in the twenty-four mystic sites
And guard yogis as a parent an only child:
I beseech you, come to this place now,

Together with the instant protector Mahakala,
And release your magical energies
That destroy all hindrances and obstacles.

Herein I shall explain the renowned oral transmission
Known as the Six Yogas of Niguma,
An ultimately profound path traveled by all mahasiddhas,
The heart essence of all the Buddhist tantras.

Firstly prepare the mind through the trainings
Of the path of three perspectives of motivation;
Then receive the initiations that ripen the mind.
Guarding the tantric commitments well,
Enter the path for accomplishing
Buddhahood in one short lifetime.
O fortunate one wishing to gain quick enlightenment,
Listen well to this advice.

The lineage of this profound transmission, known as the Six Yogas of Niguma, was originally brought to Tibet by the mighty yogi Khyungpo Naljor, who received it directly from Niguma. Niguma herself had received the transmission from the mahasiddha Naropa.

A brief account of the life of Khyungpo Naljor is found in his own writings in verse form. This account is as follows.

I, the insignificant monk Khyungpo Naljor,
Was born in the exalted Khyungpo family
In Nyemo Ramang of the Gangkarda area.
My father was Kungyal Gyaltak
And my mother Goja Tashi Kyi.

At the time I entered my mother's womb
My parents and also the people of the area
Gained signs of prosperity and happiness.
When I emerged from my mother's womb in the Tiger Year,
The Indian mahasiddha Amogha visited our house
And made the following prophecy.

"This child is a special incarnation.
One day he will travel to India,
Where he will gather the essential teachings
Of all the panditas and mahasiddhas
And help mankind to ripen and mature.
Emanating in countless forms,
He will train many disciples.

"He will teach the essential Mahayana Dharma,
Which is free from all extremes,
And into the ten directions will release
The lion's roar of the secret Vajrayana
Of bliss and emptiness inseparable.

"His body is in nature Heruka Chakrasamvara;
His speech the nature of Mahamaya;
His mind is the mighty Hevajra;
His place of emanation Guhyasamaja;
And his secret place Yamantaka.

"Yet although within his body are arranged
These five mystic mandalas,
He appears in the form of an ordinary human
In order to guide trainees to realization

And will emanate as a myriad of tantric divinities
To inspire the difficult-to-train practitioners.

"He will live for a hundred and fifty years
And at the end of his life will reveal
Numerous miraculous signs and omens.
After passing away he will transmigrate
To Sukhavati, Pure Land of Bliss,
Which is praised by all buddhas as supreme.

"From there, as a fully accomplished buddha
He will continue to turn the Mahayana wheel of Dharma.
In future generations those with faith in him
With the good fortune to practice his teachings
No doubt will meet with him in Sukhavati."

Having spoken these words the guru
Mahasiddha Amogha rose into the sky
And flew back to India.
This prophecy was revealed (to me)
By my parents when I was in my fifth year.

By the age of ten I had mastered
Reading, writing, and calculations.
Thereafter, due to the dispositions
Of my parents, I entered into study
Of the Bon tradition
And especially their teachings
Of Dzogchen, the Great Perfection;
And also Mahamudra, the Great Seal.

Then, taking a pouch of gold dust with me
And with no thought of risk to my life,
At great personal difficulty I journeyed
Seven times to India and Nepal.
Here I consulted with a hundred and fifty Indian sages
As well as with fifty mahasiddhas.

Of these, I adopted four as my root teachers.
One of these was Niguma, a second Wisdom Dakini
Who was in direct communion with Vajradhara,
The sixth-stage Beatific Form of Buddha.
Pleasing her with my enthusiasm,
I received her ultimately profound teachings.

In this way all my doubts were dispelled,
And by engaging in single-pointed practice
I gained realization of the two *siddhis*,
Conventional and supreme.

Thus, as is said here, the mighty yogi Khyungpo Naljor, who gained
both conventional and supreme realizations and actualized inconceivable spiritual liberation, visited the holy lands of India and Nepal
seven times, taking with him five hundred measures of gold. Here he
traveled throughout the ten directions in search of a teacher who had
gained final realization and had achieved direct communion with the
Enlightened Ones. All the panditas and mahasiddhas whom he met
unanimously advised him to try to meet Niguma, a female disciple
of Mahasiddha Naropa. Niguma, they told him, had achieved the
three pure stages and had the ability to communicate with Buddha
Vajradhara at will.

"Where does Niguma live?" he asked.

They answered, "If one's perception is pure, one can see her anywhere, whereas if one's perception is not pure, she simply cannot be found; for she dwells on the pure stages and has achieved the holy rainbow body. However, when the dakinis gather to make tantric feasts in the great cemetery of the Sosaling Forest, she sometimes physically appears."

Merely on hearing Niguma's name tears came to Khyungpo Naljor's eyes and every hair on his body trembled with excitement. He left immediately for the Sosaling Cemetery, reciting the Namo Buddhaya mantra of Mahakala as he went.

Eventually he arrived in the Sosaling Cemetery. Here he immediately had a vision of a dark-brown dakini. She was dancing above him in the sky at the height of seven *tala* trees. Adorned in ornaments of human bones and holding a *khatvanga* (trident) and human skull, she was dancing in all directions, and first appeared as one figure, then as many, and then again as but one.

Khyungpo Naljor thought to himself, "Surely this is Niguma," and he prostrated to her, circumambulated, and requested her to give him her perfect teachings.

The Dakini looked at him ferociously and replied, "I am a flesh-eating demoness. When my retinue arrives you will be in great danger. They will surely devour you. You must quickly flee."

Again Khyungpo Naljor prostrated, circumambulated, and requested to be given tantric teachings. The Dakini retorted, "To receive the Mahayana tantric teachings requires a great deal of gold. With gold, however, it can be done."

Khyungpo Naljor offered her the five hundred measures of gold dust that he had brought with him. To his surprise, although the Dakini accepted the gold she immediately threw it into the forest.

Khyungpo Naljor thought to himself, "Certainly this is the Dakini herself, for she discards such a quantity of gold without remorse."

The Dakini then cast a glance toward the heavens and pronounced the syllable *HRIK*. Instantly countless dakinis appeared in the sky.

Some erected three-level mandala palaces; others prepared mandalas of colored powders; and others collected the requisites of a tantric feast.

On the evening of the full moon the Dakini gave him the initiations of the illusory body and dream yoga transmissions. Then by means of the Dakini's magical ability, he was levitated into the sky, and found himself sitting on a small mound of gold dust with a host of dakinis circling in the sky above him. Four rivers of gold flowed down the mountain, one in each of the four directions.

Khyungpo was amazed: "Does this golden mountain actually exist in India, or is it merely a magical creation of the Dakini?"

The Dakini replied,

> All the things in samsaric existence
> That are colored by attachment and aversion
> Are to be seen as noninherently existent.
> Then all places are seen as a land of gold.

> When we meditate upon the illusionlike nature
> Of all the illusionlike phenomena,
> We attain illusionlike buddhahood;
> This is achieved through the power of appreciation.

The Dakini then advised him, "Accept my blessings and watch your dreams carefully."

That night he dreamed that he traveled to the land of gods and demigods. An extremely large demigod appeared to him and instantly swallowed him. The Dakini appeared in the sky and admonished him not to awaken but to hold the dream clearly. This he did, and in his dream the Dakini gave him the initiations of the Six Yogas.

The Dakini informed him, "In all of India you are the only yogi ever to receive the complete instructions of the Six Yogas in a single session of sleep." After he woke up she gave him three transmissions of the Six Yogas, a transmission of *The Vajra Verses*,[105] *The Stages of the Illusory Path*,[106] the initiations of the five tantric systems (i.e., Chakrasamvara, Mahamaya, Hevajra, Guhyasamaja, and Yamantaka), numerous associated sadhanas and instructions, the initiations of the nine-deity mandala of Hevajra, and the thirteen-deity mandala of the Well-Armed One as well as transmissions of the tantric scriptures *The Tantra of Two Forms*,[107] *The Vajra Song*,[108] *The Samphuta Tantra*[109] and associated sadhanas, the oral traditions of the Well-Armed One and Kalachakra, the whispered transmission of the four suchnesses, the traditions of the white and red Vajrayoginis, the methods of removing obscurations with the four classes of tantras, the five levels of the Chakrasamvara completion stage techniques for controlling the mystic drops of genetic force, the activities of *The Tantra of the Diamond Sky Dancer*,[110] and so forth. In brief, the Wisdom Dakini taught him countless tantras, sadhanas, and oral traditions.

Concerning this tradition, the Dakini herself personally told Khyungpo, "With the exception of myself and the mahasiddha Ivawapa, there is nobody in India today who understands these initiations and transmissions. These should be passed in a one-to-one guru-disciple transmission for seven generations. Only after these seven generations should they be given openly."

In this way the dakini Niguma transmitted the complete instruction of the Six Yogas with the root and branch traditions to Khyungpo Naljor.

This then is the source of the lineage of the profound instruction known as the Six Yogas of Niguma that gives quick and easy enlightenment in one short lifetime.

As for the actual tradition itself, this will be explained under the two headings: the preliminary practices to be meditated upon, and upon which the actual practices rely; and, in reliance upon these preliminaries, how to actually meditate upon the Six Yogas themselves, or the actual practice.

## THE PRELIMINARIES

There are two types of preliminary trainings: the general (Sutrayana) preliminaries and the exclusive (Vajrayana) preliminaries.

### THE GENERAL PRELIMINARIES

The general preliminaries refer to the methods of spiritual training that are common to or shared by both the Sutrayana and the Vajrayana. These must be accomplished before entering into the practice of the Six Yogas of Niguma.

To quote *The Tantra of Two Forms*:

> Firstly accomplish the purification practices

And so on until,

> And then train in the Middle View of emptiness.

These are the preliminaries common to both Mahayana vehicles: the Prajnaparamitayana and the Vajrayana.

> The same advice is given in *The Vajra Verses*:
> Those who are ripened by the four initiations;
> Who possess confidence and enthusiasm in practice;
> Whose minds are prepared by the preliminary practices
> Of meditation upon impermanence and death,
> Renunciation, and the shortcomings of cyclic existence:
> They gain full buddhahood in as short a time
> As six months, a year, or at least this lifetime
> By means of this supreme tantric path.

As stated above, as a preliminary to this profound path one should gain experience in the trainings of the three scopes of motivation: (i) the initial scope, which includes trainings such as meditation upon the certainty of death and the uncertainty of the time of death; (ii) the intermediate scope, which involves methods that generate a sense of renunciation and disillusionment with samsaric indulgence and give birth to the wish for liberation from samsara, by means of such meditations as those upon the frustrating and painful nature of cyclic existence; and (iii) the highest scope of motivation, which, based on the above two preliminaries, aspires to highest enlightenment as a means of benefiting all sentient beings and, in order to accomplish this, enters into the altruistic bodhisattva ways, such as the six perfections. To enter the Vajrayana one must firstly accomplish these Hinayana and general Mahayana trainings.

The stages of the preliminary trainings for cultivating the mind have been described in detail by Jowo Atisha and his disciples in their writings on the tradition of practicing the three levels of methods whereby all aspects of the Buddha's teachings may be integrated into a single meditational sitting. These can be learned from Lama Tsongkhapa's two major treatises on the Lam Rim tradition, known as *The Great*[111] and *Small*[112] *Expositions on the Stages of the Spiritual Path*.

## The Exclusive Vajrayana Preliminaries

The exclusive Vairayana preliminaries will be presented under two headings: the necessity of receiving the initiations and the necessity of guarding the commitments and vows of the Tantric tradition.

### The Necessity of Receiving the Initiations

To quote *The Vajra Verses*:

> Ripen the mind with the initiations.

As stated here, in order to take up the practices of the Vajrayana one must first ripen one's stream of being by means of receiving the initiations. This is clearly expressed in *The Mark of Mahamudra*:[113]

Anyone wishing to practice this tradition
Should firstly gain the appropriate initiations.
Then one will certainly become
A proper vessel for the secret teachings.
With no initiation there is no attainment,
Just as pressing sand produces no oil.
When tantric teachings and instructions are given
Out of pride and with no initiation,
Both teacher and disciple after death
Will certainly fall into the hells,
Even if the common *siddhis* have been attained.
Therefore take every precaution
To ensure that the initiations are received.

This same point is stressed in all the tantric scriptures. Therefore
if one wishes to enter into practice of the two stages of the Vajrayana,
one must make every effort to receive the four complete initiations
into the appropriate mandala.

The specific initiations required in order to practice this particular tradition are given in *The Tantra of the Mystic Bond*:[114]

The correct explanation is as follows:
The body practice is Hevajra,
Speech is Mahamaya,
Mind is Heruka Chakrasamvara,
Activity is Vajrabhairava (Yamantaka),
And the essential nature is Guhyasamaja.
These are the methods taught
For the sake of future generations.

These stages of yogic techniques
Are all exclusively tantric.

The initiations bring together
These five essential mandalas.

The yogi who expresses respect in this system
Should be taught these five tantric methods.
These should be hidden from barbaric languages,
For they are Buddha's most secret teachings,
Tantric methods containing the heart of the essential precepts;
And they are not ordinary ascetic practices.

In the Shangpa Kagyu tradition it is taught that if possible one should receive initiation into all five of these tantric systems.

The reason for this is that the Six Yogas of Niguma and also the Six Yogas of Naropa contain completion stage practices that do not rely upon just one specific tantric system. To the contrary, both of these traditions gather together numerous factors from both the male and female tantric systems.

In the event that one cannot or does not wish to take all five of the above initiations, one should at least receive the initiation into the Heruka or Hevajra systems. In addition, one should receive the transmissions of each of the six yogas, for these plant mystic seeds for gaining rapid insight into the individual yogas.

This latter set of six transmissions (i.e., those initiations into each of the six completion stage yogas) do not involve the four levels of initiation as does a general Highest Yoga Tantra empowerment. However, I will not go into this here in detail. The subject can be learned from other writings.

## THE NECESSITY OF GUARDING THE VOWS AND COMMITMENTS

The fundamental text called *The Root Tantra of Chakrasamvara*[115] states,

The practitioner wishing to meditate on this system
Should always maintain the tantric precepts.

And also in *The Complete Union*:[116]

Not entering into the mandala,
Abandoning the tantric commitments,
And not understanding the secret teachings
Bring no attainment whatsoever,
No matter how much one may practice.

It is taught that one gains no attainment whatsoever through tantric endeavor when one has not received the prerequisite initiations into the mandala, does not maintain the tantric precepts, and does not know the secret instructions on the two stages of Vajrayana practice.

Therefore one should listen to the tantric teachings and should maintain the general tantric precepts. Especially, one should make every effort to avoid becoming stained by the root downfalls, even at personal risk to one's life.

## The Actual Practice

The methods of meditating upon the actual practice include two topics: how to train in the generation stage methods and how to train in the completion stage methods.

## How to Train in the Generation Stage Methods

The master Nagarjuna wrote,

Abiding well in the generation stage yogas
With the wish to accomplish the completion stage:

This was said by Buddha to be
The recommended approach to Vajrayana practice.

Here one should apply oneself to (one of the five tantric systems mentioned above, such as) the five-deity Heruka mandala, and mentally purify the bases of death, intermediate state, and rebirth, mentally transforming these into the three perfect buddha kayas (Dharmakaya, Sambhogakaya, and Nirmanakaya). This ripens one's stream of being for the practice of the completion stage methods for accomplishing the actual purification and transformation.

In brief, one should accomplish both coarse and subtle aspects of the generation stage yogas for transforming these three states into the three kayas.

Moreover, it is said that one should meditate upon as complex a mandala as possible for this purpose. The degree of complexity of the mandala meditated upon in the generation stage yogas affects the degree to which one will purify these three bases (death, intermediate state, and rebirth); and the more complex the mandala meditated upon, the more powerful becomes the potency to ripen one's continuum through the completion stage yogas.

## How to Train in the Completion Stage Methods

This involves two subjects: the preliminary of emptying oneself of negativities and the actual completion stage yogas.

### The Preliminary of Emptying Oneself of Negativities

The Vajra Verses states,

Three cycles of emptying through purification
By means of the condensed essence...

Elsewhere the same text says,

> Emptying by means of the purifying syllable *AH*,
> Emptying by purifying sickness and hindrances,
> And the three signs of purification. . .

Concerning the first of these, *A Treatise on the Steps in Practice*[117] states,

> Emptying by means of the purifying syllable *AH*
> Involves three meditations and three prayers.

The term "condensed essence" in the first quotation above is explained as follows. The essence of all teachings of Buddha is found in The Perfection of Wisdom Sutras. The most extensive version of these sutras is *The Perfection of Wisdom Sutra in One Hundred Thousand Verses*.[118] This is condensed into *The Sutra in Twenty-Five Thousand Verses*,[119] and is further condensed into *The Sutra in Eight Thousand Verses*.[120] This is in turn abbreviated into *The Condensed Sutra*.[121] Finally, the essential meaning of this sutra condenses into the singular syllable *AH*.

The scripture *In Praise of Manjushri's Holy Name*[122] says,

> Thus the accomplished buddhas
> Gain buddhahood from the syllable *AH*;
> Therefore *AH* is the supreme mantra sound.

Application of the mantra *AH* as a practice involves: (I) the preliminary of guru yoga, (II) the basic method, and (III) the three signs of purification.

*The Preliminary of Guru Yoga*

Upon one's head is a jewelled throne supported by eight lions. There, seated upon cushions of a lotus and a moon, is my personal guru in the form of a white Buddha Vajradhara. He has one face and two arms. In his right hand is a vajra and in his left a bell, which he holds at his heart. Adorned with the precious ornaments and clothed in the silken garments of a bodhisattva, he is embellished with all the marks and signs of perfection and is locked in sexual embrace with the consort Vajraishvaridhatu. The white letter OM marks the crown of his head, AH his throat, and HUM his heart.

Lights emanate from this syllable at his heart, summoning forth the lineage gurus and mandala divinities, surrounded by the buddhas and bodhisattvas, as well as the dakas and dakinis of the three worlds, and the Dharma protectors and wisdom guardians. These dissolve into the root guru.

*JAH HUM BAM HOH*: They unite and become nondual.

One then concentrates on the guru as an embodiment of the objects of refuge, and makes the following prayer:

> A form embodying all buddhas,
> In nature a holder of diamond knowledge,
> The root of the Three Jewels of Refuge:
> Homage to the holy root guru.

Reciting this verse three times, prostrate to the root guru, and visualize making offerings to him while maintaining awareness of how the guru is the supreme field of merit as indicated by both scriptural authority and reason. Perform the symbolic offering of the universe and mentally send forth outer, inner, secret, and suchness offerings. Then make the following prayer:

> O precious guru, send forth your inspiring blessings to
> help me cleanse and purify from within myself the seeds of
> all negative deeds, downfalls, and weakened commitments
> created since beginningless time. Send forth inspiring
> blessings to help me pacify and eliminate all diseases and
> hindrances. Send forth inspiring blessings to help me to
> generate quick insight into the stages and paths of practice.

This is repeated three times, whereupon lights emanate forth successively from the three mantric letters at the guru's three sites—white lights from his crown, red from his throat, and blue from his heart. They come to one's crown, throat, and heart, respectively, and dissolve into these sites, giving blessings of the guru's body, speech, and mind. All three lights then shine forth simultaneously, giving the three blessings at once.

In this way the four initiations are successively gained, and one's body, speech, and mind are purified of stains, together with their subtle instincts. One gains the *siddhis* of the three vajras.

The guru then dissolves into light, which comes above one's head and enters one's body via one's Brahma aperture. Contemplate that he then reappears as a white letter *AH*, in nature light, residing near one's Brahma aperture, with oneself visualized as the tantric divinity

To know this guru yoga technique in more detail, refer to Lama Tsongkhapa's commentary to the Six Yogas of Naropa.[123]

### The Basic Method

Visualize yourself as Heruka. A white triangular *dharmodaya* appears at the level of your eyebrows, the two upper points running toward your ears and the third toward the root of your tongue. The triangle is like a balloon filled with air. It appears in the nature of blissful wisdom and gives rise to ecstasy.

Meditating in this way, recite the syllables *AH AH*. From the syllable at one's crown white liquids rain forth, in nature the wisdom of blissful emptiness of all buddhas but in the form of white nectar. This fills one's body, absorbing the negativities, downfalls, and transgressions of body, speech, and mind. These leave one's body via one's pores in the form of muddy liquid, smoky waters, pus, blood, and so forth. Thus one's continuum is cleansed of all darkness. Meditate that one's mind becomes in nature the wisdom of bliss inseparably one with emptiness.

Here, the triangular *dharmodaya* at one's eyebrow level has the form of the birthplace of the mudra, and thus symbolizes the wisdom of innate great bliss, or higher tantric consciousness, and the letter *AH*, representing the birthless, noninherent nature of all phenomena, symbolizes emptiness as an object of consciousness. Furthermore, the *dharmodaya* has the shape of the consort's vagina, thus symbolizing innate wisdom, and its three sides represent the three doors of liberation, thus signifying emptiness as an object of wisdom. Therefore the meditation has the function of purifying one's stream of being of stains and shortcomings, which is the effect of contemplating emptiness.

In other commentaries to the system this purification is effected by means of performing the Vajrasattva meditation and mantric recitation. However, as many gurus of the past have said, there is no method of purification more profound than the meditation upon *AH* given above.

As for the emptiness meditation for purifying oneself of diseases and hindrances, this is done as follows. For diseases of vital energy disturbance, visualize that a stream of nectar the color of melted butter flows from an orange-colored letter *AH* and *dharmodaya*. For diseases of heat, visualize that a stream of camphorlike nectar flows forth from a white *AH* and *dharmodaya*. For diseases of cold, visualize that copperlike nectars flow forth from a red *AH* and *dharmodaya*.

To eliminate hindrances and evil spirits, meditate that from a black letter *AH* and a *dharmodaya* there emanates forth nectar in the form of countless tiny wrathful divinities.

In each of the above meditations on eliminating diseases, the illness takes the form of pus, blood, lymph, and so forth, and is driven out of the body. In the case of hindrances and evil spirits, these leave the body in the form of worms, maggots, scorpions, and so forth. One's body becomes as pure and clear as crystal.

## The Three Signs of Purification

Thirdly, as a sign of purification of negativity and obscurations, one dreams of flying through the sky. The sign of elimination of disease is that one dreams of blood falling, and of vomiting. The sign of purification of hindrances and evil spirits is that one dreams of many insects being driven out of one's body.

## The Actual Completion Stage Yogas

The actual path to be meditated upon will be explained under three headings: (I) the nature of the basis, (II) the stages of the path to be accomplished, and (III) the manner of actualizing the goal.

## The Nature of the Basis

Here the coarse and subtle levels of the individual and common natures of the body and mind are introduced. This is necessary because in the completion stage yogas one must generate experience by means of stimulating the points of the vajra body. To accomplish this one must know the points where pressure is to be applied, and also the manner of the application. Fundamental to this process is an understanding of the essential nature of the body and mind.

In the Six Yogas of Niguma the particular places and manner of application of stimulation are the same as in the Six Yogas of Naropa, and these can be learned in detail from Lama Tsongkhapa's commentary to Naropa's Six Yogas.

### The Stages of the Path

This involves two subjects: (A) the actual path to be accomplished and (B) the methods for amplifying the power of practice.

### The Actual Path to Be Accomplished

In the completion stage yogas this refers to the Six Yogas themselves. The six are as follows: (1) the path of methods for automatically igniting the fires of the inner fire; (2) the illusory body yoga, which gives liberation from attachment and aversion; (3) dream yoga, which automatically purifies mistaken perception; (4) clear light yoga, which automatically dispels mental darkness; (5) consciousness transference, which produces enlightenment without meditation; and (6) the bardo yoga, which produces a buddha's Sambhogakaya form.

### The Inner Fire Yoga

This involves two subjects: (a) the preliminary practice of establishing a sense of the empty body by means of meditating upon the inner fire and the bodily pressure points and (b) the actual inner fire yoga.

### The Preliminary of Establishing a Sense of the Empty Body

The practice begins with a guru yoga method. This proceeds as does the guru yoga technique explained earlier. After this, one meditates on Buddha Vajradhara and makes the request to him for blessings to quickly generate within one's continuum the samadhi of the mystic fire. As before, one meditates on taking the four initiations of samadhi.

Sit in the six-point fire posture. Expel any impure airs. Arise in the form of the holy Vajrayogini, body red in color, like heated copper, holding a curved knife in one's right hand and, in one's left, a skull-cup filled with blood. The inside of one's body, and even the inside of one's fingers, are empty like an inflated balloon. In fact, one's body is seen as insubstantial and immaterial, like a rainbow in the sky.

*The Actual Inner Fire Yoga*

The inner fire yoga involves six subjects, as follows: consuming the inner fire as nutriment; using it as clothing; using it as a resting place; riding it as a magic horse; directing it for liberation from hindering forces; and utilizing it to receive the most powerful initiations.

The most important of these is the first of the six: consuming the inner fire as nutriment. This refers to (i) the general and (ii) specialized ways of working with the three main energy channels and four main pressure points.

*The General Method*

Sit in the six-point fire posture as before and meditate upon yourself as the Yogini. Just below your navel are four fires, one in each of the four directions, approximately the size of a bird's egg. Breathe in air from the two nostrils and pull in lower air from below. Bring these together at the navel.

This causes the four fires to blaze forth fiercely with a reddish hue. Extremely hot, they fill one's body with a reddish flame and give rise to the blissful inner fire. The airs from above and below are thus held together in this mystic kiss for as long as is comfortable. When they can no longer be held, they should be released gently through the nostrils.

Now visualize the central energy channel, called *uma*. It runs straight up the center of the body just in front of the spine. The thickness of a wheat straw, its upper terminal comes to the point between the eyebrows and its lower terminal to a point slightly below the navel. To its right is the energy channel called *roma*, and to its left is *kyangma*. These connect into the central channel at the bottom terminal.

At the top they run into the right and left nostrils. At the inside of the central channel where they meet at the base is a sun disc the size of half a chick pea. Upon the sun disc is a red letter *RAM* blazing with the flames of inner fire. It is the size of a mere barley seed.

Below the navel is a triangular *dharmodaya*. The wide base is on the top and its tip points downward. Inside the *dharmodaya* is an air mandala shaped like a bow and very vibrant. As before, one pulls in the airs from above and below. The airs move from below, causing the mystic fires to blaze forth from the letter RAM. Red in color and hot to the touch, they rush up the central energy channel, giving rise to the experience of blissful inner fire. As before, hold the airs at the navel for as long as is comfortable and then release them slowly through the nostrils.

### The Specialized Method

Secondly, the special way of practicing the path, which relies upon manipulating the forces in the three channels and four energy points, will be taught under two headings: citing the textual sources of the teaching and the manner of implementing the instruction.

### The Textual Sources

*The Vajra Verses* states,

> Sitting in the correct posture,
> Visualize the three channels and four energy points
> With the mantric syllables *AH* and *HAM*.
> Through the blazing and falling
> One becomes adorned instantly by the four joys.

> Then by union with the special tantric wisdom one experiences
> The samsaric and nonsamsaric joys of four types.
> Through causing the moonlike energies to descend,
> Reversing their flow, and blending the vital energies,
> One becomes adorned by nonsamsaric gnosis.

## The Manner of Implementing the Instruction

This is taught under two headings: the path of relying upon one's own body and the path of relying upon the body of another.

## The Path of Relying upon One's Own Body

The first of these is in two sections: bringing the vital energies into the central channel by means of meditating upon the inner fire; and in reliance upon having brought the energies into the central channel, the stages of generating tantric experience.

## Bringing the Vital Energies into the Central Channel

The first of these involves three subjects: meditating upon the energy channels, meditating upon the mantric syllables, and meditating upon the vase-breathing technique.

### Meditating upon the energy channels

Begin by performing the guru yoga meditations as before. Then, as is said in *Elucidation of the Summary of the Five Stages*:[124]

> One must know four subjects:
> Body, time, object, and energy.

As said here, in order to engage in the practice one must first understand these four points.

The time for the meditation is at dawn, when the mind is clear, or in the evening, when bodily heat is strong. Otherwise, if this does not agree with one's metabolism, it is acceptable to meditate whenever one feels inspired to do so.

The physical posture is as follows. Sit with legs crossed, back straight, neck inclined slightly forward, tongue against the palate, eyes toward the tip of the nose, teeth and lips held as feels natural and relaxed, hands in the meditation gesture just below the navel, body supported by a meditation band, and so forth.

As for the breath, exhale all negative air. Avoid breathing either too deeply or shallowly by simply letting the breath flow in a relaxed manner.

The visualization then proceeds as follows. Envisioning oneself as Heruka with Consort, concentrate on the energy channels. As before, the central channel runs up the center of the body just in front of the spine, with *roma* to its right and *kyangma* to its left. Each of these three channels is approximately the thickness of a wheat straw. They connect below as explained earlier.

The four pressure points are visualized in the following manner. At the navel is the wheel of emanation, shaped like a triangular Sanskrit letter *EH*. It has sixty-four petals, is red in color, and opens upward. At the heart is the wheel of truth, with eight petals, shaped round like the Sanskrit letter *VAM*, white in color, opening downward. At the throat is the wheel of enjoyment, with sixteen petals, red in color, also shaped like the round Sanskrit letter *VAM*, its face opening upward. Finally, at one's crown is the wheel of great bliss, shaped like a triangular Sanskrit *EH*, multicolored, having thirty-two petals, its mouth opening downward. Meditate in this way. One visualizes the upper chakras only for a moment, and then shifts concentration below the heart (i.e., at the navel) for as long as possible, dedicating the main part of the session to this latter concentration.

In this one should recollect the advice of Mahasiddha Ivawapa: to maintain radiance and clarity in the visualization of the pressure points.

*Secondly, meditating upon the mantric syllables*
As in (the first technique above for) the meditation upon the inner fire, one visualizes the three energy channels and four pressure points. One then arranges the mantric syllables within these. The process is

explained in both *The Tantra of Two Forms* and *The Samphuta Tantra*, and is further elucidated in the writings of various mahasiddhas such as those of Krishnacharya.

There are both elaborate and condensed methods of performing the meditation. In the elaborate method one visualizes mantric syllables at the center of each of the pressure points as well as on each of the petals. This is explained in the oral tradition. In the condensed method the syllables are visualized only on the pressure points themselves. This is described in *The Explanatory Tantra*[125] and has also been recommended by many of the mahasiddhas. I shall explain the latter tradition.

How does the meditation proceed? One visualizes that at the center of the chakra at the navel, at the middle of the central energy channel, is a sun disc the size of half a chick pea. Upon this is the Sanskrit letter *AH*, red in color, its head pointing upward. In nature it is the inner fire, emanates forth bright light, and is the size of a mustard seed. Above it is a half-moon the size of a wheat kernel. Above this is a mystic drop and a tiny zig-zag flame.

At the center of the heart chakra at the middle of the central channel is a moon disc, a blue letter *HUM* upon it, its head pointing downward.

At the center of the throat chakra at the middle of the central channel is a moon disc, a white letter *HAM* upon it, its head pointing downward. White bodhi-mind substances fall from it like snow.

Each of these syllables is the size of a mustard seed, is exceedingly bright, and is crowned by a half-moon and a zig-zag of flame.

As well, at each of the chakras the side channels wrap themselves around the central channel and in this way form knots that obstruct the free flow of the vital energies from the side channels into the central one. The meditation upon the mantric syllables aims at opening these passages. One holds this visualization, identifying one's mind with the letter *AH* at the navel. Here it should be pointed out that the inner fire is both the foundation and central pillar of the path, and that the ultimate place of residence of the inner fire is the pressure point at the navel. Therefore, it is important to concentrate single-pointedly on the syllable AH at the navel and thus stimulate the inner fire and cause it to ignite.

The way to hold the visualization is to see the visualized mystic drop and one's own mind as entering into a unity. When this is done well, the visualized drop and the visualizing mind no longer appear as separate entities. By means of blending the two and causing them to become inseparable, one gains especially subtle tantric pride. Moreover, the syllables should be visualized as being as small as possible. The smaller they are, the more easy it becomes to control the vital energies. These letters are seen as being bright and in the nature of light, for this causes mental torpor to be cut off. Also, meditating on the half-moon and zig-zag of flame and on the bodhi-mind substance falling like snow, it becomes very easy to give rise to tantric bliss.

*Thirdly, the vase-breathing technique*
This is referred to in *The Vajra Verses* by the passage, "…controlling the vital energies and blending the airs. . . ."

When one breathes in, this is done not through the mouth but rather gently through the nostrils. The air is not expelled, but is directed to the navel. Meditate that the two side channels are filled with air. Swallow silently while pressing down with the abdominal muscles, visualizing that the airs dissolve into the syllable AH at the navel. Then draw in air through the two lower passages and cup these lower airs at the navel with the upper airs. Visualize them entering the central channel while slowly exhaling through the nostrils.

The vase-breathing exercise should be performed when the stomach is neither too full nor too empty. The best time for the meditation is after the food has been digested but has not yet left the stomach.

The exercise should be done without a break, although for not too prolonged a period of time per session.

Once competence in the practice has been established, when holding the upper and lower airs in the vase position visualize as before the chakras at the crown, throat, heart, and navel, together with the knots formed around them by the side channels and letters standing at their middle. Then visualize that the lower vital energy in the chakra at the sexual site rises and strikes against the letter AH at the central channel. This in turn causes the letters HAM, OM, and HUM at the crown, throat, and heart to melt and fall to the navel, where they dissolve into the letter AH, becoming inseparably one with it. One then fixes the mind single-pointedly on the mystic drop at the navel, which has the nature of innate bliss.

Through holding the mind here the subtle flame of inner fire above the AH flares up. When one meditates like this, the light becomes especially radiant, causing the bodhi-mind substances to melt, fall, and dissolve into the syllable HUM. We should meditate in this way, concentrating single-pointedly upon the syllable AH, until signs of stability arise.

This meditation upon generating the inner fire, first of the Six Yogas of Sister Niguma, acts as a foundation stone for the other five.

In this context the scripture *Elucidation of the Summary of the Five Stages* states,

> By controlling the vital energies
> Through the yoga of inner fire,
> One arrives at great bliss consciousness

In tantric systems such as Guhyasamaja and so forth the yogi applies himself to the yoga of vajra recitation and brings the vital energies to the heart, thus releasing the knots at the pressure points. Here this is accomplished through the yoga of inner fire.

By means of the inner fire and the use of a mudra one gains control of the vital energies and, just as at the time of death, causes all energies to dissolve into the indestructible drop at the heart, giving rise to the innate wisdom of great bliss as explained in systems such as Guhyasamaja.

And just as at death the clear light arises and one then enters into the bardo, by means of the inner fire yoga we are able to generate the finest substance of energy and mind, and then from this arise in the illusory body. Thus the inner fire yoga is fundamental to the illusory body yoga.

Similarly, dream yoga is accomplished by means of controlling the vital energies and by the power of conscious intent. Of these, the former is the most important. To gain this ability we must be able to hold the clear light of sleep and, at the time of awakening, be able to direct the vital energies into the central channel. As the function of the inner fire yoga is to bring the vital energies into the central channel for the first time, the heat yoga is also fundamental to the dream yoga.

The fourth of the six yogas is the clear light yoga, of which there are two levels: semblant and actual. In the Six Yogas the clear light comes after the illusory body. The Kagyu master Mokchokpa said,

In bringing the illusory body into the clear light
One must understand four points:
Method, time, form, and object.

As intimated here, by means of understanding these four points one can manifest clear light consciousness. This refers to the actual clear light; but for both semblant and actual clear light methods one must have control of the vital energies, and be able to bring the energies into the central channel and cause them to abide there and dissolve. As with the illusory body yoga, the function of the inner fire yoga is to give this control over the energies. Thus the heat yoga is fundamental to the clear light yoga.

The sixth yoga is that of the bardo, or intermediate state. There are three forms of this yoga respectively for practitioners of high, inter-mediate, and small capacity. As is explained later (in the section on the bardo yoga), to engage in the methods for practitioners of high-est and intermediate capacity we must have gained the ability to bring the energies into the central channel and cause them to abide and dis-solve. Thus the heat yoga is also instrumental here.

Furthermore, the yoga of consciousness transference also depends upon the heat yoga, for this former yoga depends upon the power of control over the vital energies. To have power over consciousness transference one must first be able to bring the energies into the cen-tral channel. Therefore the inner fire yoga is fundamental to the transference yoga.

In general, the inner fire yoga is the basis of all completion stage practices of Anuttarayoga Tantra giving rise to the full experience of the innate great bliss, for all the completion stage yogas depend upon bringing the energies into the central channel and melting the bodhi-mind substances, and this is the special function of the yoga of inner fire.

### Secondly, the Stages of Generating Tantric Experience

This has two phases: how to cultivate experience of the four empti-nesses and how to cultivate experience of the four joys.

### How to Cultivate Experience of the Four Emptinesses

From the time one is able to concentrate single-pointedly upon the *AH* at the navel for a sixth of a complete day (i.e., four hours) with-out wandering, then wherever we fix the mind the energies will col-lect. The reason is the inseparable nature of mind and subtle energy.

The sign of having brought the energies into the central channel is that when we concentrate on the breath it passes evenly through both nostrils. The sign of causing it to abide is that, after we breathe in, the air no longer moves in the nostrils. This may be learned in detail from other sources. Thirdly, the signs of causing it to dissolve are of both coarse and subtle levels.

The coarse signs are that the earth element dissolves into water, giving rise to a miragelike appearance; water dissolves into fire, giving a smokelike appearance; fire dissolves into air, producing a sparklike sign resembling that of fireflies; and air dissolves into consciousness, giving an appearance like a butterlamp.

The subtle signs are as follows: a subtle whiteness, like the light of a full moon in the autumn sky; a subtle redness, like sunlight pervading the sky; a heavy darkness, like that of the sky after dusk (when there is no moon); and the natural hue of the sky when it is free from moonlight, sunlight, and darkness. These relate to the states of appearance, increase, near attainment, and clear light which immediately follow the dissolution of the five gross elements and precede entrance into the bardo in the death of an ordinary person.

The process is given as follows in Khyungpo Naljor's famous *Instruction on the Three Bardos*,[126] which he bases on *The Tantra of the Wisdom Dance*[127] and *The Victorious Tantra of Nonduality*.[128]

> Firstly, earth dissolves into water, then water into fire, fire into air, air into consciousness, and consciousness into clear light. The sign of earth dissolving into water is that one's bodily strength fails; when water dissolves into fire one's bodily liquids begin to dry; fire dissolving into air is marked by a loss of bodily heat; and air into consciousness is shown by the ceasing of the breath. Finally, consciousness dissolves into clear light, giving rise to a wisdom vision in three phases: appearance, increase, and near attainment.

As said here, when death comes to an ordinary person, the outer elements first dissolve, giving rise to the outer signs as described above. After the five outer dissolutions occur, the three phases of appearance, increase, and near attainment arise and cause the clear light of death to manifest.

As for the inner signs that coincide with the dissolution of the elements, *The Victorious Tantra of Nonduality* states,

> First is the miragelike appearance that, although like a mirage, brings a vision of a five-colored light. The second is like moonlight, the third like sunlight, the fourth like darkness, the fifth like a cloudless sky beyond conceptual thought, a vision of emptiness with no center or limit.

Also, Mahasiddha Ivawapa said,

The first is a sign like seeing a wild animal reflected in water, the second like smoke, the third like fireflies at night, the fourth like a lamp, and the fifth like a cloudless sky without characteristics.

Thus, as said here, firstly earth dissolves into water, which gives rise to a miragelike vision, and so forth until air dissolves into consciousness. Then the subtle energies generated by the conceptual mind dissolve into appearance, giving rise to a vision like the moonlight in an autumn sky, and so forth, until the clear light of death itself arises, giving rise to a vision like that of a clear sky at dawn. When the clear light vision arises we should retain it by means of recollecting the meaning of the emptiness teaching.

### How to Cultivate Experience of the Four Joys

One ignites the special inner fire at the navel, causing the white bodhi-mind substance to melt from within the letter HAM in the crown chakra. It descends through the central channel. Coming from the crown to the throat chakra, it gives rise to joy; from the throat to the heart it gives rise to supreme joy; from the heart to the navel, to special joy; and from the navel to the tip of the jewel it gives rise to innately-born joy. This is the order of how they descend.

*The Vajra Garland*[129] states,

> To explain the order of arisal
> Of the four joys born from the descending substance,
> When the substance leaves the wheel of great bliss
> Joy is experienced.
> When it leaves the wheel of enjoyment
> Supreme joy is experienced.
> When it leaves the wheel of truth
> Special joy is born.
> And when it leaves the wheel of emanation
> One experiences innately-born joy.

When the substance melts, descends, and arrives at the base of the channel below the navel, it touches the sensory power inside the channel and gives rise to a special sensation. This sensory power is a principal condition that, when combined with control of the drop, gives rise to a special sensory consciousness of bliss. This in turn acts as a simultaneous condition that arises in the nature of great bliss as a mental consciousness. By combining this with a recollection of the view of emptiness one can generate great bliss in the nature of insight into the emptiness nature of mind. It is this that is to be cultivated and maintained. When the experience of innate bliss generated by melting the bodhi-mind in the central channel is the actual experience, then because the energy that normally causes the substance to be ejaculated has been dissolved, the substance will not be emitted, even if one does not apply the special exercises, or *yantras*. However, beginners should apply the meditations and exercises for reversing the substances if the innate bliss causes the energies to move, or there is a danger of ejaculation. Moreover, there is no threat of disease if one brings the substance directly back to the syllable *HAM* in the pressure point at the crown, even if one does not direct it through the other points of the body.

In general there are various ways of directing the inner fire, such as to the navel, the sexual site, inside, and outside the central channel, inside the body to the extremities of the skin, and so forth. Similarly, there are various ways of melting the mystic substances. One should know the stages of these techniques and the manner of their application.

When the drops to be controlled are not inside the central channel, one must make great efforts to bring the substances back to their original sites in the upper part of the body and to spread the sensations through the channels and points.

The stages of generating the four joys by means of reversing the drop and bringing it back up the channel are as given in *The Vajra Garland*:

> Joy at the wheel of emanation,
> Supreme joy at the wheel of truth,
> Special joy at the wheel of enjoyment,
> And innate joy at the wheel of bliss:
> These are the joys in the reversed process.

This explanation is in harmony with that given in *The Mark of Mahamudra*. In both these works it is said that each of the four blisses is experienced in four ways in dependance upon the moonlike substance, thus making sixteen joys. Moreover, when the white bodhi-mind substance (i.e., male drops) moves it also causes the sunlike red bodhi-mind substance (i.e., female drops) to follow, and this is experienced in three ways in each of the four chakras, thus constituting twelve joys.

As for the four downward-moving joys, it is said that the bliss experienced is greater than that of the upward-moving joys because of the nature of the innate bliss experienced. When the innate downward-moving joy is complete then the experience becomes stable and it is not possible for the substance to be ejaculated.

This is also stated in *The Mark of Mahamudra*:

> When stability is attained
> The substance will not be emitted.

The actual manner of maintaining the experience of the four emptinesses and four joys should be studied in detail in other texts. What I have said here is but a general description.

When the meditation session is complete and you wish to arise from the innate joy and clear light vision, contemplate that you gather together the most subtle aspects of mind and energy, and shape them into the form of Heruka. This Heruka then enters into the old aggregates.

This is what is meant by becoming skilled in the method of blending the results of practice with one's actual situation.

### *The Path of Relying upon a Karmamudra, or Body of Another Person*

*The Five Stages*[130] states,

> Of all the types of illusory phenomena,
> The illusory female is supreme;
> For she reveals with clarity
> The nature of the three appearances.

As said here, by relying upon a *karmamudra* as the external condition, the yogi on the high levels of the completion stage practices is led to great bliss.

Here one relies upon one of the four types of mudra, such as the lotuslike mudra who possesses all characteristics, has been matured by tantric initiation, and has a high degree of spiritual liberation. Such a consort is known as a *mudra*, or a Wisdom Lady. For this practice one must understand the oral teachings well and have complete control of the two principal vital energies.

One enters into sexual union with the mudra, which gives rise to the special innate bliss. This causes the vital energies to dissolve just as at the time of death, inducing the clear light of mind to arise with great strength.

This is to be performed not only at the time of controlling the life energies, but also at the time of the three higher activities.

However, this practice is extremely secret and it is not appropriate to say more here. Therefore I will not go into greater detail.

This completes the section on generating the inner fire by means of stimulating the three energy channels and four pressure points.

To use the inner fire as clothing, one performs the general meditation for generating the inner fire as before. Sit on a comfortable seat, pull the knees in against the chest, drop the throat against the knees, cross the hands over the kidneys, and bring the breath under control.

To use the heat as a resting place, tuck the left foot behind the right thigh and curl up like a sleeping dog. Then bring the vital energies under control.

Riding the heat as a magic horse is performed as follows. Sit with hands on the thighs and meditate on the body as being empty. Below the navel is a sun disc, Guru Amitayus sitting upon it. He is the size of a finger in height and the color of red-hot iron. From there the channel flows upward to one's crown. It is open at the top like an opened window, and in the sky above one can see countless buddhas and bodhisattvas. From their hearts there flow forth wisdom nectars. These nectars resemble melted butter and enter one's body via one's Brahma aperture. They rain down upon Guru Amitayus, causing him to release a blast of flame that fills one's body. As before, perform the breathing exercise and *yantra* of motion.

Then, whenever you go anywhere visualize that your two arms become wings. Under your armpits and on the soles of your feet visualize light-green wind goddesses. Whenever you move, visualize that these cause you to fly and that they carry you through the sky. Perform the vase breathing twenty-one times. This will help you to travel quickly, as though carried by a magic horse.

To receive the powerful initiations, visualize white Vajradhara and Consort upon your head. Offer the mandala symbolizing the universe and request them to bestow the four initiations. From the point of their sexual union flows forth bodhi-mind nectar. This enters your body via your Brahma aperture and descends. Contemplate that in this way the four initiations are attained.

Thus is complete my explanation of the inner fire yoga.

### The Illusory Body Yoga

*The Vajra Verses* states,

> The nontrue illusory body yoga is to be
> Applied by high, medium, and small practitioners
> With an inseparable sense of appreciation.
> One's own body and also all that appears
> Are to be seen as empty manifestations
> With no sense of mundane appearance.
> Take all forms as the form of the deity.
> This brings freedom from attachment and aversion
> And brings realization of the fourteen stages.

The illusory body yoga is explained under three headings: the reason it is taught after the inner fire yoga, recognizing the hidden illusory body, and some auxiliary practices mentioned in the texts of the gurus.

*The Reason for the Order*

There is a very important reason for following up the inner fire training with the illusory body yoga. By means of the inner fire yoga as the inner condition and the use of a mudra as the external condition we are enabled to collect and dissolve all the vital energies just as occurs at the time of death, giving rise to a clear light experience like that known at the time of death. Now, just as after the moment of death a bardo body is produced from the finest substances of energy and mind, in actual practice we wish to use the subtle energy which is the vehicle of clear light as the evolving cause and the mind itself as the simultaneously-acting cause in order to arise in the form of Heruka. We have already generated a facsimile of the clear light of death through means of dissolving the elements and energies. Therefore, applying the illusory body yoga to arise in the form of a deity is most appropriate at this time.

*Recognizing the Hidden Illusory Body*

This is dealt with under two headings: the actual practice and how this is explained by the gurus of the tradition.

*The Actual Practice*

The illusory body and clear light yogas in this system of the Six Yogas of Niguma actually come from the Tantra of Guhyasamaja as transmitted and elucidated by Arya Nagarjuna and his disciples Aryadeva, Chandrakirti, and so forth, and we should study them from these sources. The tradition of their instruction is as follows.

For as long as we are unable to cause the vital energies to enter the central channel, to abide, and to dissolve, we will be unable to generate the full experience of the samadhi of the stages of appearance, increase, and near attainment leading up to the experience of final mind isolation. It is from the subtle energy and consciousness produced from final mind isolation that the nature of the illusory body is produced.

The oral tradition of the Marpa system is based upon the scripture *Elucidation of the Summary of the Five Stages*:

> First is the miragelike appearance that,
> Although like a mirage,
> Brings vision of a five-colored light.
> The second is like moonlight, the third like sunlight,
>     and so forth.
> The (illusory body) is attained after all these have manifested.

Thus this passage indicates the three emptinesses of mind isolation from which the illusory body is produced.

Elsewhere the same text states,

> The illusory body is produced
> From subtle energy and mind,
> Together with appearances.

This indicates the actual nature of the illusory body. This nature is further clarified by the quotation from *The Vajra Verses* given above:

> The nontrue illusory body yoga is to be
> Applied by high, medium, and small practitioners. . .

and so forth.

Here the words "nontrue illusory body" are used, for the illusory body to be produced is the form of a tantric deity that, although it appears as real, is in fact insubstantial and immaterial.

The second line of the passage refers to the levels of practitioners. The third line then states, ". . . with an inseparable sense of appreciation." The meaning is that it is mandatory for all three types of trainees to rely upon a guru and, showing intense trust in him, make every effort to please him in the three ways and thus receive his oral instructions and blessings.

The same passage also states,

> One's own body and also all that appears
> Are to be seen as empty manifestations . . .
> Take all forms as the form of the deity.

This means that one should arise in the actual form of a deity. This is to be done not by mere imagination but by manifesting the most subtle aspects of energy and mind and then arising as a tantric form from these.

The text states, ". . . empty manifestations with no sense of mundane appearance." This refers again to the illusory body itself.

Elsewhere the same text states,

> Meditate on whatever appears
> As being of an illusory nature.
> Abide within the illusionlike samadhi
> And see everything in that way.

The first passage closes by saying,

> This brings freedom from attachment and aversion
> And brings realization of the fourteen stages.

The subtle energy and mind which reside at the heart as the indestructible drop represent the final basis of imputation for the sense of self. By clinging to this self as truly existent and inherently real, the distorted thoughts of attachment and aversion are born. By means of this meditation, which causes the vital energies to enter the central channel, to abide, and to dissolve, and then by experiencing the semblant clear light, we arise in the actual form of a tantric divinity with the impure illusory body. Then by means of causing this form to enter into the actual clear light we arise with the pure illusory body. Thus by means of the illusionlike samadhi we become free from the chains of delusions such as attachment and aversion, and attain the fourteenth stage of perfection, actualizing the goal of buddhahood in the form of Vajradhara, Holder of Diamond Knowledge.

### How This Is Explained by the Gurus of the Tradition

Khyungpo Naljor states in his *Instruction on the Three Bardos*, which comments on the meaning of *The Vajra Verses* quoted above,

> The generation and completion stage yogas, and in particular the dream and clear light yogas, are the methods for purifying the three bardo bodies, which are the bases to be purified by the yogi.

And also *The Tantra of the Wisdom Dance* says,

> The three bardo bodies are purified
> By the generation and completion stage yogas,
> Dream yoga, and also the clear light yogas.

Moreover, *The Tantra of Two Forms* states,

> Like illusion and dream:
> This is like the bardo experience.

The meaning is that the bardo body is the base to be purified, and that the means of purifying this involves the generation and completion stage yogas. Thus the ripened form is explained as being the present body purified by meditation upon oneself in the form of a deity. The dream body is the body of instincts purified by controlling the vital energies and winds through the oral tradition teachings. Thirdly, the bardo body is said to be a mental body purified by the illusory body yoga of arising in an illusory form from the clear light of the present path. Thus the passage in *The Tantra of Two Forms* which shows the hidden meaning of the Mother Tantra teaching on the subject seems to give the most clear presentation of the topic.

The yogi Mokchokpa writes,

> The mental body becomes the illusory body
> Free from all suffering.
> This is (cultivated by) the illusory samadhi.

The nature of the illusory samadhi of the Highest Yoga Tantra system is given in the following passage:

> The illusory body has three characteristics:
> Its branches and trunk are complete,
> Like an image reflected in a mirror;
> It pervades all objects of experience,
> Like the moon reflected in water;
> And, like a rainbow in the sky,
> It is produced by pure means,
> Such as peaceful mantras and so forth.

Thus the nature of the illusory body which exists as the form of a tantric divinity complete with trunk and limbs is shown by numerous examples such as a reflection in a mirror, the moon in water, and a rainbow in the sky.

Khyungpo Naljor and also Mokchokpa both explain the bardo and illusory bodies as being mental bodies. Mokchokpa writes,

> They are both bodies of light
> Formed of five clear radiances.

Thus the nature of the illusory body is said to be formed of the most subtle aspects of the five vital energies, of which the principal one is the life-sustaining energy. In systems such as the Tantra of Guhyasamaja one meditates upon collecting the five vital energies and bringing them into the drop, which is directed to the tip of the nose. Thus in the tantras and in the scriptures written by Nagarjuna and his disciples and in the oral tradition coming from them it is clearly stated that the evolutionary cause of the illusory body is constituted of the five vital energies, of which the main factor is the life-sustaining energy.

As for the illusory nature experienced during meditation, the above text relates,

> At the time of performing meditation (we work with)
> Dream consciousness, which creates a mental body.
> When purified by familiarity with its self-appearing nature
> This can be transformed into anything whatsoever.

> Also, by meditation upon the body of a deity, which is men-
> tally created,
> One produces the rainbowlike divine form
> Which is without flesh and blood.

Moreover the illusory dream body and the illusory body experienced in meditation are to be sealed by the four inner mudras. The above text continues,

The four mudras are of two types:
Inner and outer.
Purification by the inner mudra
At the confused time of sleep is like this:

When attachment or aversion arises in dreams,
Understand the illusion as dream consciousness.
When the mental body is accomplished,
This is the *samaya* of understanding the illusion.
The illusory seal on the instinctual body
Is the fulfillment of the illusory *samaya*.

The doctrine of *karmamudra*
Means purification in the art of seeing as an illusion
Everything from a worm to a buddha.
By this the connection is cut
Between consciousness and its objects.

When we can see as illusions
The self-appearing things of the world,
This is the foundation of all excellence.
As it fulfills all actions,
It is known as the *karmamudra*.

The *dharmamudra* is explained as follows:
There arises the experience of blissful clarity in dreams
And the experience of the bliss of radiant emptiness,
Which is understood as the nature of one's own mind.

Furthermore, the master Naropa himself said,

Blissful, radiant, and nonconceptual:
These are the three innate characteristics
Constituting the *dharmamudra*.

The *mahamudra* is explained as follows:
The illusory body itself unites inseparably
With bliss, radiance, and nonconceptuality.
Because these become an indivisible entity
The experience is known as *mahamudra*, the Great Seal.

And in the text *Instruction on the Three Blendings*[131] it is said,

The experience is one of bliss,
And the illusory meaning is understood.

This reference to the three blendings is given within the context of its being experienced in meditation. Although there are many scriptures on this subject by the mahasiddhas of old, the above comments are drawn from the works of the later masters of the six-yoga systems of the Naropa and Niguma traditions.

Now I will introduce the practice as it is applied by the three types of practitioners: (a) how the highest practitioner relies upon the guru, (b) how the medium practitioner is led by reciting a scriptural passage, and (c) how the small practitioner relies on samadhi.

### How the Highest Practitioner Relies upon the Guru

The disciple of highest qualification can accomplish the training merely by relying upon the guru. This involves two subjects: (i) taking prayer as the path of the guru and (ii) taking appearances as the path of nontrue existence.

(i) Here one performs the guru yoga meditation and makes three prayers: to generate renunciation, to accomplish the illusory body and dream yogas, and to accomplish clear light *mahamudra*. One makes these three prayers while meditating on the guru as an illusion.

(ii) One transforms the impure world and its inhabitants into the Heruka mandala and its deities, and meditates on their illusory nature.

### How the Medium Disciple Trains through Recitation

The disciple of medium qualification should adopt the approach taught in *The Sutra Requested by the Noble Achintyaprabhasa*, wherein it is said,

> "All dharmas are an illusion and a dream."
> Whoever recites and recollects these words
> Becomes free from worldly bonds
> And gains buddhahood in this lifetime.

As instructed here, one should constantly meditate on the illusory nature of all phenomena and recite this truth in words: "All dharmas are an illusion and a dream." While doing so one should also maintain the vision of oneself as a tantric deity.

Niguma herself said,

> If we do not know how to meditate
> On the illusory nature of whatever appears,
> How can we ever apply the opponent forces?
> How can we overcome negativities
> Merely by trying to avoid them?
> By recognizing their illusory nature,
> Liberation arises of itself.

Therefore we should take whatever appears and meditate on its illusory nature.

*How the Small Disciple Trains by Means of Samadhi*
The least qualified practitioner should rely upon staying on his meditation seat, avoiding the numerous activities (that high and medium practitioners can engage in) such as walking about, changing places of abode, being gregarious, associating with (people holding) wrong views, and so forth. As these obstruct the path of virtue in those of small capacity, they should avoid them and instead meditate formally as much as is possible.

*Some Auxiliary Practices*
One should constantly regard the sentient creatures of the six realms as being of an illusory nature. Visualizing oneself as the tantric deity, envision the triangular *dharmodaya* below the navel. It is white outside and red inside, and contains all sentient beings. These beings are insubstantial and in the nature of light. Pull up the air forcefully from below and press it against the *dharmodaya*. Contemplate how the living beings grasp at the noninherently-existent phenomena as truly existent and thus cause themselves to wander in the miserable realms of cyclic existence. Generate compassion for them, and then meditate how they too are like illusions and like dreams that, although appearing as real, have no true existence.

Secondly is the practice of transforming diseases and evil spirits into the illusory path. Meditate that the diseases and/or evil spirits are in nature the guru and meditational deity, and how they are noninherently real, like an illusion. Breathe in through the right nostril, meditating that these negative forces are pulled down into the *dharmodaya* and there are transformed. Apply the exercises and *yantras*, etc.

The six beneficial effects of the above transformational practices are: one gains greater control over the mystic drop, becoming able to retain it during meditation; one becomes more proficient in dream yoga; all sentient beings come within one's scope of meditation; the sentient beings are matured and liberated; all things naturally arise as illusions; and one becomes able to retain memory of and control over one's dreams.

This is but a general explanation of how to practice the illusory body yoga as condensed and arranged in brief from the writings of the great masters of the past.

This is the completion of my elucidation of the illusory body yoga.

### Dream Yoga, Which Dispels Mental Darkness

This will be explained under two headings: the reason why the dream yoga follows the illusory body yoga and the actual dream yoga instruction.

### The Reason for the Order

*The Vajra Verses* states,

> Whoever overpowers conceptual thought
> Should dedicate himself intensely to dream yoga,
> Which automatically purifies the darkness of confusion.
> The excellence gained by the illusory body training
> Then automatically arises, day and night.

This is the purpose for the order of these yogas. As said earlier, the main force used in the dream yoga is the power of control over the vital energies which operate during sleep. Moreover, in the tradition of blending sleep with the tantric yogas, (the clear light that arises when) going to sleep is linked to the Dharmakaya, the dream state to the Sambhogakaya, and waking up to the Nirmanakaya. Therefore in this context the sleep yoga becomes an auxiliary branch of the illusory body yoga.

*The Actual Dream Yoga Instruction*

As said above, the main practice in the dream yoga is the control of the vital energies. In particular, the principal instruction becomes retaining the clear light of sleep. Thus it becomes necessary to say something on the two subjects of dream yoga and clear light.

The manner of cultivating the power of intention in the dream yoga is explained in the oral tradition of the gurus under six headings: (a) recognizing dreams, (b) purifying them, (c) increasing dream objects, (d) emanating within the dream, (e) being aware of the objects of perception, and (f) meditating on their thatness.

(a) The first of these begins by meditating on guru yoga and making a prayer that one may be able to retain the dream and to practice the spiritual path within the context of the dream.

The method of training in retaining dreams is twofold: during the day practicing an appropriate mindfulness meditation and at night applying the forceful method of the oral instruction.

The first of these involves regarding all objects perceived during the daytime as things of a dream. One must think to oneself, "These objects are but dream experiences and I must recognize this dream as a dream."

Practicing this mindfulness during the day will have the effect that at night when a dream occurs one will automatically think, "This is but a dream experience." The stronger becomes the instinct of the training cultivated during the day, the stronger will become one's ability to recognize the dream state when asleep.

Secondly, the forceful method of the oral tradition to be applied at night is also twofold: the method that relies upon controlling the white and red drops and the method of the nine unfailing points.

In the former of these one begins by visualizing oneself as the tantric deity and, as in the practice of the inner fire explained earlier, envisions the energy channels. At the base of the central channel upon the navel chakra is the syllable *AH* and at the crown chakra the syllable *HAM*. From the *HAM* comes a small white drop and from the *AH* a red drop. Both are in the nature of light and are radiantly bright. They come to the heart and encircle it.

We then prepare to go to sleep, making a firm resolution that, "I must recognize dreams as dreams." We bring the drops (as one) to the throat chakra and again make the above resolution, visualizing as we go to sleep that the drops (as one) remain inside the central channel at the throat chakra.

The second forceful method is that of the nine unfailing points. The nine points are constituted of three categories: three are to do with the times, which are predawn, dawn, and sunrise; three are to do with postures, which are the vajra posture, squatting, and the lion posture; and three deal with visualizations to be performed.

The first of these visualizations is as follows. Visualizing oneself as the tantric deity, at the center of the inner channel at one's throat chakra is a moon disc, and upon it stands one's root guru in the form of Heruka, dark red in color, sexually embracing a consort resembling himself. He has one face and two arms. At his heart is a sun disc, and upon this stands a blue syllable *HUM*. This syllable is in the nature of light and is the size of a mustard seed. Lights from the letter *HUM* cause the guru as Heruka to become extremely radiant.

Lights then flood forth from the guru, illuminating myself as the deity. Fix the mind on this image single-pointedly and make the resolution as before.

The second visualization begins by dissolving the world and its inhabitants into oneself. One then dissolves into the guru at one's throat. The guru dissolves into the syllable *HUM* at his heart, and this dissolves into itself from the bottom upward and then into the half-moon above it, and then into the tiny zig-zag of flame. This then disappears like a rainbow melting into space. As before, make the firm resolution to recognize any dream as a dream.

The third visualization is as mentioned in the following passage from *The Ocean of Wisdom*:[132]

> Generated at the throat of all beings
> Is the syllable AM.

Inside the central channel at one's throat is a tiny red lotus having four petals. At its center stands a letter AM, red in color, exceedingly radiant and the size of a mustard seed.

Fix the mind on it and recollect the dream resolution as before. Here it is very important to prevent the mind from wandering and to set a strong resolve not to become lost in sleep and, whenever a dream arises, to recognize whatever arises in the mind as a dream. Should you wake up in the middle of the dream, do not open your eyes. Rather, draw up the lower energies and recollect the dream, trying to keep the dream going again. This helps in the practice of recognizing the dream state and strengthens the power of increasing the intensity of dreaming.

From the point in training when one can bring the energies into the central channel by means of stimulating the mystic fire as explained earlier, when we meditate on the above three visualization processes for retaining dreams the power of holding the dream state by means of controlling the vital energies gains a special strength. In addition, in reliance upon the visualizations one gains a special ability to recognize and retain the clear light of sleep.

(b) Secondly follows the process of purifying dreams. Here there are four techniques to be mastered.

The first of these is called "purifying the mind by means of the body." One sits at the peak of a large cliff. In the sky before you visualize that you as Heruka and Consort are in the air over the cliff, an arrow's length in height. You (as Heruka) then look over the cliff, and a great fear of heights wells up within you. Think to yourself, "This is a dream," and set the resolve as before to recognize any dream as a dream. The Heruka and Consort are then visualized as falling over the cliff into nothingness.

The second technique is called "purifying the body by means of the mind." Visualize that every pore of your body contains a blue letter *HUM*. The letters have the head inside the pores and are half submerged and half protruding. These radiate forth blue lights, which fill one's body and cause it to become empty and pure.

The third method is called "purification by means of Nairatmika, the Egoless One," consort of Hevajra. In the space before you visualize the dakini Nairatmika, the Egoless One. She is blue in color and holds a curved knife and skull-cup. One recites the mantra *OM AH SVAHA*, causing blue lights to radiate forth from her body.

They enter one's own body via one's sexual organ, and then the Egoless One herself enters one's body via the same passage. She melts into light, and one's body becomes filled with a bluish radiance. It then melts into light like a rainbow disappearing into the sky. All becomes pristine emptiness.

The fourth technique is called "purification by resolution." When we recognize that we are dreaming we should think, "My ordinary body is asleep in bed and this thing appearing to me now is but a dream body. All the things now appearing in my field of perception are but the manifestations of a dream."

Thinking in this way, determine to project yourself to a Pure Land such as Tushita or Sukhavati, where one can see the faces of the buddhas and bodhisattvas and can hear their sacred teachings; or else determine to take birth consciously in the impure world in order to work for the benefit of the living beings.

(c) To increase the dream objects, take the body that appears in the dream and manifest it as two. Then manifest the two as four, and so forth until eventually you have hundreds and thousands of bodies.

(d) To eliminate death, emanate in the form of Yamantaka. To overcome the effects of serpent spirits, emanate as Garuda. To subdue the kingly spirits, emanate as Hayagriva. Practice these and other such emanations. In brief, emanate as whatever tantric deity is appropriate to the need.

One can also emanate as the various coarse and subtle elements, changing from earth to water, water to fire, fire to air, and so forth, as described earlier.

(e) If in this way one can gain proficiency in the dream yoga, one will achieve the ability to understand the phenomenal world that appears to us, such as the ways of the sentient beings of the pure and impure worlds, the death and transmigration of living beings, and so forth. However, it would seem that this practice and this ability are applicable only in the context of a particular level of the training.

(f) When you recognize the dream state, meditate on yourself as Heruka with Consort. Send lights forth from the syllable *HUM* at your heart, causing the world to melt into the mandala palace and the beings of the world to dissolve into the visualized deities of the mandala. These then dissolve into Heruka and Consort, the Consort dissolves into Heruka, he into the *HUM* at his heart, and the *HUM* into itself from the bottom upward and eventually into the zig-zag of flame above. The flame then dissolves into unapprehendable nothingness. Hold the mind here on the view of emptiness.

There are four hindrances to the practice of dream yoga. The first is to not recognize a dream as a dream. The second is to wake up from the dream when the yoga is applied. The third is to be disturbed in the dream by confusing factors such as lust caused by the drop moving to the lower chakras. Finally, the fourth is to not experience any dreams.

The remedy to the first problem is to set a firm resolution before going to sleep to recognize any dream that arises. The remedy to the second is not to open one's eyes, even if one awakens, but instead to think over and recapture the dream that was occurring. The remedy to the third hindrance is to bring the mystic drop back up to the throat chakra. Finally, the remedy to the fourth problem is to set a firm determination to dream many dreams and to recognize them when they occur. Such are the teachings of the lineage gurus.

This completes my elucidation of the dream yoga.

### The Clear Light Yoga
*The Vajra Verses* states,

> Appreciation for the guru inspires blissful radiance,
> And by the glance of samsaric and nonsamsaric bliss
> Blissful radiance united with nonconceptual thought arises.
> Preliminaries, actual practice, and concluding procedures
>     adorn the path.

Here the first line shows the cause of clear light realization. The second line indicates the distinction between semblant and actual clear light, which is made on the basis of whether or not the innate bliss perceiving emptiness arises with or without an appearance of duality. The third line shows the nature of the path of clear light. Finally, the fourth line shows the stages of entering into the preliminaries, actual practice, and concluding procedures of the clear light yoga.

The reason for placing the clear light yoga as fourth in the order of the six yogas is given by the master Mokchokpa:

> The illusory body enters into the clear light.

In other tantric systems, such as Guhyasamaja, the clear light yoga is fourth of the five phases of the completion stage, coming after the illusory body yoga. The impure illusory body is purified by absorbing it in the clear light experience.

I would like to explain something about the clear light yoga according to the oral tradition.

Many gurus have said that there are two principal methods of generating the clear light realization. The first of these is accomplished by means of meditating upon the syllable *AH*; the second, by means of meditating upon the dakini Nairatmika, the Egoless One. However, neither of these is exclusive to the completion stage of Niguma's system of Highest Yoga Tantra.

According to the Niguma oral transmission, the exclusively Highest Yoga Tantra means of the completion stage is twofold: (i) generating clear light consciousness by means of relying upon the guru; and (ii) generating it by means of the mystic syllable *HUM*. I would like to say something about these two techniques.

Visualizing oneself as Heruka with Consort, one envisions the central channel running from the tip of the jewel below to the crown aperture above. Meditate that the inside of this channel is filled with bodhi-mind substances resembling falling snow. At one's heart is the chakra of the wheel of dharma, and upon it is one's own root guru in the form of a tiny drop, in color white tinged with red. At the center of this drop is a white letter *HUM*, the size of a mere mustard seed, radiating lights the color of quicksilver that in nature are innate bliss.

Fix the mind on this letter. Light then emanates forth from it with special strength, causing the world and its inhabitants to melt into light. These melt into oneself as Heruka with Consort. Heruka (and Consort) then also melt into light from the head downward and feet upward; this is absorbed into the mystic drop described above. The drop then melts into the syllable *HUM*, and this melts into itself from the bottom upward, eventually melting into the zig-zag of flame above. This then dissolves into nothingness. Fix the mind in the sphere of the unapprehendable for some time. This causes the vital energies to enter the central channel and to abide and dissolve, giving rise to the wisdom of clear light.

This meditation can be practiced from the time one becomes proficient in the yoga of directing the energies into the central channel, causing them to abide and dissolve, and thus giving rise to the innate bliss by means of stimulating the inner fire. Here it should be pointed out that the final place of concentration in the body for giving rise to the clear light is the heart chakra, and therefore concentrating on the heart has a greater effect than concentrating elsewhere. Moreover, the wisdom of innate great bliss that is produced here is generated with special strength by means of cultivating it in the nature of the experiences of the four emptinesses and the four joys, and at that time the view of emptiness becomes especially profound, pervading both consciousness and the objects of perception.

When one wishes to arise from the clear light meditation one should do so in the form of Heruka directly from the most subtle aspects of energy and mind. This Heruka then enters into the old aggregates in the manner of a Wisdom Being entering a Symbolic Being. Thereafter, all the objects that appear are seen as emptiness, the emptiness as bliss, and the bliss as the form of the tantric deity. In the postmeditation state the objects that appear to the mind should be sealed with the wisdom of great bliss generated during meditation. By contemplating in this way, the wisdom of great bliss generated in meditation takes on a special strength.

Now a few words on how to cultivate the clear light of sleep. This can be practiced from the time we become proficient in directing the energies into the central channel and causing them to abide and dissolve through meditation during the waking state. As soon as we begin to go to sleep we should meditate on the stages of dissolution of the coarse and subtle elements as described earlier and should direct the coarse vital energies into the central channel, giving rise to the experience of the four emptinesses and the four joys. Now, the chakra at the heart is the site of the drop generated during the time of sleep, and therefore during the waking state we should meditate on causing the energies to enter, abide, and dissolve here. This is done as described earlier. Then when we enter sleep we should retain the clear light experience, and if a dream begins to occur, we should arise in the form of Heruka from the finest substance of energy and mind. On waking up from sleep we should direct this to enter into the old aggregates.

As for the beneficial effects of the clear light yoga, as these are explained clearly in systems such as the Tantra of Guhyasamaja and are well known to everyone, I will not say more on them here.

Thus is complete my elucidation of the clear light yoga.

### The Yoga of Consciousness Transference

*The Vajra Verses* states,

> In the best transference there is
> Neither practitioner nor method.
> The medium and lesser trainees
> Avoid attachment and aversion;
> By means of joy, respect, and concentration
> They throw consciousness upward
> And adorn the practice with a prayer.

I would like to say something on the techniques referred to in this passage.

This oral instruction on the transference of consciousness is a special facet of Highest Yoga Tantra. It is taught in scriptures such as *The Samphuta Tantra*, which is a common explanatory tantra to both the Heruka and Hevajra systems. It is also elucidated in *The Tantra of the Diamond Sky Dancer* and *The Tantra of The Mystic Bond*, which are tantric scriptures exclusive to the Heruka system, as well as in *The Root Tantra of the Four Seats*[133] and in *The Instructions of Manjushri*.[134] The methods of transference are clearly elucidated in these texts and one should understand the important points in practice as explained by them. A more detailed understanding of the methods can be learned from Lama Tsongkhapa's *Extensive Commentary on Consciousness Transference.*[135]

The beneficial effects of the consciousness transference technique are mentioned in *The Tantra of the Diamond Sky Dancer:*

> Killing a Brahmin every day,
> Committing the five inexpiable karmas,
> And even stealing, cheating, and sexual abuse
> Are purifed by this path.
> One is no longer stained by evil
> And goes far beyond samsaric faults.

These are the beneficial effects of the practice as explained in *The Tantra of the Diamond Sky Dancer.* The same thing is said in *The Mystic Kiss*[136] and in *The Root Tantra of the Four Seats.* Therefore one should apply oneself to the methods with enthusiasm.

As for the actual application of the transference, *The Tantra of the Diamond Sky Dancer* relates,

> Perform transference when the time comes.
> To do so earlier is to kill a deity.
> As a result of killing a deity
> One will certainly burn in hell.
> Therefore the wise make effort
> To know the signs of death.

As said here, one should make observations for the signs of death and, when they occur, apply the longevity methods. When these do not work and the signs of death are not turned away, the time has come to apply the actual transference yogas.

*The Four Seats* relates,

> The best time to train in the transference yogas
> Is before one is afflicted with illness.

As advised above, it is best to apply the training techniques before becoming too weak with illness. Once severe illness has set in one will not be able to master the trainings, no matter how strong one's wish may be.

*The Tantra of the Diamond Sky Dancer* states,

> One ties the doors with the vase breathing
> And purifies the door of the central channel.

*The Four Seats* and *The Samphuta Tantra* say much the same thing. By means of the vase-breathing technique one causes the vital energies that operate in the doors of the senses to be withdrawn and directed into the central channel. This must be accomplished in order to effect the transference competently. One closes off eight of the nine paths of exit of consciousness, leaving open the Golden Passage, which is the Brahma aperture at the crown of the head. It is through this Golden Passage that one will make the transference to accomplish rebirth as a knowledge holder of the tantric path.

Four transference methods are taught in the oral tradition: the transference of Dharmakaya Thatness, the transference of the guru's blessings, the transference of a divinity's great union, and the transference of the Unfailing Dakini. From amongst these it is the transference of the Unfailing Dakini that most teachers recommend these days. Therefore I will explain this fourth method.

Begin by performing a guru yoga meditation as explained earlier. Offer strong prayers to be able to accomplish the transference yoga to whatever Pure Land is desired. Sitting in the vajra posture, with legs crossed and the hands placed on the thighs, visualize yourself as Heruka with Consort, the central energy channel running straight up the center of your body. This channel is the thickness of a wheat straw and runs from the Brahma aperture above to a point four finger-widths below the navel.

At the base of this channel is a triangular *dharmodaya*, white outside and red inside, with two of its points toward the two kidneys and the third point in the direction of the sexual organ.

Inside the lower aperture of the central channel is one's own mind in the form of a white letter *AH*, by nature radiance. It seems extremely light and delicate, as though it could be blown away by the slightest breeze. Hold the mind here for some time.

Above your head visualize either a white or red Vajrayogini. Her appearance is as described in the standard manuals. Perform the usual steps of summoning and absorbing the Wisdom Beings, invoking and receiving empowerment from the Initiation Deities, becoming crowned by the buddha who is the family lord, making offerings and prayers, and performing the mantric recitation. Consider that this visualized Vajrayogini is inseparably one with one's own root guru.

Then offer the following prayer:

> O Mother Yogini, please guide me to the Pure Land of the Dakinis, the Land of Bliss and Void. Meditational deity Vajrayogini, please guide me to the Dakini Pure Land of Bliss and Void. Holy Guru Vajrayogini, please guide me to the Dakini Pure Land of Bliss and Void. Buddha Vajra-yogini, please guide me to the Dakini Pure Land of Bliss and Void.

One now draws in the airs from above and below and directs them to the syllable *AH* previously described, pressing upon the *AH* from above and below. One meditates on the *AH* in this way while holding the airs in the vase technique.

Lights in the form of hooks emanate downward from the heart of the Vajrayogini visualized above one's head. They strike against the syllable AH and pull upward on it. Simultaneously make a movement with the lower spine, causing the lower airs to rise. Say the sound of the letter HIK, and visualize that the white syllable AH enters the central channel and shoots upward, coming to the Brahma aperture. Then bring the airs downward again, visualizing that the AH accompanies them downward and comes to rest at its former abode at the base of the channel. Repeat this process as many times as possible.

At the conclusion of the practice a stream of wisdom nectars issues forth from Vajrayogini's heart and dissolves into the syllable AH. As before, perform the vase-breathing exercise.

Repeat the process seven or twenty-one times.

It is well known that overly practicing the transference yoga can shorten one's lifespan. Consequently the vase-breathing technique together with the meditation upon the flowing nectars is applied as a means to prolong life.

The signs of progress in the practice are as follows: A blister forms on the crown of the head, an itch occurs above one's Brahma aperture, a drop of pus and blood is emitted from the Golden Passage, and so forth.

As said earlier, when the time comes for actual application of the transference method (i.e., at the time of death), one should abandon all attachment to possessions and material things.

Should one wish to perform the transference in conjunction with the use of mystical substances, this is described in the oral tradition as follows:

> One's own and a female's fluids
> Lead energy and mind upward.
> Salt opens the mouth of the channel
> And brain guards against hindrances.

As indicated here, one takes a small quantity of each of these substances, places them in one's palm and recites many mantras. The substance is then applied to the Brahma aperture. This has been taught by the gurus of old. This method is known as "transference by the power of intention." In it there is no need for transference by the power of the energies. However, even though this method produces rebirth in a Pure Land, there is no way to determine the specific Pure Land in which one will take rebirth.

One then meditates on and prays to the Vajrayogini above one's head. The visualization proceeds as before. The energies push up from below and one sounds the letter *HIK*. One's mind in the form of a white letter *AH* shoots up the central channel and out the Brahma aperture. It enters Vajrayogini via the passage of her sexual organ, which is red in color. The *AH* comes to her heart and dissolves into it. Meditate that the mind becomes one with the wisdom of bliss and void of Vajrayogini, inseparable in nature from the root guru. When we meditate in this way we fulfill all four points of the transference training.

Here I have not spoken about the fine details of the points in the oral tradition. These may be learned from other sources.

Thus ends my elucidation of the transference yoga.

### The Bardo Yoga

*The Vajra Verses* states,

> One should know the eighty stages of dissolution
> Such as form, sound, earth, water,
> Appearances, sensory experiences, and so on.

There are three ways to practice the bardo yoga. These are in the perspective of the capacity of the trainee: highest, medium, and small.

When an ordinary person dies the elements of his/her continuum dissolve into one another and the clear light of mind temporarily arises. The trainee of highest capacity takes this clear light of death and applies the yoga of final mind isolation from a tantric system such as Guhyasamaja. Then, instead of entering the bardo, he/she arises in the actual form of a tantric deity such as Heruka, embellished by all the signs of perfection. This is accomplished by means of the illusory body yoga, third of the completion stage yogas in systems such as the Tantra of Guhyasamaja. Here, mind becomes clear light and the vital energies that act as a vehicle of the clear light consciousness become the illusory body. This is the enlightenment to be gained by those who have no instincts of tantric practice from previous lives. It is called "mediocre enlightenment" (the best enlightenment being not that gained at death, but that gained in this lifetime, which is achieved by those with tantric instincts from previous lives).

The practitioner of medium capacity, because of the strength of having meditated in this lifetime, has the ability to bring the vital energies into the central channel and experience the signs of entering, abiding, and dissolving the energies. Then, when at the time of death the twenty-five coarse elements dissolve and the clear light of death arises, which is the foundation or mother clear light, he/she blends this with the son clear light, which is the clear light of the path of meditation. One generates the foundation clear light into the clear light of the path.

Lama Tsongkhapa states in his *Book of the Three Convictions*,[137]

> Because the foundation clear light of death is the mother clear light, in order to be able to blend it with the son clear light we should, during waking consciousness, be able to bring the vital energies into the central channel where they will abide and dissolve. Within this sphere we should meditate on the four emptinesses and especially upon the emptiness of all phenomena. If we can do this and also blend the two clear lights, even in times of deepest sleep,

then at the time of death we will be able to accomplish the practice competently.

In this training there are numerous levels of application in accordance with the level of insight of the trainee.

After the clear light vision passes and one enters the bardo, one should visualize oneself in the form of a tantric deity, even if one has already arisen in an ordinary bardo body. Here again there are many levels of practice in accordance with the level of the trainee.

Such are the trainings for practitioners of high and medium capacity. Now to say something about the training for practitioners of small capacity.

Firstly, they must gain familiarity with the methods for recognizing the bardo experience. Then, when the clear light of death arises, they should visualize that it is transformed into the clear light of the path. Consequently, when the bardo body arises, they are able to apply the bardo techniques to it. This has been taught by the gurus of old.

Thus is complete my elucidation of the bardo yoga.

### The Methods for Amplifying the Power of the Training

With the exception of the Tantra of Kalachakra, which contains the tradition of three cycles related to mental application, all other Highest Yoga Tantra systems must implement the special techniques for amplifying the power of practice in order to make the transition from one yogic level to the next.

This is necessary, for example, at the completion of the coarse and subtle phases of the generation stage yogas in order to actualize the eight common *siddhis* (such as flying, being able to pass through solid substances, etc.). Then it is necessary in the completion stage yogas firstly in order to manifest the impure illusory body.

Secondly, the illusory body yogi requires these methods in order to manifest the actual clear light and to achieve the stage of a trainee's great union. Then, thirdly, the yogi at the trainee's great union stage requires the methods to actualize the great union beyond training. These three completion stage activities, and the three yogic phases associated with them—form, formless, and totally formless—can be studied in detail from Lama Tsongkhapa's writings on the subject.

*The Manner of Actualizing the Goal*
*The Vajra Verses* states,

> Whoever applies him/herself to the path
> Attains the state of perfect buddhahood
> In six months, a year, or at least within this lifetime.

And elsewhere, the same scripture relates,

> Through practice of this supreme path
> The wisdom of blissful emptiness automatically arises
> And one attains enlightenment in this lifetime
> Or, at the very least, in the bardo;
> Or one goes to the Dakini Pure Land.

Thus as is stated here, the practitioner of highest capacity, who is likened to a precious jewel, attains enlightenment in this very lifetime.

Lesser practitioners attain enlightenment in the bardo, or at least within seven or sixteen lifetimes. In brief, the practice of this unexcelled path very rapidly gives birth to the innate bliss of the mind and body possessed of seven characteristics concomitant with enlightenment gained through tantric methods.

This bliss, united with the clear light wisdom perceiving the final meaning of emptiness, produces the stage beyond all trainings. One is then able to benefit countless beings by sending out emanations in an unbroken stream in order to work for the benefit and upliftment of the world until the realms of samsara have been emptied.

When the sun rises, the stars flee;
And similarly, it is my sincere wish
That this commentary, written
To explain the full meaning of the points
In the practice of the Six Yogas of Sister Niguma,
May elucidate the inner meaning of the tantras
And cause wrong attitudes to flee and hide.

The subject is the heart-essence of the Wisdom Dakini,
The secret path of the mighty Buddha Vajradhara,
Which has come down in an unbroken lineage
From Naropa, his disciple Sister Niguma,
And Khyungpo Naljor, master of the eight powers—
A lineage known as "the seven precious gems."

Because of studying, contemplating, and polishing
This sublime path, a wish-fulfilling gem of practices,
And by flying the banner of single-pointed application,
May the glorious state of full enlightenment,
Which fulfills the purposes of self and others,
Be quickly and surely attained.

Through any goodness that may arise
From my elucidating this supreme tantric path,
May the spiritual mud of living beings be washed away
And may they gain the vajra mind
Free from every obscuration.

May I myself take direct responsibility
For the beings sinking in the ocean of samsara,
Who are extremely coarse and vulgar;
May I become skilled in the tantric path,
Which has a vast range of methods for the deluded.
May all be guided to the city of enlightenment.

The Colophon: This treatise on the Six Yogas of Sister Niguma, entitled *A Transmission of the Wisdom Dakini*, has been written by the
Buddhist monk Gendun Gyatso at the repeated request of numerous
practitioners from central and southern Tibet. It is based on *The
Vajra Verses* as explained in the commentaries of various Kagyu masters, as well as upon the writings of the masters Khyungpo Naljor and
Mokchokpa. In addition, it takes into account the oral transmissions
coming from Lama Tsongkhapa and his spiritual sons.

I have written it out of respect for these illustrious masters of the
past and especially out of respect for the master who taught it to me,
(my father) Dorjechang Ananda Dhvaja, the dust of whose feet I place
proudly upon my head. May it cause the enlightenment doctrine to
prosper and thrive.

# CHAPTER FOUR:

# The Third Dalai Lama's

## *The Tantric Yogas of the Bodhisattva of Compassion*[138]

### GYALWA SONAM GYATSO (1543-1588)

AVALOKITESHVARA

# Translator's Preamble

ALTHOUGH all Tibetan yogic training aims at or culminates in the Highest, or Anuttara, Yoga Tantra systems, and the practices accord in nature with those described by the Second Dalai Lama in the previous chapter, Tibetans also love the more simple tantric applications of the Kriya, Charya, and Yoga Tantra classes.

The Avalokiteshvara Tantra is a favorite from amongst these. The six-syllable Avalokiteshvara mantra—OM MANI PADME HUM—might almost be considered the national song of Tibet. Every Tibetan recites several thousand of it on a daily basis, and many do the retreat in which six million recitations are completed. Most Tibetan temples have an enormous prayer wheel near the entrance, stuffed with millions of this mantra, and visitors who enter should turn the wheel a few times, to release the power of OM MANI PADME HUM. One hears it wherever one goes in Tibet, and indeed in most of Central Asia.

However, the actual meditation system is much more complex than the mere recitation of mantra might suggest. The Third Dalai Lama outlines some of this complexity in the text that follows.

As he states in the opening verse, two principal lineages of the Avalokiteshvara Tantra were popular in Tibet: that descending from the Indian female mystic Bhikshuni Shrimati and that descending from the mahasiddhas. His text outlines the practice for the second of these two traditions. As for the first of the two lineages, that of Bhikshuni Shrimati, I discuss this in my book *The Female Budddhas* (Santa Fe:

Clear Light Publishers, 2003) and readers can refer there for more information.

The Third Dalai Lama divides the training into seven stages: (1) the preliminaries, (2) the yoga with symbols, (3) the yoga without symbols, (4) the yoga for between sessions, (5) the yoga of sleep, (6) the yoga of consciousness transference, and (7) the yoga for attaining enlightenment in the bardo. The second and third of these—the yoga with symbols and the yoga without symbols—are the Kriya, Charya, and Yoga Tantra equivalents of what the fourth class of Tantra calls the generation and completion stage yogas, and thus, together with the fourth topic, could also be called "the main body of the training." The fifth, sixth, and seventh could also be called supplementary or branch trainings.

The Third Dalai Lama gives the greatest amount of detail on the second of these seven sections, "the yoga with symbols."

Earlier in this book, in Chapter One, the Thirteenth Dalai Lama discussed the Kriya tantras. He stated, "The three families of tantras in the Kriya division are: the supreme family of Vairochana, also called the Tathagata family... the intermediate Padma family ... and the fundamental Vajra family. . . . One should enter into whichever of these is suitable to one's personal karmic predispositions, receiving initiation into either a powder (i.e., sand), cloth, or meditation mandala."

The Avalokiteshvara Tantra belongs to the second of these three categories of the Kriya Tantra division, i.e., the Padma (or "Lotus") family.

The Thirteenth Dalai Lama then outlined the principal themes of the meditations known as "the yoga with symbols" as practiced in the Kriya tantras. There he said,

> Concerning the actual yogas (i.e., the yoga with symbols),
> firstly there is the *dhyana* of four branches of recitation:

(a) The self-basis, or generation of oneself as a mandala deity. This involves meditation upon the six deities (or stages of arisal as a deity): suchness, mantric sound, mantric letters, emanated forms, mudras, and symbol (i.e., the actual deity).

(b) The other-basis, which means generating the supporting and supported mandala and deities in front, sending forth praises and offerings, etc.

(c) The mental basis, in which one meditates that one's mind rests on a moon disc at one's heart.

(d) The audial basis, wherein one concentrates upon the seed syllable and mantra rosary on that moon disc, and then does the mantra recitation. . . .

These are the practices known as "the yoga with symbols," the first stage of the Kriya Tantra yogas.

If we look carefully at the Third Dalai Lama's presentation of the Avalokiteshvara yoga with symbols, we will see the various stages of Kriya Tantra meditation as outlined here by the Thirteenth Dalai Lama.

The first of his comments described how the yoga with symbols involves ". . . meditation upon the six deities." These six are not six different buddha or deity forms, but rather refer to six stages of arising as the mandala deity. The principal method of the yoga with symbols involves the dissolving of the ordinary sense of self and then rearising with the reidentification as oneself as the mandala deity, in this case Avalokiteshvara, and this is performed in six stages.

The first of the six is called "the ultimate deity," and refers to the recitation of the "purification in emptiness" mantra, together with the accompanying visualization. This mantra appears at the beginning of almost every daily sadhana, or meditation method. Here the entire inanimate universe is visualized as dissolving into light and the light into the animate beings; the animate is then dissolved into light, which dissolves into oneself. One's own body then dissolves into light from head down and feet up, and into the mantra seed at one's heart. Finally, this dissolves into a vast, infinite, radiant voidness.

The Third Dalai Lama gives the instruction for this in a verse:

> Recite the *Svabhava* mantra and contemplate its meaning
> To purify in emptiness the objects of perception.
> Everything is seen as being empty
> Of possessing inherent being.

One rests the mind in this state of infinite radiance free from any forms and concepts, devoid of all duality, for as long as possible.

Then from the vast radiant emptiness one arises as firstly a mantric sound, then a mantric letter, then emanated forms, then a "mudra" (i.e., the formal symbol of the buddha family), and finally as symbol (i.e., the actual deity).

The Third Dalai Lama's text describes these various stages of spiritual unfoldment. When they have been completed, one goes on to the other steps listed in the quote from the Thirteenth Dalai Lama above, i.e., the other-basis, the mental basis, and the audial basis (which is the mantra recitation).

Readers will notice that the Third Dalai Lama writes in a somewhat skeletal style. He does this on purpose, so as to emphasize the importance of the living oral tradition. Traditionally a practitioner would approach a high lama holding the lineage and request the lama to read and explain the work. The lama would then take a few days or even a few weeks to slowly work through the lines, perhaps spending an entire day unpacking the meanings of a single word. In this way the experiential oral tradition would bring the text to life, and instill a vibrant sense of the meditation technique within the mindstream of the practitioner.

As the Third Dalai Lama points out in his opening verse, the lineage serving as the source of inspiration for his text is known as "that of the mahasiddhas."

In general the term "mahasiddha" refers to any person who has attained realization of the tantric path. "Maha" is "great" and "siddha" means "accomplished in power." The power referred to here is tantric in nature, and includes the eight ordinary powers, such as levitation and so forth, as well as the extraordinary power of the wisdom of blissful and radiant voidness.

In particular, however, "mahasiddha" refers to the unconventional Indian tantric masters who appeared in India between the sixth and eleventh centuries. Usually antisocial, unwashed, rude, and sometimes even seeming to border on mystical madness, they appeared at a time when mainstream Indian Buddhism had become formula-driven rather than experiential. Most of them began their lives as monks or nuns, but became disillusioned by the tedious pace and slow progress of the staid monastic lifestyle. Later in life they dropped out of the monastic doldrums, and opted instead for an unconventional lifestyle filled with sex, alcohol, and meat-eating. Most of them lived in small jungle or riverside communities that engaged regularly in tantric feasts involving all three of the above simultaneously.

The more famous among the mahasiddhas attained enlightenment in one lifetime. Eighty-four of these are honored as a set by Tibetans, and books of inspirational stories of their extraordinary exploits are popular with Tibetan laypeople and monastics alike.

Most of the Buddhist tantric lineages extant in Tibet were passed through or transformed by the visionary experiences of these mahasiddhas. The Avalokiteshvara tradition presented by the Third Dalai Lama is a good example. As with the other mahasiddha traditions, it extracts quintessential elements from the complex structures of the basic tantras taught by the Buddha and organizes these into steps for easy practice. For this reason these lineages are often known in Tibetan as *men ngak*, or "living oral traditions."

In my preamble to the previous chapter I mentioned how the name "Dalai Lama" was not used during the lifetimes of the First or Second incarnations, and in fact came into existence only during the lifetime of the Third.

In fact the name was born from controversy. The first Dalai Lama had been given the ordination name Gendun Drubpa, and the second was given Gendun Gyatso. Thus both had "Gendun" as a first name. Most monks believed that this was in fulfillment of an ancient prophecy, and that all Dalai Lama incarnations would have "Gendun" as the first portion of his name, with the second portion being different for each incarnation.

The controversy over the name "Dalai Lama" began when the Second's chief disciple, Panchen Sonam Drakpa, was appointed as the tutor to the child who was recognized and enthroned as the young reincarnation. Rather than give him the first name "Gendun," as was expected, at the boy's ordination ceremony the Panchen named him Sonam Gyatso. The elders were flabberghasted, but nothing could be done.

When Panchen Sonam Drakpa repeated the "Gyatso" portion of the Second's name, rather than the "Gendun" portion, history was changed. Later, when Sonam Gyatso traveled to Mongolia in 1578 at the invitation of the great Mongol king Altan Khan, the Khan became overwhelmed by the Master's spiritual presence and declared him to be the supreme guru of all Mongols. He issued a proclamation to this effect, referring to the Master by the second portion of his name, or Gyatso, which means "Ocean." "Ocean" translates into Mongolian as "Dalai." Thus the name "Dalai Lama" was born.

Tibetans rarely used it, however, preferring to retain the epithet "Jey Tamchey Khyenpa," by which both the First and Second incarnations had been known. Later, after the Fifth Dalai Lama was made king of Tibet in 1642, they added several other epithets, any of which could be used. The three most popular were Gyalwa Rinpochey, or "Precious Victor," Kundun, or "Presence," and Yishin Norbu, or "Wish-fulfilling Jewel."

As for the epithet "Dalai Lama," Mongolians continued to use it over the centuries that followed, and later the Chinese learned it from them. The British picked it up from the Chinese, and the rest of the world learned of it from the British.

I originally read this exquisite little text in the mid-1980s with my good friend and spiritual mentor Sharpa Tulku, who over the years has been a constant source of encouragement, guidance, and inspiration.

# The Third Dalai Lama's Text

## Prologue

Two especially popular lineages of the tradition
Of the Avalokiteshvara tantric yogas
Have come to Tibet from India:
That of the nun Bhikshuni Shrimati,
Who was blessed by the Arya;
And, secondly, that known far and wide as the
Ear-whispered guidelines of the mahasiddhas.
Here I will give a summary of the latter practice.

## I. The Preliminaries

One must first receive the appropriate initiations
From a qualified lineage holder
And must also receive the profound
Oral transmissions and precepts.
In addition one must learn and observe
The levels of commitment and discipline.

## II. The Yoga with Symbols

Firstly arrange an altar
With an image of Arya Avalokiteshvara

Or representations of the body, speech, and mind
Of the buddhas of the three times.
In front of it place a meditation seat
Upon which the practice will be performed.

Begin each meditation session
By preparing the mind for the profound path
Through meditating upon guru yoga.
Then perform the Vajrasattva meditation and
Mantric recitation in conjunction with
Application of the four opponent forces
That purify the mind of obstacles,
Negative karmic tendencies, and spiritual failings.
These are the preliminaries that prepare
The mind for the actual yogas.

The actual body of the meditation
Is conducted as follows.
Recite the *Svabhava* mantra and contemplate its meaning
To purify in emptiness the objects of perception.
Everything is seen as being empty
Of possessing inherent being.
Within the sphere of emptiness appears
A stainless lotus bearing a moon disc,
Your mind in the form of the syllable *HRIH*
Standing upright at the moon's center.

*HRIH* transforms into a white eight-petalled lotus
Bearing the syllable *HRIH*.
This syllable emanates brilliant rays of light
That fulfill the needs of the world.
These reabsorb into *HRIH*,

Which melts into a ball of light.
From this ball of light you emerge suddenly
As Arya Avalokiteshvara, your body
White as a dazzling snow mountain.

You have four hands, of which the
Inner two are folded together at your heart
In the gesture of great compassion.
As for the outer two, that on the right
Holds a crystal rosary and
That on the left, a white lotus.

You are adorned with the silken robes and
Precious ornaments of a bodhisattva hero,
And your legs are folded in the vajra posture.
A white *OM* marks your forehead,
A red *AH* marks your throat, and
A blue *HUM* marks your heart.
Also at your heart is a white syllable *HRIH*.

Lights radiate forth from *HRIH*, summoning forth
In the form of Arya Avalokiteshvara
The masses of divinities of the immutable
Body, speech, and mind of the Enlightened Ones.
These are absorbed into your body,
Which thus becomes the abode
Of all meditational divinities.

Upon your head appears Guru Amitabha,
The Buddha of Boundless Light.
Then the root and lineage gurus are summoned
And dissolve into him.

Thus he becomes the abode
Of all the holy gurus.

Similarly, at your heart the syllable *HRIH*
Stands on a moon disc.
Around it is arranged the string
Of the six-syllable mantra
*OM MANI PADME HUM.*
The various heart and proximate mantras
Are summoned forth. They dissolve
Into *HRIH* and the six-syllable mantra,
Which become in nature all mantras.

The entire external world that acts as the vessel
(For the living beings) transforms
Into the divine mandala palace;
The living beings that fill the vessel
Transform into exalted Avalokiteshvara;
And all the limitless sounds that arise
Transform into the six-syllable mantra.
Your mind becomes in nature
The wisdom of emptiness inseparable from compassion.
Practicing awareness of the three embodiments
And the three mystical transformations
In this way while meditating single-pointedly
And reciting the six-syllable mantra
Is the stage known as the yoga with symbols.

## III. THE YOGA WITHOUT SYMBOLS

All phenomena that appear and exist
Should be seen as objects of a dream,

Like illusions, mere appearances,
And hallucinations.
Although they appear, not an atom
Of them is established as inherently real.
Meditating in this way is known
As the yoga without symbols.

## IV. THE YOGA FOR BETWEEN SESSIONS

Then by reciting the three seed syllables
Of OM, AH, and HUM,
Ordinary food, clothing, and shelter
Are dissolved into emptiness
And the skies become filled respectively
With ambrosia, divine raiment, and mandala palaces.
Holding this practice of deity yoga in mind
And remaining free from mundane perception
While interacting with the world
Is the yoga to be applied
Between meditational sittings.

## V. THE YOGA OF SLEEP

At night when you go to bed
See yourself as the tantric divinity
Avalokiteshvara, the Bodhisattva of Compassion.
Buddha Amitabha, the embodiment of all gurus,
Is seated above the crown of your head.
At the center of your heart is the syllable HRIH,
Embodiment of all meditational deities.
Then as you go to sleep

These two transform into mystic drops
And unite at the heart.
Maintain this vision in the mind.
Then, after the clear light of sleep dawns
And the drop moves to the throat center,
Observe any dreams that occur
And transform them by means
Of special meditations on sleep.
Such is the oral tradition teaching
Known as "the great sleep yoga."

## VI. The Yoga of Consciousness Transference

At the base of the central energy channel
Is a mystic drop, reddish white in color.
Inside it is your own mind in the form
Of a white drop the size of a mustard seed.
Pull upward on the lower energies
And wrathfully utter the syllable *HIK*.

Like a shooting star the drop suddenly
Comes to the center of the heart,
Where it dissolves into the heart of
The mandala deity Arya Avalokiteshvara.
Thus your mind becomes in nature
Inseparably one with Avalokiteshvara.

Your mind in the form of Avalokiteshvara
Then moves up the central channel
And comes to the Brahma aperture
At the crown of your head.

Lights in the form of hook-rays
Emanate from the heart of Amitabha Buddha,
Who is seated above the crown of your head.
These radiate downward,
Strike against your mind as Avalokiteshvara,
And pull it upward.

It leaves your body via your crown aperture
And dissolves into Guru Amitabha's heart.
By means of his miraculous powers
Amitabha then rises into the sky
And flies directly to Sukhavati,
The Pure Land of Bliss.

Such is the profound yoga
For the transference of consciousness
Whereby even those of strong negative karma
Can gain the exalted state of liberation.

## VII. The Yoga of Bardo Accomplishment

Lastly, here is the method for practicing
The yoga for gaining enlightenment
In the bardo, or state
Between death and rebirth.

Like a flash of lightning in a cloud
And like a fish rising from
The depths of a pond,
The clear light of death manifests
And subtle consciousness and energy

Enter into the bardo state.
Transform the body into the divine nature
Of a tantric deity and mystic mandala;
Transform speech into the mandala of mantras;
Transform the mind itself into awareness
Of the transcendental nature of Suchness.
Remain inseparable from these three mandalas.
In this way you can control your own destiny,
Consciously directing your mind to a rebirth
In a pure realm, or as a human or celestial being,
And can thus achieve once more a physical form
Most appropriate to dwelling in the ways of Dharma.
This is the nature of the yogic technique
To be applied in the bardo
For the sake of achieving
Higher rebirth and enlightenment.

## VIII. CONCLUSION

Thus is complete a brief explanation
Of the essential states in practice
Of the profound path of Avalokiteshvara,
A most sublime tantric method.
It was written by the Buddhist monk
Sonam Gyatso Palzangpo
At the request of a faithful disciple
Who asked for a simple and easily understandable
Outline of the Avalokiteshvara yogas
That nonetheless would be
Both complete and clear on the
Principal points of the system.

This sacred yogic method is a treasure,
A lotus garden from which living beings
May find the honey of enlightenment
And accomplish the highest joy.

In this short text I have opened the gates
To the supreme Mahayana palace,
A palace usually locked in secrecy.
It is my hope that by doing so
The profound knowledge contained therein
May be carried far and wide
For the goodness and welfare of the world.

# CHAPTER FIVE:

## The Fourteenth Dalai Lama's
### *Concerning the Kalachakra Initiation*[139]

GYALWA TENZIN GYATSO (B. 1935)

THE FOURTEENTH DALAI LAMA

# Translator's Preamble

A s WE SAW in the Introduction, Vajrayana practice is a culmination or extension of the Sutrayana trainings. Therefore in this short essay the Dalai Lama begins his introduction to the nature and purpose of the Kalachakra initiation by creating a context between the Kalachakra system and Sutrayana topics like the four noble truths, the two levels of reality, the four Indian schools of Buddhist philosophy, and so forth. Here he follows the traditional presentations of lineage masters such as Buton Rinchen Drubpa of the Zhalu School and Tsongkhapa of the Geluk School, both of whom are important in the Kalachakra lineage of transmission. The mainstream Gelukpa lineage of the Kalachakra Tantra comes into the Gelukpa from the Zhalu.

Readers familiar with Tibetan Buddhist literature will know that the Geluk School is often referred to as "The Yellow Hat School," or *Zhaser* in Tibetan. The Seventh Dalai Lama signed several of his works with the epithet "The Yellow Hat Lama Kalzang Gyatso." By contrast, all other schools of Tibetan Buddhism are referred to as "The Red Hats," or *Zhamar*. The name comes because of the color of the mahapandita hat; early Tibetan schools wore red, whereas Tsongkhapa and his Gelukpa successors wore (and continue to wear) a yellow version of it. Most formal portraits over the centuries of the Dalai and Panchen Lama incarnations usually depict them in this famous yellow pandita hat. The present Dalai Lama usually dons it on ceremonial occasions. Even those Dalai Lamas who never earned the geshey degree, and thus were not qualified to carry the title "maha-pandita," are usually depicted as wearing it.[140]

Ask any Tibetan lama about the history of this yellow hat and he probably will reply that Tsongkhapa introduced it as a declaration of his "reformation" of Tibetan Buddhism. I have heard several dozen lamas give Tsongkhapa as the source of it. The same claim is made in numerous Western scholarly books.

The reality, however, is that the yellow hat was introduced by the Zhalu master Buton Rinchen Drubpa almost a century before Tsong-khapa's use of it. Tsongkhapa therefore used it as a signal that he was primarily endorsing Buton's lineages.

Buton is also one of the greatest Tibetan writers on the Kalachakra system, and his *Collected Works* is a treasury of knowledge on the sys-tem. Tsongkhapa considered Buton's presentation to be so thorough that he wrote almost nothing on the system himself, and instead ded-icated his Tantric pen to enormous treatises on systems such as the Guhyasamaja Tantra, the Heruka Chakrasamvara Tantra, and the Six Yogas of Naropa. Of course his *Ngakrim Chenmo*, or *Stages on the Mantra Path*, is his magnum opus on the Buddhist tantras as a whole.[141]

After discussing the Sutrayana doctrines that are used as prelimi-naries to the Vajrayana in both the Zhalu and Geluk Schools of Tibetan Buddhism, the Dalai Lama goes on to introduce some of the *kye cho*, or "special characteristics," of the Kalachakra Tantra.

Anyone receiving initiation into any of the Highest Yoga Tantra systems takes a precept to honor the nineteen *samayas*, or sacred pledges, associated with the five buddha families: Akshobhya, Vai-rochana, Ratnasambhava, Amitabha, and Amoghasiddhi. The five buddhas, as we see in other chapters of this book, are linked to the five sections of the mandala—the four directions and the center—and represent the transformation of the five elements and five skand-has into the five wisdoms and five enlightenment aspects.

Several of these nineteen *samayas* of the five buddha families involve doing a practice three times during the day and three times during the night, such as generating the mind of Refuge in the Three Jewels, bringing vajra (male energies) and bell (female energies) together in harmony, and so forth. In the olden days people would honor these nineteen *samayas* by actually doing the practices.

In more recent centuries, however, the tradition of actually doing the nineteen practices has been replaced by reading a liturgy that encapsulates the nineteen. Because many of them mention "three times during the day and three times during the night," the liturgy is usually chanted three times in the morning immediately after waking up, and three times at night before going to sleep. The specific type of liturgy is known in Tibetan as *Tundruk Naljor*, or "Six-Session Yoga," because of being read six times in this way.

Hundreds of Tibetan texts of this nature have been written over the centuries. For example, the Seventh Dalai wrote one that uses Milarepa as the central focus; he wrote that for people who make the Six Yogas of Naropa their principal practice. The lineage of the Six Yogas of Naropa descends through Milarepa.

A small Six-Session Yoga liturgy focusing on Kalachakra in the visualization was distributed to the 350,000 people who attended the Dalai Lama's Kalachakra initiation in Bodh Gaya during January of 1974. It had been written by Khangsar Dorjechang (1888-1941), one of the greatest Tibetan lamas in the first half of the twentieth century. I translated and published that small text as a pamphlet[142] for the Westerners who attended, and also later included it in *The Practice of Kalachakra*.[143]

I have attached Khangsar Dorjechang's Six-Session Kalachakra Yoga at the end of this chapter because of its association with the Dalai Lama and his 1974 initiation. It is an excellent example of the kind of tantric liturgy employed by casual practitioners today.

# The Fourteenth Dalai Lama's Text

## THE SEARCH FOR INNER HAPPINESS

THE NOTION OF "I" is a mere projection on the four or five psychophysical aggregates which make up the person. Yet this sense of "I," which is possessed by us all, even the smallest insect, innately seeks to find satisfaction and to avoid misery.

In order to establish desirable states of happiness and to eliminate undesirable states of frustration and sorrow, the various kinds of living beings apply themselves, according to their individual capacities, to the activities that will achieve these goals.

The happiness which is to be produced and the sorrows to be eliminated are of many types. For example, people gain a type of happiness from food, shelter, and social success, and they experience much suffering when these are taken from them.

However, were one to ask whether the limits of joy and sorrow end here, the answer is to the negative. No matter how much food, shelter, and social success one has, these external conditions alone will not produce a lasting happiness if the mind is disturbed by spiritual unease.

This indicates that in addition to concerning ourselves with physical and environmental well-being, we must try to create an inner basis of peace and spiritual balance.

Which happiness is stronger, that arising from external conditions or that arising from inner spiritual harmony?

When one has the latter, then suffering does not arise in the mind even when the external conditions of happiness fail to converge. Alternatively, when one is bereft of inner peace, the most pleasant external situation is unable to bring happiness to the mind.

## The Spiritual Solution

In this sense, the inner state of the mind is much more important than external conditions.

Therefore, it is essential that we ourselves know the means by which a state of inner peace is created and cultivated. Not only would this benefit us individually in a very immediate, practical, and down-to-earth sense; but also in this era when there is so much social tension on the earth, when the nations of the world are themselves so intensely concerned with competition and with efforts to overpower one another—even at the threat of nuclear devastation—it is most urgent for us to try to develop spiritual wisdom.

At present the world is not lacking in technological or industrial development. What are we lacking? A basis for inner harmony and joy.

Were we to cultivate the gentle pleasures of a loving and compassionate mind inspired by wisdom, the result would be that we would continually experience peace and happiness, even when confronted by external hardships, and we would have a pacifying effect on our chaotic environment rather than merely being caught up in and perpetuating it.

On the other hand, when our mind is bereft of spiritual qualities and instead we are controlled by inner forces such as greed, jealousy, aggression, pride, and so forth, then even the most positive external conditions will fail to bring any significant comfort to the mind.

Hence this inner peace and joy not only benefit the individual who develops them, they also benefit the entire human community, and by extension this entire world in which we live.

182 : THE FOURTEENTH DALAI LAMA

## THE FOUR NOBLE TRUTHS

What does Buddhism have to contribute to the human quest for spiritual knowledge?

The root of the Buddhadharma is the teaching of the four noble truths discerned by the Enlightened Beings. These four are: the nature of suffering, its causes, liberation from or the cessation of suffering, and the path to such liberation.

The truth of suffering invokes the topic of the various levels of hardship, frustration, and pain that we living beings experience and that we must learn to recognize. Usually we mistake suffering, especially in its subtle forms, and misidentify it as pleasure or entertainment. When the nature of suffering has been understood, the mind takes on a quality of indifference toward it.

Therefore after speaking of suffering the Buddha taught its source, its cause.

First of all we must investigate the question of whether the undesirable states of suffering that we experience arise from causes, or if they arise without causes. Secondly, if they have causes and these can be identified, can they also be eliminated? These are important questions.

When one perceives that in fact there are various ways to eliminate all inner causes of misery, one gains a certain conviction in one's own spiritual potential. From this is born a mind that will work for liberation.

Therefore, the Buddha taught the third truth—of cessation, or the liberation from suffering.

By understanding that a state of inner illumination totally beyond suffering can be generated, one appreciates the fact that liberation is something to be achieved within the mind itself, and not through any other object. Once the stains and aberrations of one's own mind have been purified in the mind's own final nature, liberation is achieved.

This being so, we should cultivate the liberating techniques within our own mindstream and eradicate all distorting factors and obscurations, such as attachment and the other delusions, that so strongly influence our present mode of existence. We must reverse deluded habits of thought born from misunderstanding reality, and actualize the pristinely clear level of mind.

Here "pristinely clear mind" refers to the consciousness that has totally eradicated the mental habits of incorrectly apprehending objects of knowledge.

To accomplish this, one must generate an awareness of emptiness, the way things actually exist. When this awareness arises, the mind that mistakenly apprehends its objects can be put to rest.

We should use our ability to destroy from within ourselves the confused habits of thought of wrongly perceiving things—or seeing them other than the way they exist—by generating this awareness of the ultimate mode of existence of reality.

The Buddha taught that by generating this awareness of the ultimate mode, and then meditating on it single-pointedly, all forms of mental distortion are destroyed.

## Approaches to Truth

This ultimate mode of things has been explained by various means in order to suit the individual capacities and needs of the various kinds of disciples.

The Buddha's words suggest themes for four different trends in philosophical thought. In India these developed into four major schools. In this way the Buddha provided a diverse range of paths to spiritual growth and enlightenment. Trainees should begin their spiritual careers by first gaining proficiency in the simpler methods before going on to the higher.

In Tibet we regarded these four schools as offering, from the lower to the higher schools, a diversity of philosophical and spiritual attitudes that the trainee can work with in a disciplined sequence, beginning with the lower and going on to the higher.

When put to the test of reason, it soon becomes obvious that several important doctrines accepted by the lower schools fail to withstand the rational scrutiny of an intensive investigation. A number of crucial faults become evident.

We should always carry reason and investigation as our tools. Critically examine all teachings that you hear. You must discern which of them are intended to be taken directly, and which are lower doctrines given by the Buddha in accordance with a specific time and need, and therefore are in need of interpretation.

Any teachings which, when tested, reveal logical flaws must be approached with the attitude that they require a nonliteral interpretation.

Of the four schools of Indian Buddhist thought, the most direct description of the ultimate nature of being is found in the Madhyamaka, or Middle View School. This ultimate nature is a phenomenon they call emptiness.

We should therefore try to understand this school's teachings on the ultimate nature of being by carefully studying and meditating on its authoritative traditions.

## METHODS OF APPLICATION

In order to be able to generate inner spiritual forces which are strong enough to destroy the various mental distortions, one must engage a powerful method. The more powerful the method, the stronger becomes one's application to the view of emptiness. When one's method is strong, one's meditations on emptiness become very powerful and one's ability to destroy mental and spiritual distortion is intensified.

On the basis of the vastness of the methods used, the Buddha's teachings are divided into two main vehicles: the Bodhisattvayana and the Shravakayana, generally known as the Mahayana and Hinayana, respectively.

In the Bodhisattvayana method one meditates that everything one does is for the benefit of living beings. Once it has been understood that all living beings, just like oneself, want happiness and dislike suffering, the attitude which assumes responsibility for their well-being arises. This attitude is an amazing, wonderful, and most courageous force, more precious than anything else in existence.

When one uses it as a basis for one's meditation upon the ultimate mode of things, the forces that destroy delusion and distortion are easily cultivated.

What are the methods of meditating on this altruistic and compassionate aspiration to highest enlightenment in conjunction with meditation on emptiness as explained in the great Madhyamaka works?

These are classified in accordance with the coarseness or subtlety of the level of consciousness performing the meditation. Factors such as the subtlety, the force, and nature of one's mind and so forth strongly influence one's experience of the view of emptiness.

How so? The coarse levels of consciousness will not produce an experience of emptiness as quickly as will the subtle; and whether the coarse or subtle mind engaged in meditation is doing so on the basis of a union of method and wisdom also affects the impact of the practice. A meditation in which method and wisdom are not held in union will not produce tremendous results. When the mind is absorbed in method and wisdom conjoined, meditation on emptiness is most effective.

According to the schools of Buddhist thought that accept six spheres of consciousness (the five sensory consciousnesses together with a purely mental consciousness), there is both a coarse or ordinary level of consciousness that can perform meditation on emptiness on the basis of method and wisdom combined, and a subtle level of consciousness able to perform this meditation. Once one has cultivated a subtle level of consciousness propelled by the vast aspiration to highest enlightenment and applies it to realization of emptiness, the meditation becomes extremely powerful and is able to instantly destroy the host of destructive mental traits.

## THE TANTRIC PATH

Where can be found the practices of the coarse and subtle levels of consciousness that counteract delusion by means of undivided method and wisdom? This leads to the subject of the Buddhist tantras.

According to the *Tantra of the Two Forms*[144] (of the Hevajra cycle), there are four classes of tantras: Kriya, Charya, Yoga, and Anuttarayoga. Kalachakra belongs to the last of these four.

In the three lower Tantra classes one generates a coarse consciousness combining method and wisdom, and then meditates on emptiness.

The yogic techniques for engaging the powerful, subtle levels of consciousness focused in meditation born from the inseparability of method and wisdom are found only in the texts of Highest Yoga Tantra.

To generate this subtle level of consciousness one must first eliminate the agitation of the coarse level of conceptual thought. Many methods for effecting this end have been taught.

One such method found in the Highest Yoga tantras involves arresting the deceptive projections of conceptual thought by means of channeling the vital energies of the nervous system. In a second method one cuts off the movements of conceptual thought and engages in totally nonconceptual meditation in order to eliminate the elements that distort the mind.

## THE KALACHAKRA TRADITION

A number of different approaches to this yogic path have been expounded. Here I will speak briefly about the meditative techniques found in the Kalachakra system, which belongs to the Highest Yoga Tantra class. It is a tantric system with several unique characteristics.

Generally, Highest Yoga Tantra systems are of two types: "buried tantras" such as Guhyasamaja, and "clear tantras" such as Kala-chakra.[145] The difference between these two styles appears in the fourth initiation. In the buried tantras the fourth initiation is revealed in a very concealed or hidden manner, whereas in the clear tantras it is presented openly.

Although basically all the individual systems found in the Highest Yoga tantras are equally profound, they each have their own approach which renders them more effective as a practice in accordance with the specific nature of the individual practitioners, their karmic tendencies, and so forth. If one practices the Highest Yoga Tantra system most appropriate to one's situation, the effect will be far more powerful than meditating on any other system of the same Tantra class.

It is important that the practitioner engages in the system most suited to him or her. To demonstrate this metaphorically, a sick person takes a medicine appropriate to the specific illness and to the general condition of his or her being. In the same way, all systems in the Highest Yoga tantras are equally powerful, but a difference between them appears in their application to the physical, psychic, and karmic situation of the individual practitioner.[146]

This is obvious from the different ways in which people experience the manifestations of the subtle consciousness and energies, such as in the visions of smoke and so forth at the time of death.

The yogic path of Kalachakra provides a very special method for those who have the correct body, mind, and karmic predispositions. These special qualities become apparent after one has completed the imagined generation stage yogas and engages in the unfeigned completion stage practices. Here again the Kalachakra system reveals a unique presentation of the six yogas that constitute the completion stage.

In the discussion of the Kalachakra generation stage yogas, which ripen and mature the mind for the completion stage, it is traditional to introduce the topic of the three Kalachakras: Outer, Inner, and Alternative.

Outer Kalachakra comprises the elements of the universe in which we live. Inner Kalachakra is the psychophysical aggregates, the sensory and psychic capacities of the living being, and so forth. Thirdly, Alternative Kalachakra is the path of the generation and completion stage yogas, the yogic methods that have the power to purify the above two Kalachakras.

Outer Kalachakra is generally explained in the context of this universe. Then, when one meditates on the mandala, Inner Kalachakra is seen as the body, faces, hands, feet, and so forth (of Kalachakra and Consort), as well as all the surrounding deities of the mandala, conceived as symbols of the stars, planets, constellations, and so forth. From this we can know that Kalachakra has a special connection with all the living beings of this world system.

## THE KALACHAKRA LINEAGE

From the point of view of the personage at whose request the Kalachakra doctrine was expounded, unlike any other tantra Kalachakra was taught at the request of Suchandra, spiritual chieftain of the fabulous land of Shambhala.

It is said that in order to benefit the subjects of the ninety regions of his country, Suchandra traveled to India and requested just such a teaching from the Buddha. Kalachakra therefore has a special relationship with Shambhala.

From Suchandra the lineage has been passed down through a line of seven spiritual leaders, beginning with Suchandra himself, and twenty-one kalkin masters, beginning with Manjushri Yashas. (We are presently in the era of the twenty-first kalkin.) In the coming of the twenty-fifth kalkin, the special connection that the people of this earth share with Kalachakra will manifest strongly in world events.

In general, the Kalachakra system, like any Highest Yoga tantra, is meant for practitioners of the highest faculty. Nonetheless, because of the above considerations it was the tradition in Tibet to give the initiation openly to very large gatherings.

Although Shambhala is a place located somewhere on this planet, it is a place that can be seen only by those whose minds and karmic propensities are pure. This is how it remains hidden from the everyday world.

The Buddha taught in accordance with the predispositions of mental focus and the qualities existing within the practitioners. It is said that for general trainees he taught the paths of the Shravakayana and Pratyekabuddhayana, that is, the ways of the Hearers and the Solitary Sages; and for the practitioners of a more vast karmic predisposition he taught the Bodhisattvayana, or the general Mahayana. Finally, for the few of highest potential and faculty he taught the Tantrayana, which is also known as the Vajrayana. Here he manifested in various forms, sometimes as a monk and sometimes as a tantric deity, to teach the three lower of the four classes of tantras. Then in the forms of various mandala deities embodying the inseparable union of method and wisdom he taught the Highest Yoga tantras.

Because these teachings were given in mystical manifestations of the Buddha to those in transcendental states of purified karma and perception, it does not matter much whether or not any specific tantra was expounded during the life of the historical Buddha himself.

However, in fact *The Kalachakra Root Tantra*[147] was set forth by Buddha Shakyamuni himself during his very lifetime.

The principal recipient of Buddha's original Kalachakra course, Suchandra of Shambhala, transcribed the teaching (into *The Kalachakra Root Tantra)* and also composed a clarification of it entitled *A Commentary to the Root Tantra.* Later, Manjushri Yashas, the first kalkin master, composed an abridgement entitled *The Abbreviated Kalachakra Tantra.*[148] Manjushri Yashas' son and spiritual successor, Kalkin Pundarika, then composed an extensive elucidation of *(The Abbreviated Kalachakra Tantra)* entitled *The Great Commentary: A Stainless Light.*[149]

Consequently knowledge of the yogic and philosophical systems of the Kalachakra tradition became widespread throughout Shambhala.

Eventually Chilupa, a master from eastern India, traveled to Shambhala in search of the Kalachakra tantric doctrines. On the way he met an incarnation of the bodhisattva Manjushri, and received from him the initiation, scriptures, commentaries, and oral transmissions of the Kalachakra system.

Chilupa eventually passed the lineage to the Bengali-born master famed as Pindo Acharya. In this way in India it was propagated by such illustrious masters as Kalachakrapada the Elder; Kalachakrapada the Younger; the Nalanda sage Manjukirti; the Tibetan monk Sangyey Yeshey, who had come from Kham Province of Tibet, worked his way up the hierarchy of Bodh Gaya Monastery,[150] and became its abbot; and the Nepali pandit Samanta Shribhadra.

In this way the lineage gradually spread throughout India and Nepal.

The Kalachakra tradition came to Tibet in a number of lines of transmission. One of the most important of these was that of the Tibetan yogi Rva Chorab, who traveled to Nepal to study the Kalachakra doctrines under Samanta Shribhadra. He later invited this teacher to Tibet, where they translated many of the major scriptures related to Kalachakra. Rva Chorab passed the lineage to his principal disciple, Rva Yeshey Sangyey, and eventually it came to Buton Rinchen Drubpa. Another important lineage is that of Dro Lotsawa, that also came to Buton. Buton united and transmitted these two lines of transmission, as well as systematizing and elucidating the tradition as a whole.

Thus the lineage has been passed from generation to generation until the present day.

## ATTENDING A KALACHAKRA INITIATION

The higher meditations of the Kalachakra tradition can be practiced only by a select few. But because of past and future events, and in order to establish a strong karmic relationship with Kalachakra in the minds of the people, there is now a tradition of giving the initiation to large public gatherings.

The following are qualifications of someone who wishes to receive the Kalachakra transmission for actual practice.

The first qualification is that of bodhichitta, the aspiration to highest enlightenment, which cherishes others more than oneself. Here it is said that the best disciple dwells in an unfeigned experience of this sublime mind; the medium disciple has had a small glimpse of it in his or her meditations; the lowest should have at least an appreciation for and interest in developing it.

The second qualification is given in terms of the special insight training, i.e., one's experience of emptiness. Here it is said that the best disciple has an undistorted experience of the nature of ultimate reality as explained in the Madhyamaka or Yogachara Schools of Mahayana thought; the medium disciple has a correct understanding based on study and reason in general; and the lowest disciple should at least have appreciation for and interest in learning the philosophical views of either of the two above-mentioned schools.

In addition, a disciple seeking the Kalachakra initiation should have a feeling for and interest in this particular tantric tradition. The purpose of initiation is to plant specific karmic seeds in the mind of the recipient; but if he or she does not possess the openness born from a basic degree of spiritual interest, it will be very difficult for the seeds to have any impact.

Should anyone wish to attend an initiation ceremony merely as a blessing, that is to say, in order to establish a karmic relationship with the Kalachakra lineage, initiation can be given on this basis to those who can appreciate and respect the opportunity. People attending solely within that perspective should not imagine taking on the commitments or disciplines of the system, such as the bodhisattva or tantric precepts. Rather, they should feel that they are present solely for purposes of enjoying the spiritual inspiration that the event provides.

Even if one has more faith than knowledge, and does not comprehend the principles of the path combining method and wisdom as explained above, the seeds of initiation can still be firmly planted in the mindstream of a trainee if he or she has even a small basis of spiritual conviction.

Therefore this is the minimum qualification required to attend the Kalachakra initiation. One should have at least a small particle of spiritual interest, even if one is not a formal practitioner.

## Cultivating a Daily Practice

For those who attend the initiation and wish to cultivate a daily training, it is common to begin by performing a six-session guru yoga method. A number of texts of this nature exist. This type of practice presents a concise review of the important points in the generation stage yogas of the Kalachakra path within the context of a guru yoga prayer and meditation. Practices of this nature are called "six-session yogas" because they are meant to be recited and contemplated three times during the day and three times at night. If this is not possible, then one should try to read and meditate on the guru yoga text at least once each day, blending the meaning of the words with one's mindstream.

This is how we should begin our training. However, we should not limit our practice to this level of endeavor alone. To best fulfill the purpose of the initiation, we should take a six-session guru yoga method as the basis of our daily meditation and then month by month, year by year we should try to constantly expand our minds in knowledge of the practice.

At the beginning we should study in depth the nature of the Kalachakra path, its generation and completion stage yogas, paying special attention to those aspects that we find most difficult to understand. Then, having heard and reflected upon the instructions, we should try to generate realization of them within our own stream of being.

As explained above, at the moment our minds are bound by habitual modes of perception, modes that are distorting and impure. We must dissolve these impure patterns of thought and this false posturing into the Dharmadhatu reality, the nature of emptiness.

Should we accomplish that task then we automatically fulfill the purposes of Buddhadharma, of the Mahayana, of the Vajrayana, of Highest Yoga Tantra, and of having received the Kalachakra initiation.

Although the path to enlightenment is a somewhat rigorous undertaking, it is well worthwhile. The wise, therefore, energetically apply themselves to it.

# Khangsar Dorjechang's (1888-1941) Six-Session Yoga: *A Kalachakra Guru Yoga Method*[151]

*Namo Guru Kalachakra Bhyah*

Herein lies a spiritual method capable of inspiring every happiness and spiritual quality, a guru yoga meditation focusing upon glorious Kalachakra.

(The Preliminaries)

Begin by constructing a clear visualization of the objects of refuge. Then as a preliminary to the actual meditation upon the spiritual master as inseparably one in nature with glorious Kalachakra, recite the verse for turning the mind to refuge and for arousing the compassionate bodhi-mind, and the verse of the four boundless thoughts (of compassion, love, joy, and equanimity):

To the Buddhas, the Dharma, and the Sangha
I turn for refuge until enlightenment is gained. By the merits of my
   practices, such as the six perfections,
May buddhahood be attained for the sake of all. *(3x)*

May all sentient beings have happiness and its causes;
May they be free of suffering and its causes;
May they never be separated from that happiness which is
   without suffering;

And may they be free from attraction to the near and aversion to
  the far. *(3x)*


(The Actual Meditation)

In the sky before me
Is a lion-throne of precious substances.
There, on cushions of lotus, sun, moon,
And the planets *rahu* and *kalagni*,
Is the embodiment of all refuge objects,
My root guru in the form of glorious Kalachakra,
Body blue in color, having one face,
His two hands holding a vajra and a bell.

Sexually embracing his consort Vishvamata,
He stands in the posture of haughtiness,
His two feet trampling a white and a red deity.
White OM marks his crown; red AH, his throat;
And blue HUM, his heart.

Lights emanate from HUM at his heart.
They invite all objects of refuge: gurus,
Meditational deities, buddhas, bodhisattvas,
Shravaka arhants, pratyekabuddhas,
Dakas, dakinis, and Dharma protectors.
These are absorbed into Kalachakra and Consort, and they become
In nature all three objects of refuge
Collected into one entity.
In deep respect I pay homage with all three doors;
All material and mentally created things I offer;
I acknowledge every negativity and failing
Accumulated since beginninglessness;

And in the goodness of both ordinary beings
And transcended masters I rejoice.
O masters, remain in samsara until it is emptied
And turn the wheel of knowledge.
Pray, firmly stay until the end of the world.
All goodness I dedicate to the peerless enlightenment.

The body, speech, and mind of both myself and others,
Our wealth and our masses of goodness
Of the past, present, and future,
And the precious mandala of Mount Meru and so forth,
Together with Samantabhadra's peerless offerings,
I mentally claim and offer (as a mandala)
To the gurus, meditational deities, and Three Precious Gems;
Out of compassion please accept them
And bestow upon me your transforming powers.

Now recite the name mantra (in this case, of His Holiness the
Dalai Lama) as many times as possible: *OM AH GURU VAJRADHARA
VAGINDRA SUMATI SHASANADHARA SAMUDRA SHRIBHADRA
SARVA SIDDHI HUM HUM.*[152]

O rain of benefits and spiritual happiness,
King of jewels, *chittamani*, fulfiller of wishes,
To you, teacher and meditational deity,
All sources of power combined,
I make this request.
Inspire the stream of my being
With your transforming powers and blessings.

By the strength of this single-pointed request,
The constantly sympathetic one

Comes to the crown of my head
And dissolves into me. I myself become glorious Kalachakra,
With all faces and arms.

(The Kalachakra Mantric Recitation)

At your heart visualize either a sun disc bearing the letter *HUM*,
or else a moon disc bearing the syllable "Possessor of Ten Powers."
In either case these are encircled by the *mantramala*.

    As you recite the mantra, visualize that light rays go out from
these, accomplish the two purposes (of self and others), and then
collect together and dissolve back into the *mantramala*.

    The mantra to be recited is as follows: *OM AH HUM HOH
HAMKSHAHMALAVARAYA HUM PHAT.*[153]

(The Concluding Prayer)

By the meritorious energy of this practice
May I never become separated from,
But in life after life be cared for by,
The spiritual masters and meditational deities,
And have the fortune to attain the supreme path.

By having full confidence in the kind masters,
The foundation of all joy and goodness,
Source of every spiritual attainment,
May I delight them with the offerings
Of respect, service, and effective practice.

The opportunities of a human form—
So meaningful, hard to gain, and easily lost;
The sufferings of the lower realms—

So intense and long-lasting:
Knowing this may I live in accord
With karmic law and the precepts of refuge
By constantly living within the guideline
Of transcending the negative and cultivating the good.

No need to speak of the misery of the lower realms,
Even the pleasures of the higher worlds
Are little more than honey on a razor's edge.
In order to gain liberation from this round of becoming,
May I establish within myself the three higher trainings
Of discipline, meditative concentration, and wisdom
And then increase their forces evermore.

May I always dwell within the compassionate bodhi-mind,
The aspiration for enlightenment to benefit the world,
And diligently train in the bodhisattva ways—
The six perfections and four means of benefiting—
And quickly complete the collections of merit and wisdom.

Having thus trained the mind
In the fundamental practices of exoteric Mahayana
And having properly entered into the gateway of the
    peerless Vajrayana
By receiving the appropriate initiations,
May I honor the tantric precepts and commitment
As deeply as I cherish my very life.

Whenever preconceptions of mundane appearance arise,
They should be transformed into the wisdom of bliss and emptiness.
May I single-pointedly practice to fulfillment

The central concept of Tantra's two yogic stages,
This ear-whispered lineage of the great mystery.

May I come before the sublime countenance
Of the illustrious Lord of Shambhala in the
Wondrous land of purity, and quickly actualize
The state of great union, the inseparability
Of the empty body male-and-consort
And the unchanging great bliss.

In the future, during the ripened era of
Raudra Chakri, "The Wrathful Holder of the Wheel,"
May I take birth amongst the foremost disciples
And complete the sublime path of the Primordial Kalachakra,
Becoming a supreme adept, a friend to all.

May I never ever be separated from the spiritual masters;
May I always have access to their enlightenment teachings;
May I accomplish the ten stages and five paths
And quickly attain the state of Buddha Vajradhara.

The merits of having engaged in this practice
I turn into causes for the fulfillment of the deeds
And prayers of the buddhas and bodhisattvas,
And to the upholding of Dharma, scriptural and insight.

The Colophon: This (Tibetan) text is one of ten thousand printed for free distribution at the Kalachakra initiation given by His Holiness the Dalai Lama in Ladakh in 1976, and was adapted from the short guru yoga method composed by Kyabjey Khangsar Dorjechang.

# Chapter Six:

## The First Dalai Lama's

### *Notes on the Two Yogic Stages of Glorious Kalachakra*[154]

#### Gyalwa Gendun Drubpa (1391-1475)

KALACHAKRA

# Translator's Preamble

IN CHAPTER ONE of the present volume the Thirteenth Dalai Lama points out that the Anuttarayoga Tantra systems such as Guhyasamaja, Chakrasamvara, and Vajrabhairava are in a category known as *be gyu,* or "hidden tantras," whereas the Kalachakra is an Anuttarayoga tantra in a category called *sel gyu,* or "clarified tantras."

He writes, "Another important Anuttarayoga Tantra system is that known as the Kalachakra, a tradition that presents the Anuttara path in a manner markedly different than the presentation found in all the other Anuttarayoga systems.... The clarified tantra of the Kalachakra tradition is usually mentioned separately from the other Anuttarayoga systems, for its infrastructure is considerably different than those of the mainstream traditions such as Guhyasamaja, Vajrabhairava, Heruka Chakrasamvara, and so forth."

In the Second Dalai Lama's treatise on the Six Yogas of Niguma (Chapter Three of this volume) we saw quintessential elements from the five tantric systems in the first of the above two categories—the Guhyasamaja, Vajrabhairava, Heruka Chakrasamvara tantric systems, as well as Mahamaya and Hevajra—brought together into a structure organized for easy application. These Anuttara tantric systems are also sometimes referred to as mainstream tantras because they all use a similar language and approach.

The Kalachakra might not be as mainstream, but it is as well known and perhaps even more popular than the others, because of one unique feature. The "hidden tantras," such as Guhyasamaja and Chakrasamvara, have strong practice traditions, and usually initiation into their mandalas means that one must take an oath of daily practice. This usually means a commitment to recite one of the sadhanas, which can take anywhere from a half hour to several hours each day. Thus most Tibetans are reluctant to attend such initiations.

The Kalachakra, however, is unique in that it is often given in public to large groups of people. For example, the present Dalai Lama has given it on almost two dozen occasions, often to crowds numbering in the hundreds of thousands. Usually there is no major practice commitment associated with it, but only the option of reciting a few mantras a day.

The reason for the openness of the Kalachakra, as opposed to the far more exclusive policy of the mainstream tantras—an exclusiveness enforced by this imposition of an arduous daily practice—is usually stated to be karmic propensity. Everyone has a karmic connection with Kalachakra, whereas this is not the case with the mainstream tantras. The reason is that the emphasis in the mainstream tantras is placed upon bodily energies, energy pathways, and so forth. Each of the mainstream tantras takes its own yogic approach to these subjects, and thus practitioners will have a greater propensity for the practice of one of them over the others.

With Kalachakra, however, the "Outer Kalachakra" refers to the universe in general. The Thirteenth Dalai Lama puts it like this in Chapter One of the present volume: "'Outer Kalachakra' comprises the six elements of earth, water, fire, air, space, and wisdom; the world of Mt. Meru, the four continents, and the eight subcontinents and so forth, together with everything above, below, and in all the directions; and also all objects of smell, sight, taste, touch, sound, and dharma."

In other words, Outer Kalachakra is the world in which we live; and because all human beings have a strong karmic connection with this world, all are equally open to attending a Kalachakra initiation.

However, there nonetheless is a strong practice tradition associated with the Kalachakra system, and the First Dalai Lama presents the nuts and bolts of this tradition in straightforward fashion in his treatise. This practice, however, is adopted by the few, rather than by the many. For example, during the three decades I have spent around the Tibetans, I have met hundreds of practitioners who have undertaken the three-year retreat in conjunction with the mainstream tantras, but have met only one who has done this long retreat on the Kalachakra system. Millions receive the initiation, but few take up the practice.

The text is quite important to the Dalai Lama legacy in that it established a precedent of Kalachakra practice for the lineage. Indeed, the Second Dalai Lama claimed to have attained enlightenment through the Kalachakra yogas, which he received from the controversial master Khedrup Norzang Gyatso, often referred to in literature as "the Mad Yogi of the Olkha Mountains." He mentions this in a poem he wrote in praise of this great guru, found in his collection of mystical songs:

> O most holy root guru, through your kindness
> I mastered the yogas of the two tantric stages
> Of glorious Kalachakra, king of the tantras,
> As well as its branches, like astrology,
> That facilitate higher knowledge....
>
> You helped me to see the great inner enemy,
> The "I"-grasping habit that sees things as real,
> And to see its limitlessly harmful effects.
> You also showed me how to destroy it;
> So now everything manifest in the sphere of perception
> Effortlessly arises within the path of the void.

The Dalai Lama link with Kalachakra practice became somewhat weakened during the lives of the Fourth, Fifth, and Sixth incarnations, and during this time the tradition became fragmented and almost extinct. However, the Seventh Dalai Lama had his elderly guru Ngawang Chokden, who later became known to history as the First Reting Rinpochey, travel throughout Central Asia collecting together the various threads of the tradition. Ngawang Chokden then passed them to the Seventh, who revived the legacy. This service to the Kalachakra transmission is referred to in historical literature as one of the four great deeds of the Seventh Dalai Lama.

The Seventh inspired numerous monasteries throughout Central Asia to create departments dedicated exclusively to the study and practice of Kalachakra. Many of these were in Kham and Amdo, in eastern Tibet.

Of course with the present Dalai Lama giving the initiation on so many occasions, half a dozen of which have been in the West, a practicing Western Kalachakra tradition has also begun to emerge. It will be interesting to see how this evolves.

A few remarks on the First Dalai Lama's life and works might be in order, in that he is the source of the Dalai Lama tradition. He was born as one of four sons to a poor family of goat herders in Tsang, Southwest Tibet. His biography speaks in depth of the large number of auspicious signs surrounding his birth, and how even in infancy he showed extraordinary signs of spiritual maturity. Consequently when his father died a few years later, his mother placed him in Nartang Monastery under the care of an uncle, Geshey Choshey by name. Many Western books erroneously state that he was a nephew of Lama Tsongkhapa, founder of the Gelukpa School of Tibetan Buddhism, presumably because they mistake Tsongkhapa for this uncle.

Nartang was one of the great centers of learning in Tibet at the time, and the boy blossomed. By the age of twenty he had become the shining star of young graduates. The Nartang abbot advised him to make pilgrimage to the spiritual centers of Central Tibet and further his studies in the great monastic centers there. He readily accepted, and shortly after arriving in the Lhasa area he encountered the illustrious Lama Tsongkhapa. Lama Tsongkhapa immediately recognized the potential of the young monk, and prophesied that he would bring great benefits to Dharma and living beings.

The First Dalai Lama remained at Tsongkhapa's side for the next four years, receiving many initiations, transmissions, and teachings from him. When Tsongkhapa passed away in 1419, the Dalai Lama continued his training for a further decade under Tsongkhapa's principal disciples, including Gyaltsap Jey, Khedrup Jey, and Sherab Sengey. The third of these three was the disciple to whom Tsongkhapa had entrusted most of his tantric lineages, and the First Dalai Lama took him as his principal guru. The two made many retreats together over the years to follow, until the eager trainee achieved his enlightenment. By the time of his death at the ripe old age of eighty-four, he had become one of the most beloved teachers and saints in Central Asia.

One of his major works was the establishment of Tashilhunpo in Shigatse, near his birthplace in Tsang. Tashilhunpo became one of the six great Gelukpa monastic institutes of Tibet, and remains as such even today. He was also deeply revered for his numerous writings, many of which are still studied in the great monastic universities.

Although he did not write on the Kalachakra tantric system, he frequently taught it, and thus was instrumental in its preservation and dissemination. Fortunately an enterprising disciple took notes at one of his Kalachakra discourses, and these were later incorporated into his official corpus of Collected Works. It is this text that is translated in this chapter.

I originally read and translated the text in the mid-1980s under the guidance of the very wonderful Kyabjey Lati Rinpochey of Ganden Shartsey Monastery, with the assistance of my good friend Tepo

Tulku. Kyabjey Rinpochey is one of the most learned, accomplished, and highly realized Tibetan lamas alive today, and his kindness in taking time to unpack the richness of the First Dalai Lama's words was beyond compare.

# The First Dalai Lama's Text

Homage to the feet of the Lama
Inseparably one with Primordial Kalachakra

HERE THE EXPLANATION of the two yogic stages in the practice of the Kalachakra path will be presented under two headings: a presentation of the general nature of the paths and practices leading to enlightenment, and an explanation of the individual paths and stages.

## THE GENERAL NATURE OF THE PATHS AND PRACTICES

One should first refine the mind by means of the ordinary Sutrayana methods. In specific, cultivate a definite understanding of the pure view of emptiness. Then seek out the complete initiations that ripen the mind and permit one to enter into the extraordinary Vajrayana path. Thereafter, as intensely as one cherishes one's life, one should cherish the disciplines and commitments of the Tantric path, as elucidated at the time of initiation.

With this as the basis one engages in the coarse and subtle yogas of the generation stage, which mature one's being for practice of the completion stage. Finally, when these generation stage yogas have been taken to fulfillment one enters into meditation upon the completion stage, together with its six yogic branches.

The result is the attainment of complete buddhahood in the form of Kalachakra and Consort.

## THE INDIVIDUAL PATHS AND PRACTICES

This will be presented under two headings: the initiations which make one into a proper vessel for Tantric practice; and, having become a proper vessel, the paths upon which one is to meditate.

### THE INITIATIONS WHICH MAKE ONE INTO A PROPER VESSEL FOR TANTRIC PRACTICE

This involves four subjects: the mandala into which initiation is given, the number and stages of initiation, the nature of the individual initiations, and the purpose of initiation.

### THE MANDALA INTO WHICH INITIATION IS GIVEN

The (Indian) mahasiddha Tilbupa (Skt. Ghantapada) writes,

> There are three types of mandalas used as the basis of initiation: those made from colored particles, those painted on canvas, and those visualized in the body.

The Guhyasamaja Tantra[155] and also (Acharya Abhayakaragupta's) The Vajra Rosary of Initiation Rites[156] mention the mandala of *dhyana*, or meditative application, as a fourth alternative.

The Kalachakra tradition differs somewhat from these mainstream traditions, as is explained in The Treatise on the Initiations:[157]

> There are seven initiations. The mandala should be constructed and these should be given. The basis is a mandala made from colored particles.

As clearly stated (by Naropa) in *A Commentary to the Treatise on the Initiations*,[158] the Kalachakra empowerments are to be given solely on the basis of a mandala made of colored powders. It is sufficient to use just the simple form of the mandala, known as "the mind mandala." Accordingly, in (the master's preliminary activity of) generating the mandala by means of the propitiatory recitation, it is sufficient to use a text of only the mind mandala. There is no need to perform the (extensive) invocations of all three mandalas (i.e., of body, speech, and mind).

## THE NUMBER AND STAGES OF INITIATION

Generally it is said that there are eleven initiations: the seven of entering like a child, together with the four standard Highest Yoga Tantra initiations—vase, secret, wisdom, and fourth.

These latter four are given twice, the two phases being called the "higher" and the "higher-than-higher" initiations. However, as the names and nature of these are the same in both phases, they are grouped together. That is, both vase initiations are counted as one, and both secret as one. Both wisdom initiations, together with the fourth initiation of the first set, are also counted as one, as they all share the same nature. Finally, the fourth initiation of the higher-than-higher phase is counted by itself as the fourth initiation (for it alone reveals the full meaning of enlightenment).

These two phases (of four initiations) are preceded by the seven initiations of entering the mandala like a child enters the world. This process of spiritual rebirth is likened to the birth and stages in the growth of a child, such as washing, piercing the ears, giving earrings, encouraging the child to laugh and smile, and so forth. Thus are their names derived.

The initiation ceremony begins with the usual preliminaries (of taking refuge, generating the bodhi-mind, etc.), analyzing the disciple, and so forth. One is then brought to the mandala and given the seven initiations of a child. These are followed by the four higher and then the four higher-than-higher initiations.

During the initiation ceremony one assumes the pledge of secrecy and thereafter if one reveals the secrets of Vajrayana to the uniniti- ated or to the spiritually immature, one's mystic link with the Vajra- yana is broken.

Similarly, if the guru confuses the stages of initiation, he creates the root downfall of speaking the higher secrets to the uninitiated; for the ceremony will be invalid and consequently even though the disciples hear the procedures they remain without initiation.

## THE NATURE AND PURPOSE OF THE INITIATIONS

The seven initiations of entering like a child are each followed by the sprinkling of vase waters. Therefore they are also called the water ini- tiations. The four faces of Kalachakra, which represent the vajra body, speech, mind, and wisdom, reveal the nature of these initiations.

Firstly the disciples are shown the white face of vajra body, which is in the north. This causes them to generate the vajra body. The four consorts residing in the mandala that has been produced from col- ored powders bestow the water initiation, and the five Tathagatas bestow the initiation of the vajra crown.[159]

Next they are shown the red face of vajra speech, which is in the south. This causes them to generate vajra speech. The ten powerful goddesses then bestow the initiation of the silk headdress, and Kala- chakra and Consort bestow the initiation of vajra and bell.

The disciples are now shown the black face of vajra mind, which is in the east. This causes them to generate the vajra mind. The heroes and heroines of the mandala then give the initiation of discipline, and the male and female Wrathful Ones give the initiation of the name

Finally the disciples are shown the yellow face of wisdom, which is in the west. This causes the vajra wisdom to be generated within them. Vajrasattva and Consort give the initiation of permissions.

Anyone who attains these seven initiations and takes the practice of the generation stage to fulfillment shall become a master of the seven stages in this very life. Even if one is not able to complete these generation stage yogas before death strikes, this attainment will definitely be achieved within seven lifetimes.

The main purpose of these seven initiations is to transform the spiritual aspirant into a vessel suitable for practice of the generation stage yogas, and to provide a path for the cultivation of meditative stability. However, the initiations of the silk headdress and of the vajra and bell also have the function of transforming the disciple into a vessel capable of successfully practicing the completion stage yogas, which gain control over the ten energies flowing through the secondary channels of the body and redirect them into the *dhuti*, the central channel.

The next set of initiations, known as the four higher initiations, have both generation and completion stage associations.

For example, the nature of the vase initiation is as follows. The disciple is (symbolically) given a mudra possessing the appropriate characteristics. He (visualizes) holding her in his arms, stroking her breasts, and so forth.

The great bliss that arises confers the vase initiation. Thus it is associated with the initiation of a master and is explained as the yoga of transforming ordinary lust into a force of enlightenment.

The reason it is given the name "the master's initiation" is revealed by the following scriptural passage (from *The Abbreviated Kalachakra Tantra*[160]):

> The masters regard sensuality as (a potential path of) purification.

The four phases of the first set of four initiations that follow are much the same as their counterparts in the mainstream Highest Yoga tantras, although there are a few exceptions. For example, even though the secret initiation in the first set (of four) is much the same as in other Highest Yoga Tantra systems, there is the distinction that here in Kalachakra when the blindfold is removed from the disciple's eyes he is told to look at the outspread vulva of a knowledge dakini. This arouses fierce passion, which in turn gives rise to great bliss. This bliss introduces the nature of the secret initiation. (In other words, the initiation is not bestowed by the power of the red and white substances, as they are in the mainstream tantras.)

Also, the fourth initiation (of the first set of four) differs from the fourth initiation given in the mainstream tantric systems. Here it is called by the name of a fourth initiation, but in fact is closer in nature to the third, that of wisdom awareness. The disciple (visualizes being) given a knowledge dakini and entering into sexual union with her. The sexual substances come to the tip of the jewel, and the bliss thus aroused confers this fourth initiation. (As this bliss is in the nature of the wisdom initiation), this fourth initiation is called "the worldly fourth initiation" (for it does not reveal the final meaning of enlightenment).

The first three of the higher-than-higher initiations that follow are as in the previous set, with the exception that on each occasion the visualized sexual union is performed with nine consorts rather than only one. The manner of inducing (the bliss that confers) the initiations is much the same. However, here the fourth initiation, which reveals the full meaning of what is to be accomplished and what transcended, possesses the full characteristics of a fourth initiation and thus is called "the nonworldly fourth initiation."

## THE PATHS TO BE MEDITATED UPON

This will be presented under three headings: the vows, commitments, and disciplines to be maintained by a Kalachakra initiate; on the basis of this training, how to meditate on the generation stage yogas; and, having thus ripened one's stream of being, how to meditate upon the completion stage yogas.

## THE DISCIPLINES AND COMMITMENTS TO BE MAINTAINED

These should be known from either the long or short versions of *A Treatise on the Root Downfalls*.[161]

## THE GENERATION STAGE YOGAS

The degree to which one accomplishes the generation stage yogas is the degree to which one prepares the basis to be purified and ripens one's mindstream for the higher yogas (of the completion stage). The meditator who has accomplished the generation stage yogas will have little difficulty in mastering the yogas of the completion stage. Thus its purpose is one of speed in the attainment of enlightenment.

However, meditation upon Solitary Kalachakra alone is not enough to bring about the desired purification, even on the coarse level. Taking a complete mandala (of body, speech, and mind), or one such as the mind mandala, which uses symbolism revealing all stages of evolution and dissolution of the world, the basis to be purified, we should apply ourselves to the three Kalachakras to be understood—Outer, Inner, and Alternative—and meditate upon the four stages of the Kalachakra generation stage yoga, which uses spiritual symbolism based on the natural processes of evolution and dissolution (i.e., how the world comes into existence and then disintegrates, and how sentient beings enter the world and then leave it).

Of the three Kalachakras mentioned above, Outer and Inner Kalachakras are the bases to be purified, whereas Alternative Kalachakra refers to the yogic practices that effect this purification and produce the three purified results.

Outer Kalachakra comprises the outer world, which is the vessel supporting the living beings. Thus it includes the planets of this solar system, as well as the sun, moon, stars, and so on.

Inner Kalachakra refers to the living beings of the world, such as human beings, who are born from a womb and who possess the six elements. Here the basis to be purified includes the aggregates, spheres of perception, channels, mystic drops, and so forth of these beings. These are all incorporated into the symbolism of the path.

One meditates upon these two Kalachakras in order to free them from obscurations.

These are the Outer and Inner Kalachakras, the bases to be purified. Because they are thus associated with the path and its results, they may be subsumed under the classification of Alternative Kalachakra.

In this context, Alternative Kalachakra has three aspects: the methods of purifying the internal bases, those for purifying the external bases, and the methods of proceeding in the generation stage yogas as a means to prepare the mind for the completion stage.

(A characteristic of the Kalachakra generation stage practice is that) the wheel of protection is not applied to the basis of purification. Instead one begins by paying homage to the visualized Field of Merit. This is a spiritual metaphor for how sentient beings generate the positive karma that produces rebirth with a special form in future lives.

One then recites the passage, "Because there is no inherent existence there is no inherent meditation. Meditation that grasps at inherent existence (of meditation) is not real meditation. Similarly, the things that we perceive are all nonexistent." Having pronounced this, one meditates on the stages of dissolution of the dual appearance of the world and its inhabitants, and then concentrates directly on the four doors of liberation (emptiness, signlessness, wishlessness, and nonactivity).

This is a spiritual metaphor for the dissolution of the physical elements during the death of someone who has created much positive karma and whose death is followed by the conscious experience of clear light.

One then proceeds with the five purifications, or "enlightenments." This begins with the visualization of the spacelike *dharmodaya*, or "source of phenomena," which symbolizes the basis of existence. In Kalachakra this is represented by empty space, and is symbolized by the sexual organ of a woman. (Just as we humans issue forth from the sexual organ of our mother, all phenomena manifest from within empty space, and the mandala of Kalachakra issues forth from the blissful wisdom of emptiness.)

Inside of this is the air mandala, which is related to the area between the crown and forehead of the consort. Above the air mandala is the mandala of fire, associated with the area from the forehead to the throat. Above this is the water mandala, associated with the area from the throat to the heart. Above this is the mandala of earth, associated with the area between the heart and navel of the consort. Above this is Mount Meru, associated with the area from the navel to the anus. Above this is a lotus, associated with the area between the secret place and secret lotus of the consort.

Above this is a moon, sun, and *kalagni* disc. These are associated with the three energy channels leading to the lotus of the consort, called "the conch," and which direct the energies causing solid and liquid wastes, as well as the sexual substances, to move. Then above this is the vajra tent, symbolic of the father's act of placing his vajra in the secret place of the consort.

Inside the vajra tent is the inconceivable mansion, the secret place of the consort; and inside this the vowels and consonants of the Sanskrit alphabet stand upright upon cushions of moon and sun discs. From the moon(s) and sun(s) arise the white and red bodhi-mind substances, symbolic of the mixing of sperm and ovum in the secret place of the consort.

Between the moon and sun appears the letter *HUM*, like the outline of the hare in the moon, symbolic of the entrance of a bardo being into the newly fertilized ovum mixture. This is marked by a black letter *HIH*, symbolizing the vital energies (produced by the fusion of sperm and ovum) which act as the vehicle of consciousness (symbolized by the syllable *HUM*). These all merge together and transform into the letter *HAM*, symbolic of the growth of the body in the womb of the consort. The letter *HAM* then transforms into light and reemerges as complete Glorious Kalachakra.

This process, until the complete generation of the deities of the supremely victorious mandala (i.e., first of the four generation stage meditations), symbolizes the complete evolution of the fetus, including the five aggregates, five elements, six sensory powers, six spheres of perception, five powers of action, and their five functions. This process is given a spiritual context by the twenty stages called "the twenty enlightenments."

When the meditation enters the phase known as victorious activity (i.e., second of the four generation stage meditations), Vajravega arises from the wisdom-energies at one's heart and emanates forth. Instantly the wisdom-winds stir, summoning the Wisdom Beings, who merge with the previously visualized Symbolic Beings, becoming of one taste with them.

This stage of meditation until the completion of the victorious activities practice represents the growth of the body and the experience of sexuality.

One then engages in "the yoga of the drop." Here one focuses on the multicolored consort, consecrates the vajra of the male and the lotus of the female, and meditates that they enter into sexual union.

This causes the letter *HAM* to melt and fall from its abode at the crown. Gradually it descends (through the energy centers of the body), inducing the four joys successively. Finally it arrives at the tip of the jewel, where it is retained.

This is the yoga of the drop of simultaneously-arising bliss and (primordial wisdom of) emptiness (i.e., third of the four generation stage meditations).

The drop is then drawn back up to the crown, and one meditates within the sphere of bliss and emptiness. This is "the subtle yoga" (i.e., the fourth generation stage meditation).

Having generated the mandala and completed the four generation stage meditations in this way, one then proceeds to recite the mantras and so forth.

The conventional symbol for these experiences is a sixteen-year-old maiden with a special sensitivity for sensual ecstasy.

## THE COMPLETION STAGE YOGAS

The explanation of the completion stage yogas will be given under three headings: the characteristics of the vajra body upon which the yogas are concentrated, a general explanation of how these six yogas are used in this application, and an explanation of each yoga individually.

### The Characteristics of the Vajra Body

The first of these involves three subjects: the abiding channels, the flowing energies, and the bodhi-mind substances that are to be directed.

### The Abiding Channels

The discussion of the energy channels involves three subjects: the nature of the six main channels and the six main chakras (energy centers) at which these converge, how these energy centers are stimulated through the six-branched yoga, and an outline of which of the six yogas is applied to which of the six energy centers.

### The Six Channels and Six Energy Centers

The three main energy channels are called *roma*, *kyangma*, and *dhuti*. These begin at the tip of the sexual organ, proceed back to the anus, and then run straight up the center of the body with an occasional slight bend. Eventually they come to the inside of the cranium and then curve down, terminating respectively at the top of the nostril passages and at the pillar between these.

These three are divided into upper and lower portions.

The upper central channel, called (the planet) *rahu*, and also *nyi-pang* and *avadhuti*, begins just above the navel. Associated with the element space, it is greenish in color, and its main function is to cause the descent of vital energy in the body.

To the right of this is *roma*, also called *rasana* and *nyima* (the sun). Red in color, it is associated with the element fire, and its main function is to cause female sexual fluids (i.e., hormones) and blood (ovum) to descend.

To the left of this is *kyangma*, which is also called *lalana* and *dawa* (the moon). White in color, it is associated with the element water, and its main function is to cause the male fluids to descend.

All three of these energy channels are dominated by the life-supporting energies flowing within them.

Below the navel, the central channel curves to the right and comes to the tip of the sexual organ. Here it is called (the flower) *kundarma*, *dungchen* (the conch), and (the planet) *kalagni*. Associated with the element of primordial wisdom, its color is blue and its main function is to cause male hormones and sperm to descend.

The left channel also curves to the center and comes to the tip of the organ. Called *lug* (the sheep), it is black in color and is associated with the air element. Its main function is to cause waste fluids to descend.

The right channel curves to the left and comes to the anus. Its name is *marser* (crimson), and it is associated with the earth element. Yellow in color, its main function is to cause feces and wastes to descend.

All three of these channels are conditioned by the downward-moving energies flowing within them.

Sometimes through incorrect meditation the downward-moving

energies (that reside in the lower channels) are caused to flow into the upper channels, and the life-supporting energies (that reside above) are forced to flow down into the lower, giving rise to many unpleasant and dangerous conditions, such as violent disease.

If such dramatic effects can be produced through (incorrect) meditation, then why should correct application not have similarly powerful results in the opposite direction—results such as eliminating physical diseases and destroying the causes of death?

In the Kalachakra system the six energy centers, or chakras, are as follows.

The first is located just below the crown aperture of the skull and has four petals of energy channels. The second is at the forehead and has sixteen petals. The third is located at the throat and has thirty-two petals. The fourth, which has eight petals, is at the heart. The fifth has sixty-four petals and is located at the navel. The sixth has two branches: the first at the anus, with thirty-two petals, and the second at the center of the sexual jewel, with eight petals.[162]

At the energy centers the left channel coils clockwise around the central channel, and the right counterclockwise, thus forming two knots that obstruct the free flow of vital energies.

One should also know how these channels converge at the centers and how they influence the flow of vital energies. This may be studied in larger commentaries.

The nature and binding effect of these knots upon the subtle energies of the body, and the consequent repercussions on consciousness, are explained in detail in the "Chapter on Wisdom" of *The Abbreviated Kalachakra Tantra*.

In other tantric systems it is often said that when the side channels form knots around the central channel, they do so very tightly, leaving no space whatsoever in the coils. In Kalachakra, however, one visualizes the knots as being loose and as having space between the coils.

### How the Energy Centers Are Stimulated

There are many different methods for generating tantric experience by means of drawing the male and female substances as well as the vital energies through the center of the chakras as explained above and for opening the central channel from top to bottom. These may be learned in detail from larger commentaries. The essence is as follows.

### The Six Yogas and Six Energy Centers

When practicing the first two yogas—those of individual withdrawal and *dhyana*—one successively concentrates the drops and energies at the upper aperture of the central channel. During the yogas of energy control and subsequent mindfulness one focuses these at the navel. The yoga of retention brings them into the central channel running through the center of all six energy centers. Finally, by means of the yogas of samadhi the energies are concentrated from the base to the top of the central channel.

### The Flowing Energies

The Kalachakra literature does not speak of five root and five secondary energies (as do the mainstream tantras such as Guhyasamaja and so forth). Yet it too speaks of ten subtle bodily energies, and these share the same nature (as the ten in the mainstream systems). In fact the ten (in both systems) are actually subsumed under the five root energies. In this tradition (i.e., Kalachakra) it is said that the all-pervading energy flows mainly through the gates of the nostrils.

Where are these first energies generated and where do they abide?

Ten energy channels converge at the heart. The two apertures of the central channel, above and below the knots at the heart, are the respective sites where the life-sustaining and downward-moving energies first arise and then abide.

As for the pathways of their flow, the life-sustaining energy mostly flows in the three upper channels and the downward-moving through the three lower channels.

Similarly, the petals to the east and southeast of the heart are the sites of the equally-abiding and "turtle" energies. The south and southwest are the sites of the upward-moving and pristine energies. The north and northeast petals are the sites of the all-pervading and divinely predisposed energies. The western and northwestern petals are the sites of the *lu* and *norlegyal* energies. These are the sites where they first arise and where they abide.

These then flow through the major ten channels. The channels themselves subdivide into many smaller passageways, which pervade the entire body like a fine network of interconnected tunnels.

### The Bodhi-Mind Substances to Be Directed

This involves three subjects: how at the time of conception the body is formed from the white and red bodhi-mind substances, or white and red drops; how these evolve during one's life; and how they move at the time of death.

The Kalachakra tradition speaks of the droplike substances in three ways: the drops generated on the four occasions (waking, dreaming, deep sleep, and sexual excitation); the drops of body, speech, mind, and wisdom; and the drops of form, sound, thought, and primordial wisdom. These terms have the same referents, and an understanding of their basis, nature, and functions is indispensable to the completion stage practices. Therefore the topic is usually introduced at this point in the presentation.

The site of the drop of the waking-state occasion, the body, and form is at the forehead. The site of the drop of the dream state, speech, and sound is at the throat. The site of the drop of deep sleep, mind, and thought is at the heart. Finally, the site of the drop of sexual ecstasy, wisdom, and primordial wisdom is at the navel.

Again, the procedure for working with these drops is to bring them down from above through the central channel to the center of the tip of the jewel, beginning with the waking-state drop and eventually uniting with the drop of primordial wisdom.

Moreover, when the drop of the fourth occasion melts (i.e., sexual ecstasy) and the collective substances are brought through the energy centers at the navel and jewel, one experiences an especially intense great bliss. The reason for this is that the drop of the fourth occasion is first generated at these two points.

The forehead and the jewel are the main sites of the white bodhi-mind substances, and here the red substances are weaker. The actual abode of the white substances, which act as the basis increasing the male energies, is the chakra at the forehead.

The main sites of the red bodhi-mind substances are the energy centers of the navel, secret place, and throat. Here the force of the red substance dominates and the white is weaker.

At the energy center located at the heart the two substances (white and red) abide with equal strength.

As explained in *The Vajra Rosary Tantra*,[163] the drops formed from the white and red droplets that abide in each of these energy centers are visualized as being the size of a sesame seed.

In the Kalachakra tradition all obscurations are categorized within the drops of the four occasions. As for how the obscurations are linked to the drops, here it is said that the drops are focal points for the extremely subtle energies and states of consciousness, and the instincts of the obscurations actually abide upon them. These instincts give rise to both the obscurations to liberation (or the host of eighty-four thousand delusions) and the obscurations to knowledge.

Thus although the drops are composed of atoms (and therefore cannot actually function as a basis of obscuration, in that they act as focal points of the subtle energies and states of consciousness which carry the instincts of obscurations), to speak of them in this way is reasonable.

The drops of both the waking and fourth occasion states are at the navel. Through generating either or both of them one stimulates the according instincts and experiences the according occasion (i.e., wakefulness and/or sexual ecstasy).

Concerning the drop at the heart, it is said to represent the basis of the body in which one experiences deep sleep.

The way in which the drops of deep sleep, dream, and waking occasions cause us to experience these three events is as follows.

When the coarse energies absorb into the chakras of the central channel at the jewel and heart, one experiences deep sleep. When these energies arise and enter into both the throat and secret place, one experiences very clear dreams for a prolonged period of time. Should these energies move to the navel and forehead, one awakens from sleep and is able to perceive the manifest objects of the external world.

Thus in the course of our day-to-day experience our mindset arises in synchronicity with these inner changes. This suggests that control of these energies and drops has a great effect on our stream of being, and that if one is able to apply the skillful yogas of the Tantric path, one can control one's states of consciousness on this primordial level and transform them into qualities of buddhahood. This powerful technique of working with the subtle energies and energy centers is found exclusively in the Highest Yoga Tantra systems.

For ordinary beings the drops of the four occasions—waking, dream, deep sleep, and sexual ecstasy—carry the potencies that induce perception of the impure objects of the world, the potencies that cause confused appearances and sound, the potencies giving rise to obscurity of mind and ignorance, and the potencies arousing dissipating bliss.

These potencies are purified by the Kalachakra yogas. To be specific, they are transformed into the empty body, unconfused sound, nonconceptual wisdom, and unchanging bliss. These are cultivated to perfection, giving rise to the vajra body, speech, and mind of a buddha, and to fully manifest primordial wisdom.

How do the six yogas purify the bases?

The stains generated on the occasion of the waking state are purified and transformed into a similitude of the path by a concentrated application of the combined yogas of individual withdrawal, *dhyana*, and subsequent mindfulness. The drop of sleep is purified and transformed into the path through the yoga of energy control and retention. The drops of sleep and sexual climax are purified through the combined yogas of subsequent mindfulness and samadhi, and are thus turned into the nature of the path.

The first of these purifications—the yoga of individual withdrawal—eliminates the stains of the drop generated in the waking state of the forehead and transforms it into the nature of the path. The yoga of subsequent mindfulness eliminates the stains of the waking drop at the navel and, used in another way, also purifies the stains of the drop of sexual ecstasy. As explained earlier, the drop at the navel carries the potencies of generating both waking state and sexual ecstasy experiences (so this combined yogic approach is necessary).

### A General Explanation of How the Six Yogas Are to Be Applied

Upon what original tantric texts and later Indian commentaries do we base the Kalachakra doctrines of the six yogas and the manner in which they work with the drops, energies, channels, and so forth?

It seems that the extensive version of *The Kalachakra Root Tantra*[164] (that Buddha taught to Suchandra) remained in Shambhala and never appeared in either India or Tibet. Only that section of *The Kalachakra Root Tantra* entitled *The Treatise on the Initiations* has come down to us today. Naropa wrote an important commentary to this, and the two are often studied together.

Other important early Kalachakra texts (written in Shambhala and India) are *The Abbreviated Kalachakra Tantra* (by Manju Yashas of

Shambhala); the threefold collection known as *Trilogy of the Bodhi-sattvas*[165] (i.e., *The Great Commentary: A Stainless Light,*[166] *The Vajra-garbha Commentary,*[167] and *The Vajrapani Commentary*[168]); the treatise on the six yogas by the mahasiddha Anupamarakshita,[169] whom we Tibetans call Pemetso; and the commentary to that by Suryashri.[170] There are also the (four) works of Shavari: one on the six yogas,[171] one on his personal insights, his summary, and his approach to the ultimate.

### Opening Discussion of the Six Yogas

The opening discussion of the six yogas will address three topics: a general introduction to the six yogas, the certainty of their number, and the certainty of their order in practice.

### How the Six Are Introduced

The first of these subjects involves four topics: the names of the six yogas, how these six yogas function as the four branches of approach and accomplishment, how they are grouped into the threefold vajra yoga and the threefold virtue, and how they are grouped into the three branches (of attainment).

The names of the six yogas are: individual withdrawal, *dhyana,* energy control, retention, subsequent mindfulness, and samadhi (or absorption).

As for the second topic (of how the yogas function as approach and accomplishment), here the yogas of individual withdrawal and *dhyana* are the approach. The yogas of energy control and retention serve as the proximate accomplishment. The yoga of subsequent mindfulness serves as the accomplishment; and the yoga of samadhi is linked to the great accomplishment, the attainment of the state of a mahasiddha, a mighty tantric adept.

The third topic involves the threefold vajra yoga and the threefold virtue. These are explained as follows. In the beginning of practice the yogas of individual withdrawal and *dhyana* serve as the virtuous vajra body yoga. In the middle, the yogas of energy control and retention serve as the virtuous vajra speech yoga. Finally, the yogas of subsequent mindfulness and samadhi serve as the virtuous vajra mind yoga.

When these are spoken of as four rather than the three vajras, this is effected by subdividing the last category into two, at which time the yoga of subsequent mindfulness is associated with the vajra mind, and the yoga of samadhi is linked to primordial vajra wisdom.

The six yogas can also be otherwise arranged into three branches, wherein the yogas of individual withdrawal and *dhyana* combine as the branch that accomplishes form; the yogas of energy control and retention combine as the branch that accomplishes higher energy; and the yogas of subsequent mindfulness and samadhi combine as the branch that accomplishes bliss.

To explain what this means in easily understood terms, the idea is that we apply the yogas of individual withdrawal and *dhyana* in order to produce a previously unknown form, and then by means of making this accomplishment firm, we stabilize the (substitute) empty body. Therefore these two yogas are said to be branches accomplishing form.

We then engage the yoga of energy control and apply the special techniques in order to direct the life sustaining and downward-moving energies to the navel energy center, where they are brought together and used to gain control over the other energies. After this, the yoga of retention is applied to bring the energies of all the six centers to the navel as before. Therefore these two yogas serve as branches producing higher energy. They are also therefore sometimes referred to as the branch establishing control over the vital energies.

Thus the yogas of individual withdrawal and *dhyana* reveal the empty body, and the yogas of energy control and retention bring the vital energies under control. That uncontrived yogi applies subsequent mindfulness to his own empty body and attains the ability to arise in the form of Kalachakra and Consort. At that time there appear the forms of the various empty-body *shaktis*. This is known as "empty-body mahamudra." The yogi, who has arisen in the form of the empty-body deity, then sexually unites with these goddesses, giving rise to the extraordinary, supreme, unchanging bliss. This is the fruition and final experience of the yoga of samadhi, and it is for this reason that the fifth and sixth yogas are grouped together as the branch producing bliss.

### The Number of the Yogas

As we can see from the above description, by accomplishing the first four yogas one engages the fifth (the yoga of subsequent mindfulness) and gains the ability to arise in a qualified empty body. The strength of that attainment in turn provides the basis for success in the sixth and final yoga, that of samadhi.

Thus (the six yogas by themselves have the power to generate the attainment of full enlightenment, and so) there is no need to supplement them with various assortments of other practices, nor to practice anything on top of them. On the other hand, to omit any of them will impair the system's potency (to produce enlightenment).

### Their Order in Practice

The six yogas are practiced in the order listed above. That is, one gains proficiency in the first before proceeding to the second, and so forth. To practice the later yogas before accomplishing the earlier ones will not produce the desired results. It is the impact of each one that carries the yogi successively across the stages of the path, and that prepares one for the next yoga to be approached. It is important to understand how this process works, and to engage in the training accordingly.

The Kalachakra doctrine of the extraordinary empty body is

somewhat similar to the illusory body doctrine of the mainstream Yoga Tantra systems, although the basis of this accomplishment must be effected by means of the first of the six yogas, that of individual withdrawal. The second yoga, that of *dhyana*, then makes this attainment firm. The empty body which has thus been produced by these two yogas, which are categorized as the branch accomplishing form, becomes one's extraordinary body (used as the basis supporting the mind in meditation). The third and fourth yogas—those of energy control and retention—are then applied in order to gain control over the subtle energies. Next, in reliance upon the external condition of a mudra, one applies subsequent mindfulness to one's own attainment and arises in the empty-body form of Kalachakra and Consort. This gives rise to the bliss that is the yoga of samadhi abiding in union.

Here the empty body produced by the yoga of subsequent mindfulness is similar to the third-stage illusory body attainment of the completion stage yogas of mainstream Tantric paths such as Guhyasamaja (i.e., the "impure" illusory body).

Moreover, the yoga of samadhi is similar to the yoga of great union in the other systems, although there are significant differences within the boundaries of the stages and how they are said to be accomplished. For instance, (in Guhyasamaja and so forth) the yoga of great union is associated solely with the arya stages, whereas in the Kalachakra tradition the yoga of samadhi also includes non-arya stages. From the time one first engages the yoga of samadhi until the time this yoga is fulfilled, one experiences the twelve levels as a result of the 1,800 dissolutions produced by the 21,600 moments of unchanging bliss. The first of these levels begins on the ordinary (i.e., non-arya) stage.

According to the illusory body doctrine in systems like Guhyasamaja, the basis of the accomplishment is established by the very first yoga, namely that of body isolation. This is then gradually intensified by means of the yoga of speech isolation, until eventually one comes to the third stage and arises within an illusory body.

If we compare this to the process of the empty body discussed in the Kalachakra tradition, here a stabilized similitude of this special body is first produced by the second yoga, that of *dhyana*. This accomplishment is gradually intensified from that point until the yoga of retention; but the empty body itself is not actually produced until the fifth yoga is applied, that of subsequent mindfulness. The empty body produced here has very little equivalent on the stage of the yoga of individual withdrawal (for this one is utterly nonmaterial).

Having applied the yoga of subsequent mindfulness, in the occasions that follow one relinquishes all physical attributes and arises solely on the basis of the Kalachakra empty body.

*An Explanation of Each of the Yogas*
Here each of the six yogas will be explained in turn, beginning with the yoga of individual withdrawal.

1. *The Yoga of Individual Withdrawal.* This will be explained under seven headings: (*a*) the meaning of the name of the yoga, (*b*) the place for performing the meditation, (*c*) the time for the meditation, (*d*) ascertaining the position of the body, (*e*) the manner of glancing, (*f*) entering the suchness of mind, and (*g*) the signs of progress.

(*a*) The yoga of individual withdrawal is so called because its main function is to cut off the individual activity of vital energies in the six sensory organs and the six spheres of sensory perception, and to withdraw these energies into utter stillness, and then individually release them.

As is said in the "Chapter on Accomplishment" (of *The Abbreviated Kalachakra Tantra*), "In the yoga of individual withdrawal the vital energies are not allowed to divert into the objects or object perceivers." The meaning is that the currents of energies to the diverse sites of sensory perception and to their objects are severed.

This is also stated in *The Treatise on Severing the Connections:*[172]

> The method is not the simple application of attentive
> mindfulness (as is the case of the Sutrayana path). Merely
> holding the mind in one-pointed concentration upon a
> mental object is not enough to withdraw the subtle ener-
> gies from the organs of sensory awareness. Holding the
> mind on a second object does not have the power to cause
> (the energies) to withdraw from other activity.

The reason is that a mere mental application is not strong enough
to eliminate the activity of the subtle energies in the sensory spheres
and so forth.

Therefore in the Kalachakra yogas it is said that one should stimulate the points of the vajra body, causing the vital energies upon
which consciousness rides to be diverted into the central channel.
Here they enter, abide, and dissolve, giving rise to a yogic experience
wherein sensory consciousness is turned back from moving toward
the sensory objects, and the connections to the individual subjects
are severed.

(*b*) The place for practicing this meditation is an extremely dark
room.

(*c*) As for the time of the practice, it is said that the yoga is to be
applied when the earth energies course more strongly in the right
nostril. This is a period when one's system is in a natural posture of
withdrawal, so to apply the yogas of individual withdrawal at this
time easily produces results.

(*d*) The position in which one should sit to perform the yoga of
individual withdrawal is either the vajra or *sattva* positions. The

hands are formed into vajra fists, with the finger knuckles facing upwards and the back of the hands pressed tightly against the two major arteries of the thighs. The elbows are kept tightly against the body and the back totally straight.

One should sit in this position without moving for the entire session, regardless of what pains come into the limbs, eyes, and so forth.

(*e*) Progress in the yoga of individual withdrawal is accompanied by the ten signs. These must arise inside the *avadhuti*, the central channel.

As is said in the "Chapter on Wisdom" (of *The Abbreviated Kalachakra Tantra* by the Shambhala kalkin Manju Yashas):

> . . .until one sees a black outline emanating stainless light inside the channel of time.

Also, *The Great Commentary: A Stainless Light* (by Kalkin Pundarika of Shambhala) states,

> . . .until the signs appear in the *avadhuti*, the channel of time.

Also, the "Chapter on Wisdom" (of *The Abbreviated Kalachakra Tantra*) states,

> The signs do not appear externally, such as in the sky. The eyes are partially closed, a glance cast upward, and the signs observed in the central channel.

*The Great Commentary* adds,

> One glances at the vajra path. When the vital energies enter
> into the center of this and only emptiness is experienced,
> one beholds the signs, such as smoke.

The meaning (of this passage) is that by bringing the vital energies
into the central channel, holding them there, and then dissolving
them, one gradually attains the ten signs of progress, such as smoke.

As said above, the eyes and the mind should focus upon the central channel at the point where it passes through the energy center of
the forehead. This is pointed out in the "Chapter on Accomplishment" (of *The Abbreviated Kalachakra Tantra*):

> In the first of the ten yogic applications the yogi perform-
> ing the propitiation casts the wrathful glance of the wheel
> bearer. This glance, the destroyer of demons, enters into
> the path of nectar and reveals the signs of progress in the
> six-branched yoga.

*The Great Commentary: A Stainless Light* adds,

> The (words) "wheel bearer" refer to the wrathful glance
> (that the yogi casts) toward the crown protrusion, his eyes
> partially closed and looking upward. This causes the signs
> to appear.

Thus during the yogas of individual withdrawal and *dhyana* the
casting of the upward glance is said to be crucial to the practice.
*The Great Commentary: A Stainless Light* continues,

> ... in the expression "the glance that destroys demons," the
> destroyer of demons is the (drop of) swirling nectar. The
> glance moves to the place of the nectar, meaning that it
> moves toward the forehead chakra.

What this is talking about is the droplet of bodhi-mind substance, likened to *kunda* nectar, that resides in the central channel at the chakra of the forehead. Casting the glance there means focusing on the site of the droplet of nectar.

The reason for casting the glance at this spot is that by the yogas of individual withdrawal and *dhyana* one newly produces the empty body and then makes this attainment firm. As was said earlier, the drop of the waking state is located at the energy center at the crown, and it is this drop that carries the potencies that give rise to the appearances that characterize the waking state. By focusing on this and entering into meditation, the experiences of the various objects that manifest to the mind on the basis of this drop are severed. When this occurs, images of empty-body deities begin to arise at this site.

As for the signs themselves, *The Guhyasamaja Tantra* states,

> The first is like a mirage, the second like smoke, the third like the flickering of fireflies, the fourth like a butterlamp, and the fifth like the space of clouds. These are the five signs that appear.

In Kalachakra, the first two signs arise in reversed order. Also *The Arali Tantra* states,

> The eyes are held half closed and a glance cast upward at the point between the eyebrows.

The meaning is that the yogi casts a glance up to the center of the eyebrows and focuses the mind one-pointedly on the empty space of the upper aperture of the central channel, thus concentrating the vital energies.

Here the expression "mind focused on space" is used. This "space" refers to that inside the upper aperture of the central channel. Awareness should not be allowed to wander elsewhere. The word "space" here does not suggest that we place the awareness on the nature of external space; it is suggesting something altogether different. This is "the space inside the upper aperture."

(*f*) (At a later stage in the practice,) when we apply the yogas of energy control and retention (i.e., the third and fourth of the Kalachakra six yogas), the vital energies are brought under control and directed into the central channel. This causes the fires of the mystic heat to blaze upward and to melt the bodhi-mind substances, giving rise to great bliss. This consciousness of great bliss then becomes the subjective mind that is directed into meditation upon the object of suchness.

However, here when we are still in the stages of the first two yogas—those of individual withdrawal and *dhyana*—our purpose is solely to newly create a substitute for an empty body, and then to make that accomplishment firm. It is not to establish a meditation upon suchness as a cause sharing the nature of the Dharmakaya, but rather simply to establish a similitude of the empty body.

(*g*) Many stages of signs appear during the yogas of individual withdrawal and *dhyana*, beginning with those that arise when one concentrates the energies at the doors of the organs and so forth. At this point in practice, the signs seem to arise in one's meditation hut.

Next one brings the energies into the central channel for the first time. The signs of this experience seem to appear at various places throughout the body, but not inside the central channel itself.

The signs that seem to arise inside the upper aperture itself are those that indicate (progress in the production of) the empty body at the site of the upper aperture.

The scriptures state that four signs arise during the day and six during the night, elucidating the manner of their appearance with certainty. The signs appear consecutively, and the third must arise before the fourth, etc. (for their appearance to be significant). Each stage of yogic experience must be made clear and firm before proceeding to the next.

In the Guhyasamaja yogas the first sign to appear is that like a mirage. In the Kalachakra yogas, however, the first to appear is the smokelike apparition. There are a number of reasons for this, linked to the place, time, and manner in which the specific yogic techniques are applied, and the manner in which the observation (for signs) is made.

In the Kalachakra system, the signs such as smoke and so forth that arise when the yogi begins to newly create the special empty body arise in the order they do because they signify the successive diversion of the ten energies that flow through the "petals" of channels that converge at the heart.

First the vital energies passing through the four petals of the four intermediate directions at the heart chakra—the *rupel, tsangpa, lhachin,* and *norlegyal* energies—are successively arrested, beginning with those of the southeast channel and moving around to the northwest "petal." From this one experiences the four signs: those of smoke, a mirage, flickering (like that of) fireflies, and a butterlamp. Then beginning in the east and moving around to the west, the energies flowing through the channels of the cardinal directions are arrested. These are the equally-abiding, upward-flowing, all-pervading, and *lu* energies. One perceives the signs that are like (the appearance in the sky of the planet) *kalagni,* the moon, the sun, and (the planet) *rahu.*

One then cuts off the flow of the life-sustaining and downward-moving energies that course above and below, thus experiencing the signs of lightning and the drop.

This phase of the completion stage yogas, which gives rise to the experience of these signs of controlling the ten energies in the production of the (substitute) empty body, is made possible by the foundations that were laid earlier in the generation stage yoga. This involved the meditation on the eight *shaktis*, who were contemplated as being in the nature of the knots in the channels at the heart and navel, together with the petals of the chakra of bliss at the navel. In the generation stage yogas (these eight become ten by counting them together with) Kalachakra and Consort, (thus symbolizing the control over all ten energies). Here Kalachakra represents the element of space and the Consort symbolizes primordial awareness. Their sexual union is the joining of the upper and lower apertures, and the union of the two principal energies.

In this way the generation stage yogas make one into a vessel for the completion stage practices. This meditation upon the ten vital energies of the student as the powerful goddesses is also linked with the initiation of the silk headdress.

At the end of appearance of the ten signs there arises the image of a shimmering black outline, the thickness of a hair, in the drop. This signifies the production of (the basis of) a Sambhogakaya form possessed of the five certainties. Here the certain time is at the end of the completion of the arisal of the ten signs, and the certain place is inside the central channel. The certain nature is that this body is not based upon either coarse or subtle atoms but is produced purely by the appearance arising in the mind. The certain body is that of Vajrasattva, the Diamond Being. Finally, the certain aspect is the blissful kiss of the inner male and female forces. Thus the five certainties achieved here are not the same as those discussed in other scriptures.

The form that is created at this level of practice, which gives rise to the ten signs, can be perceived (i.e., the experience of it generated) at any time one so desires. This brings the powers of the yoga to their full capacity, and prepares the yogi for entering into the yoga of *dhyana*, second of the six completion stage branches.

The reason for practicing the yoga of individual withdrawal in both daily and nightly yogic sessions is that different signs are more easily attained at different times. In the actual stages of practice, for instance, the empty body is said to be more easily attained in darkness and difficult to generate in brightness.

To explain the stages in simple terms, if (the sensory organs of the practitioner are stimulated by) vivid appearances (from the environment) at the time the glance is cast and the observation for signs made, that yogi will not be able to cut off the interfering effects of those appearances. As a result, it is difficult at those times to arise in an empty-body form. This interference does not occur in times of darkness.

The measure of accomplishment in this (the yoga of individual withdrawal) is well known from the descriptions found in *The Abbreviated Kalachakra Tantra* and in *The Trilogy of the Bodhisattvas*.

The scripture *The Vajragarbha Commentary* comments that the experience is like a direct sensory perception. At that time the appearance of the five (types of sensory) objects arises directly within the mental consciousness.

2. *The Yoga of Dhyana.* The physical position for performing the yoga of *dhyana* is as previously explained (i.e., for the yoga of individual withdrawal).

At the time of actual application of this yoga one fills the skies with "certainties," such as the various empty-body forms that previously appeared in the drop, as well as with "uncertainties," such as the symbols and so forth. These are then dissolved into one another, until eventually they all are absorbed into the Sambhogakaya form described above. One establishes special divine pride within this sphere of meditation, until it arises effortlessly. The strength of this is increased until eventually one's mind spontaneously projects the divine pride marked by complete certainty.

When this achievement has been made firm, the yoga of *dhyana* is fulfilled and one is ready to enter into the third of the six yogas, that of energy control.

The yoga of *dhyana* comprises five limbs. These are called con-
ceptualization, experience, joy, bliss, and one-pointedness.

The meaning of these is given in Naropa's *A Commentary to the
Treatise on the Initiations*:

> Seeing merely the nature of the coarse empty body is con-
> ceptualization; seeing deeply into the nature of the subtle
> empty body is experience. The feelings associated with the
> mental consciousness which arises from the pliancy of
> mind thus effected give rise to joy. The feelings associated
> with the physical consciousness arising from the pliancy of
> body give rise to bliss. Finally, the images of mind that arise
> in the form of Vajrasattva possessing the five certainties are
> inseparably mixed with the inner nature of one's own
> mind, giving rise to a consciousness which is an insepara-
> ble unity of form and consciousness. This is the branch of
> one-pointedness.

The first two of these five branches combine as the practice of
vipashyana, or special insight meditation. The last three combine as
shamatha, or meditative tranquility. Thus the yoga of *dhyana* essen-
tially is the samadhi which is the inseparable unity of vipashyana and
shamatha, or insight and tranquility.

3. *The Yoga of Energy Control.* The yoga of energy control is associated with the branch that accomplishes higher energy. In this context
the term "energy" refers to the subtle winds. The meaning of the
words "energy control" is that one arrests the flow of energies moving in the right and left channels.

The reason for engaging in this yoga is that although previously
one generated the divine pride of the inseparable nature of one's own
mind and the empty bodies beheld in the central channel, the interference of the peripheral energies sustained a sense of distance

(between the two). By arresting the movement of these energies one gains the ability to dwell firmly in the unfeigned pride of Vajrasattva's form. Moreover, in addition to the methods previously taught for stimulating the energy centers, here in the yoga of energy control we especially focus on the center of the navel chakra and apply the techniques that ignite the mystic heat, causing it to blaze forth with special strength. It flares up the central channel, melts the substances of bodhi-mind, and gives rise to an experience of unprecedented great bliss.

A second need for the yoga of energy control is in the work with the life-sustaining and downward-moving energies, and in specific with the process of bringing them to the navel chakra and blending them. This was not accomplished by the earlier yogas. Here we meditate on these two energies, apply the yoga of energy control to them, and effect the blending.

The two main techniques used in the yoga of energy control are the vajra-recitation and the vase-breathing methods.

The first of these, the technique known as the vajra recitation, which includes the methods for concentrating, retaining, and dissolving the vital energies, is as explained in *The Vajrapani Commentary* and so forth.

As for the order (of the two, vajra recitation and vase breathing), one begins by applying the vajra-recitation technique until one's essential nature becomes clear and the bodily elements relaxed. This causes the vital energies to flow especially smoothly. One then changes to the meditation upon vase breathing.

Concerning the manner of application of the vajra-recitation technique, some Tibetan yogis have said that when the breath energies flow evenly through both nostrils they should be visualized as entering into the two side channels and also the central channel. They advise that they should then be visualized as entering, abiding, and dissolving in the form of the three letters OM, HUM, and AH.

There is also talk of how vajra recitations focused successively on each of the three main energy channels are the vajra recitations of vajra body, vajra speech, and vajra mind. None of this is particularly meaningful.

In our tradition, the vajra recitation of the three mantric syllables is as explained in *The Commentary to the Praise of Chakrasamvara*[173] and also in (Naropa's) *A Commentary to the Treatise on the Initiations.* Here when one meditates upon the yoga of energy control one casts the glance eliminating demons, and watches for the metaphoric and certain signs as explained previously in the yoga of individual withdrawal. One observes the empty-body images unified with the vital energies.

At the time the energies enter inside (i.e., as you inhale), meditate that the energies arise with the vibrance of the syllable *OM*. This is brought to the chakra at the forehead, at the center of which abides the empty body that was previously produced through the first two yogas. These are then brought down to the navel chakra, at the center of the *dhuti*.

At the time the energies abide (that is, when the breath pauses between inhalation and exhalation), meditate that the energies arise with the vibrance of *HUM*. This and the empty body together are brought to rest at the center of the navel chakra.

Then as the energies are released (i.e., when you exhale), meditate that the energies arise with the vibrance of the syllable *AH*. The strength of the flowing energies causes the empty body to move up the path of the central channel to the upper aperture.

If one meditates repeatedly in this way, the inhalation and exhalation periods gradually decrease in length and the periods of retention increase until one eventually is able to retain the application of the empty body and the vital energies inside the *dhuti* at the navel chakra for prolonged periods of time. Finally one gains the power of completely cutting off the flow of energy (i.e., breath) passing through the nostrils, and is able to abide unwaveringly in meditation at the center of the navel. This marks the boundary wherein the yoga of energy control has been taken to fulfillment. One is now ready to proceed to the vase-breathing technique. From this point onward, whenever the energies (and breath) move, one should see them as flowing inside the central channel itself.

As for the method of applying the vase-breathing technique, this is as follows. The life-sustaining and downward-moving energies are brought to the lower aperture of the central channel, and to the center of the navel chakra. Here with the force of the mind they enter the drop that carries the potencies inducing the experience of sexual ecstasy. These two energies, together with one's own mind and the special empty body, are blended into one taste, and this state of consciousness is carefully maintained. One then meditates on vase breathing. This is what is meant by the scriptural passage,

> The energies that course above and below
> Are brought together in a kiss of the mind.

Meditating in this way, one forms a vase with the energies and ignites the fires of mystic heat inside the central channel at the navel chakra. This gives rise to the four joys descending from above (induced by the descent of the drop through the four principal chakras). When one has achieved the power to generate this experience at will, the yoga of energy control has been fulfilled. One should then engage in the yoga of retention.

4. *The Yoga of Retention.* The meditations that constitute the yoga of retention employ the vase-breathing technique in much the same way as it was utilized in the previous yoga.

As for the place and the stages of the practice, firstly the place is explained.

Here it is said (that to establish the environment of the practice) one begins with the meditation of dissolving the elements in the manner they dissolve at death. Firstly inside the central channel, or *dhuti*, at the heart chakra, as the earth element dissolves into water; then inside the throat chakra, as water dissolves into fire; next inside the forehead chakra, as fire dissolves into air; then inside the crown chakra, as air dissolves into the space element; and finally inside the center of the chakra at the secret place, as space dissolves into wisdom. At each of these sites one meditates within the framework of the experience of the inseparable nature of two principal energies, the mind, and the empty body, as was done in the previous yoga. Practicing in this way one eventually achieves the ability to move the vaselike collection (of energies, mind, and the empty body) to each of the chakras and to retain it at these sites. One also achieves the ability to induce the four joys of (the drop) ascending from below. At this time one should focus in meditation upon bliss and emptiness in inseparable union.

As a preliminary to this stage of endeavor one generates the strong thought, "I myself will arise in the form of Kalachakra and Consort." The force of this determination activates the predispositions in the mind for arising in an empty-body form or its similitude.

The presentation of the Kalachakra yoga of retention is similar to that of the clear light yoga as found in other tantric systems such as Guhyasamaja. However, its unique features here involve the extraordinary methods of separating the drop of the four occasions from obscurations. One should understand these well.

When one has achieved the ability to blend at one time the two main energies, one's mind, and the empty body into an inseparable entity inside each of the six chakras, and to retain the object of meditation (i.e., the threefold collection) at will, the yoga of retention has been carried to fulfillment. One is now ready to engage in the yoga of subsequent mindfulness.

5. *The Yoga of Subsequent Mindfulness.* The yoga of subsequent

mindfulness, also known as "vajra mind yoga," is associated with the branch for producing bliss.

The etymology of its name is given in *The Great Commentary: A Stainless Light:*

> The scripture (*The Abbreviated Kalachakra Tantra*) states, "One first recollects the image of the form, and then secondly applies a mindfulness to it. Thus there are said to be two." The meaning of this passage is that there are two mindfulnesses, one applied first to the image of the empty body previously accomplished and then a second kind that comes later.
>
> (To say something about each of these two:) Earlier when practicing the yoga of *dhyana* we produced a similitude of the empty body; this was the first (object of) mindfulness to be cultivated. After that one achieves a more qualified empty body; this is the second (object of) mindfulness.

In the latter phase of the yoga of retention one arose in the form of a sensual empty-body deity in union with consort, and achieved the power to effortlessly establish divine pride. The sensual empty-body "Male and Consort" deities filled the universe with luminosity emanated forth from their pore apertures, and then entered into union. However, this did not give rise to the unchanging bliss. Therefore the attainment remained on the level of a similitude of an empty body.

One persists in the meditation until the mind spontaneously arises in the empty-body form of Kalachakra and Consort. This causes lights to emanate forth from one's pores, arousing the desire of the empty-body *mahamudra* deities, such as the multicolored consort and the ten powerful goddesses. One then practices sexual union with these *mahamudra* empty-body deities and achieves the unchanging great bliss. When one has achieved the full power of this mudra inducing the unchanging bliss, the yoga of subsequent mindfulness has been fulfilled.

As for this practice, *The Abbreviated Kalachakra Tantra* (by Manju Yashas of Shambhala) and also (its principal commentary) *The Great Commentary: A Stainless Light* (by Pundarika of Shambhala) list four types of mudras: *karmamudra* (action seal), *jnanamudra* (wisdom seal), *mahamudra* (great seal), and *samayamudra* (commitment seal).

The first three of these give rise to the unchanging bliss; the fourth mudra is explained as the bliss that arises in dependence on what was accomplished by the former three.

*Karmamudra* is explained as the practice performed with a maiden possessing the physical attributes of a woman, such as beautiful hair and so forth, with whom one has a strong karmic link. Here the maiden herself has the ability to induce the full experience by means of her skillful embrace, without reliance on the powers of meditation.

*Jnanamudra* is a maiden created through the power of one's own mental projection.

As for the *mahamudra*, this refers to the empty bodies that actually arise as consorts from the appearances within one's own mind.

One relies upon (one of) these three types of mudra, and when the experience of bliss arises it causes the bodhi-mind substances abiding in the upper sites to descend. They come to the tip of the jewel, where they are retained and are not allowed to slip away, change, or to move (to other sites).

Concerning these terms (of falling, moving, and changing bliss arising from the movement of the drops), *The Great Commentary: A Stainless Light* states,

*Karmamudra* is the maiden who gives the falling bliss.
*Jnanamudra* is the maiden who gives the moving bliss.
*Mahamudra* is the maiden who gives the unchanging bliss.

How is this so? If the yogi is unable to control the movement of the drops solely through the power of meditation, he takes up the practice of *karmamudra*. Because the *karmamudra* gives him the power to direct the vital substances to the tip of the jewel, she is called "the maiden who bestows the falling bliss."

Union with the *jnanamudra* causes the drops to fall from the upper energy centers to the tip of the jewel; but as they cannot be retained motionlessly, they are directed through various other points of the body. Thus she is called "the maiden who brings the moving bliss."

One sits in union with the *mahamudra*, which causes the substances to melt and come to the tip of the jewel. Not only are these to be prevented from slipping, they must also be prevented from flowing into other sites. Thus it is said, "the maiden who brings unchanging bliss."

The yogis who actually arise within the empty body of Kalachakra and Consort are of three types: sharp, middling, and dull.

The first of these rely exclusively upon *mahamudra*. They are able to experience the unchanging great bliss solely through union with her. The second must first rely upon *jnanamudra* to generate a basis of bliss through which they are able to enter into *mahamudra*.

Practitioners in the third category, i.e., those of dull capacity, must first rely upon a *karmamudra*, or actual physical consort, in order to induce the experience of bliss. Only then can they proceed to the *mahamudra*.

In this way, all three types of yogis eventually come to the *mahamudra*. They enter into sexual union directly with the *mahamudra*; the drop of white substances that abides in the crown in the form of a syllable *HAM* is caused to melt and fall to the chakra at the tip of the jewel. Simultaneously, the red drop moves to the energy center at the crown. The two substances are then retained and are not allowed to change to other sites (i.e., to move to other chakras). The presence of the two drops in the two chakras is made firm until the supremely unchanging bliss is experienced. The first time this unchanging bliss arises from the stabilized presence (of the two drops in the two chakras, in reverse placement) is the border demarcating the fulfillment of the yoga of subsequent mindfulness. One is now ready to move on to the sixth yoga, that of samadhi.

6. *The Yoga of Samadhi.* When one thus simultaneously brings the white and red substances to the tip of the jewel and chakras of the crown protrusion (i.e., one brings the white drop down to the tip of the sexual organ and the red drop up to the crown) and retains them there with stability, this gives rise to a momentary flash of stabilized bliss. Of the 21,600 factors which make up our coarse form, one is dissolved. Simultaneously, of the 21,600 karmic energies coursing through the nostrils, one part of (one of the twelve sets of) 1,800 is halted.

When (in the first set) 1,800 experiences of bliss have been fulfilled and 1,799 of the vital drops piled up, one attains to the "great supreme dharma" stage of the path of application (i.e., the fourth and final stage of the second level of the path to enlightenment). A further one part of the 1,800 such moments places one on the stage of an arya, the path of direct vision (third level of the five paths to enlightenment).

If in this way one can draw 21,600 (white) male drops, the supports of bliss, to the tip of the jewel, and stack them in a stable column that extends up to the crown chakra, and if one also can bring 21,600 red drops up and form them into a red column beginning at the crown (chakra) and extending down to the tip of the jewel, on the basis of each of the (21,600 sets of red and white drops) one experiences a moment of stabilized bliss. In this way 21,600 moments of "supported" unchanging bliss arise. Each of these cuts off one part of the 21,600 karmic winds, and this in turn causes the utter dissolution of one of the 21,600 factors of the physical body.

One's form aggregate, together with the elements and objects connected with it, becomes freed from obscuration. One transcends all obscurations to knowledge and simultaneously in this very lifetime attains the state of enlightenment in the aspect of the Primordial Buddha Kalachakra.

*The Abbreviated Kalachakra Tantra* states,

> When one realizes the body, speech, and mind produced by the path of the Kalachakra yogas, one's body transcends ordinary substantiality, becomes as clear and lucent as the sky, and manifests all the major and minor signs of perfection. One's mind fills with supreme bliss and enters into an eternal embrace with the innately unmoving wisdom.

The meaning here is that the Kalachakra yogi accomplishes enlightenment in one lifetime in such a way that his or her body attains the characteristics of the form of Kalachakra and Consort, a vast empty body adorned with all the marks and signs of perfection, a body similar to space itself. It is "clear and lucent" because it is intangible and immaterial, being empty of a mundane atomic structure.

This is the bodily attainment. As for the mental attainment, its essential nature is compassion arising as the supreme, unmoving, unchanging bliss locked in eternal union with the one taste of wisdom perceiving the emptiness of noninherent existence, the "emptiness without characteristics."

When in this way the body and mind are experienced as an inseparable entity based on the supporting empty body and the supported wisdom of unchanging bliss, this is what is meant by "Primordial Kalachakra." From amongst the branches of the six-branched yoga of the Kalachakra system, it represents the sixth yoga, that of samadhi.

In the Kalachakra literature one sees a lot of discussion focused on the topics of "emptiness with characteristics" and "true emptiness without characteristics."

In the first of these, the mind directly perceiving the empty body arises within an appreciation of a subtle light of dual appearance. It is nonetheless called "emptiness" because in it the object of negation, the coarse and subtle atomic structure of the body, has been eliminated and is altogether empty of physical matter.

In the second case (i.e., emptiness without characteristics), this refers to the mind directly perceiving the emptiness of its object of negation, namely the emptiness of inherent existence. Because that mind has reversed all dual appearance it is called "without characteristics."

Thus (in the Kalachakra tradition), the discussion of the empty body as explained above, wherein the wisdom of emptiness is brought into one taste with supreme, unchanging great bliss, is a substitute for the clear light and illusory body doctrines found in the other Highest Yoga Tantra systems (that is, the empty body substitutes for the illusory body doctrine, and the one-tasteness of unchanging bliss and wisdom substitutes for the clear light doctrine). The assembling of these two (i.e., the empty body and the unchanging bliss absorbed in the wisdom of emptiness) within the stream of one's body and mind substitutes for the Great Union (of the clear light and illusory body) spoken of in the other Highest Yoga tantras.

In Kalachakra, however, the yogi goes through twelve successive levels, known as the "twelve Kalachakra stages," each of which comprises a series of extraordinary events. On each of these twelve stages one undergoes 1,800 (moments of) the wisdom of bliss and emptiness, which arise from 1,800 experiences of unchanging bliss. These arrest 1,800 subtle energy currents, cause 1,800 (of the 21,600) factors of the physical body to dematerialize, and eliminate 1,800 delusions (i.e., the "share" of that particular "level"). At the same time one stacks 1,800 drops.

The complete presence of one set of 1,800 factors constitutes one of the twelve Kalachakra stages leading to enlightenment. Traversing all twelve of the stages means that 21,600 of each of the factors have been experienced.

In brief, first one establishes the empty body of male and consort at the (chakra of) the secret place, and then stage by stage brings it up through the other chakras, from the navel to the crown.

With the exception of the doctrine of the empty body, the Kalachakra presentation of the manner of traversing the paranormal stages of the path is quite like the presentation found in the *Lam Drey* teaching (of the Sakya School of Tibetan Buddhism).

O hark!
This brief treatise on the six yogas
Of Primordial Buddha Kalachakra's completion stage
Draws from the ancient Indian scriptures
And presents their thought without error.

Requested by several of my disciples,
I, Gendun Drubpa, taught it to stimulate my mind;
And to express my respect for the practice
And teachings of the great yogis of old.

May it benefit those of a similar predisposition.
May any small merits that it has
Cause living beings to enter the Diamond Vehicle,
That they may be filled with the glory
Of supreme bliss and the wisdom of emptiness, and
Attain to the state of Primordial Buddha Kalachakra.

# CHAPTER SEVEN

## The Fifth Dalai Lama's

### *Hayagriva-Sealed-in-Secrecy Methods for Healing* (as read by the Great Thirteenth)[174]

(Ritual Manuals for a longevity initiation and for a healing initiation and the consecration of medicines, in accordance with the revelations of Gongpa Zilnon Zhepa Tsal, the Fifth Dalai Lama)

GYALWA LOBZANG GYATSO (1617-1682)

HAYAGRIVA

# Translator's Preamble

THE FIFTH DALAI LAMA (1617-1682) was perhaps the most mystical of all the Dalai Lamas, in that he seemed to spend much of his time in a state of trance. During these trances many gurus of past ages, as well as mandala deities, buddhas, and bodhisattvas would appear directly to him and give him secret transmissions, initiations, and teachings. As the Thirteenth Dalai Lama says of the Great Fifth later in this chapter, he "was continually absorbed in the wisdom dance that experiences all appearances as pure vision."

Like the Dalai Lamas before him, the Great Fifth united the Nyingma and Sarma Tantra lineages—the Old and New Tantra Transmissions—within the stream of his practice. In terms of modern sectarian classifications, the former are somewhat united today as Nyingma. The latter refers to the Kadam, Sakya, Kagyu, Zhalu, Rvaluk, and Geluk.

Although these tantric systems are much the same in content, the Old Schools tend to classify their lineages into "Distant" and "Close" lineages. The former term refers to the original transmissions that came to Tibet from India, whereas the latter refers to lineages born from the visionary experiences of their most talented lineage masters. Often the lineage masters who act as the source of Close lineages are called *terton*, or "treasure revealers." Such revelations might come in dreams (*mi lam terma*), in deep meditation (*gong ter*), or as full-blown sensory experiences (*dak nang*). Many also appear as *bey ter*, or "concealed treasures." *Dak nang* revelations are perceived almost in the manner of seeing a piece of theater. Most of the Great Fifth's revelations came in this form.

Most Nyingma masters of the past four or five centuries have tended to rely more upon the "Close" than upon the "Distant" lineages.

The two texts translated in this chapter belong to the category of Close lineages, and both descend from the Fifth Dalai Lama. The Thirteenth Dalai Lama read them as part of a set of initiation ceremonies that he gave when returning from his visit to China in 1909. A member of his entourage took notes on the occasion, and as a consequence the two texts were later published together under one title, with the Thirteenth's commentary blended into the Fifth's texts.

Thus in the form the texts appear here they could perhaps best be entitled "The Thirteenth Dalai Lama's Reading of Two Lineages Descending from the Fifth Dalai Lama." They are included in the Thirteenth's *Collected Works*.

The first of the two is part of a cycle of twenty-eight *dak nang* texts, or "pure visionary revelations," that were channeled by the Great Fifth during the middle period of his life. The twenty-eight as a set are known as *Zabcho Gyachen*, or "The Profound Dharmas of the Sealed Transmission," and are related to the mandala of the Sealed-in-Secrecy Hayagriva. The Thirteenth tells the story of how the Great Fifth received the revelation of the particular text he is reading. The text itself is a ritual manual for a longevity initiation presented in the form of a guided group meditation led by the Great Thirteenth and based on the text by the Great Fifth.

The story behind each of the twenty-eight *Zabcho Gyachen* texts from the Fifth Dalai Lama is much the same. In each case the Great Fifth falls into a trance, and the legendary eighth-century master Padmasambhava appears to him in one of his many forms, usually surrounded by various lineage masters as well as a host of mandala deities, dakas, and dakinis. Padmasambhava (or one of the lineage masters inspired by him) then pronounces the words of the mystical revelation.

In our text here Padmasambhava appears as Tsokyey Dorjey, "The Lake-Born Vajra," an epithet of the great guru inspired by the fact that as a baby he was discovered in a lotus pond by the King of Uddiyana, the Swat Valley of modern-day Pakistan. The king subsequently adopted the boy and raised him as his own. The child became known to history as Guru Padmasambhava, "The Lotus-Born Guru."

Most of the twenty-eight texts in the Great Fifth's *Zabcho Gyachen* cycle have healing through meditation as their theme, and are presented in the form of ritual manuals. As a result, they generally were used by the Great Fifth and the subsequent lineage masters as texts for one-day ceremonial events, usually when they went on teaching tours. Tibetan laypeople love this kind of event. One gets to spend an afternoon in the presence of a great teacher, practice ceremonial meditation with him, hear him teach, and then leave with a sense of having achieved both healing and spiritual transformation. Usually initiation substances are given out and eaten during the course of the event, often in the form of sweet barley balls or the like. Tibetans love this part of the ceremony, and usually carry a portion of these substances home to give to family and friends who could not attend the actual event. Often fights break out in the crowd when the substances are distributed, so enthusiastic are the people to receive their share of the culinary blessings. At one ceremony I attended in India in the early 1980s, three people were crushed to death by the overly zealous crowd as they pushed forward *en masse* to receive the initiation snacks.

The second of the two texts in this chapter, which in the Thirteenth's *Collected Works* is tacked on to the end of and published together with the *Zabcho Gyachen* text mentioned above, is a Hayagriva ritual for a healing initiation and the consecration of blessing medicines. As the colophon states, the Zhabgon Droden Dekyiling Monastery in Nagchu maintained an annual tradition of producing Hayagriva healing medicines, and the Thirteenth was passing through the region during the time of this event. They requested him to participate. He did so by firstly giving the Sangwa Gyachen initiation, and then by leading a Fifth Dalai Lama ritual for consecration of medicines.

The Thirteenth's *Collected Works* puts the two above texts together, with a single colophon for both. The first is an actual text written by the Great Fifth based on his visions, although here it is presented with notes from the Great Thirteenth's reading on that occasion. The second seems to be an initiation manual the Great Fifth wrote based on a Hidden Treasure tradition that he had received. Again, it is presented with interwoven notes from the Thirteenth's reading.

It is not possible to know more about the Fifth's two works at this date. All I have encountered is this treatment by the Thirteenth.

Traditionally the Great Fifth's *Collected Works* were kept in twenty-eight volumes, with twelve being dedicated to his outer teachings, eight to his inner teachings, and a further eight to his secret teachings. That last group of eight has never been published as a set of woodblock prints, the traditional way in Old Tibet that a lama's writings were made available for public consumption; and it is in this part of his *Collected Works* that these two texts would have been placed. Presumably the secrecy surrounding these eight volumes was maintained in order to ensure the sanctity of the legacy.

Of course many of the individual works found in these eight volumes have been published over the centuries for use in particular ceremonies; and high lamas wanting to use or study any of them would have been allowed to commission a handwritten version. Most Tibetan monasteries kept a number of monk scribes on hand solely for this work of transcribing important texts in their libraries.

The story of how the Thirteenth Dalai Lama happened to be in

Nagchu at the time is of interest. Every Tibetan lama hopes to make a three-year retreat at least once during his lifetime, and the young Thirteenth was in the second year of his first such undertaking when the British invaded his country. The Nechung Oracle was invoked by the Tibetan government, and during his trance proclaimed that the Dalai Lama should be taken out of the country for safety. As a consequence, the Thirteenth broke off his retreat and left for Mongolia (he entered a second retreat of this nature a decade later, which he successfully completed).

Even though the British retreated from Tibet a few months later, the Dalai Lama was now on the road, and invitations to visit and teach came from many quarters. Consequently what had been planned as a brief sojourn ended up being a four-year teaching tour. As well as visiting Mongolia, he traveled and taught extensively throughout China, including the sacred Wutaishan, or "Five Peaks," the mountain range a few hundred miles west of Beijing that is famed for meditation practice and is associated with the bodhisattva Manjushri. Indeed, the meditation hermitage built in honor of the Thirteenth's visit still stands on Wutaishan, having somehow miraculously survived the Communist destruction of the 1960s and 70s.

The two texts with the Thirteenth's comments were published with a single colophon at the end placing a context on both. This colophon states,

In the Earth Bird Year of the Fifteenth Sexagenary (i.e., 1909), the Thirteenth White Lotus Holder (i.e., the Thirteenth Dalai Lama) was on his way back to Lhasa after having visited the Manchu Empress in Beijing. The Tibetans were celebrating his return to the Land of Dharma, and were filled with joy.

While passing through Nagchu he stopped at Zhabgon Droden Dekyiling Monastery. This monastery maintains a tradition of annually performing a vast tantric ritual for the consecration of ambrosial medicines as a method of contributing to the happiness of all beings. The monastery was engaged in this ritual event when the Great Thirteenth arrived, presided over by the great master Drubkhang Tulku, whose mindstream had been ripened by study and practice of the hundreds of sutras and tantras over many previous lifetimes. Drubkhang and the other practitioners requested the Great Thirteenth to stay for some time and lead them in their meditations and rites, and to lead the empowering ceremonies of Hayagriva coming from the Great Fifth Dalai Lama. The Thirteenth consented. The two above texts (i.e., translated below in this chapter) were edited from notes prepared from that occasion.

Readers may note that the Great Fifth did not sign the texts in his *Zabcho Gyachen* cycle with his commonly known name of Ngawang Lobzang Gyatso, but rather used the secret tantric name Gongpa Zilnon Zhepa Tsal, "The Playful Laughing Mystic Out-shining All Others." The "Out-shining" aspect of the name indicates that it was given to him by a Nyingma master, for "Zilnon" is found as a component of several of the epithets of Padmasambhava.

This particular lineage from the Great Fifth continues to be very popular, and has been given by the present Dalai Lama on numerous occasions.

I read these texts with two very wonderful tulkus: Ven. Amchok Rinpochey of Ganden and Ven. Sharpa Rinpochey of Sera.

# The Fifth Dalai Lama's Transmission

## Part One: A Longevity Initiation

> Homage to the immortal Guru Padmasambhava,
> Embodiment of the three buddha kayas,
> He born magically from a lotus;
> And homage to the nine Heruka deities
> Of the most secret Hayagriva mandala.
> With reverence I bow to them
> And request their inspiring blessings.

### (I) The Preamble

Here, from among the many *dak nang*, or "pure visionary transmissions," of the Fifth Dalai Lama that are related to the mandala of Yangsang Gyachen, or the Sealed-in-Secrecy Hayagriva, is a ritual text on longevity initiation in accordance with the mystical tradition coming from Lama Tsokyey Dorjey Kusum Rikdu, the Lotus-Born Guru Padmasambhava, who is an emanation of the three buddha kayas.

The master who is leading the rite should begin the practice early in the morning. He commences with the usual procedures of taking refuge, generating the bodhi-mind, and so forth as outlined in the standard texts. He then performs the self-initiation rite, together with the *tsok* (tantric feast) offering.

The disciples are invited to enter the room. They symbolically wash, flowers are given out and then offered, the *torma* (sacrificial cake) for the removal of hindrances is offered, and the protection circle is established.

When these preliminaries have been completed, the master explains the Dharma in general and then in particular. (That is, he first explains the general nature of the Buddhist path and then says something about this particular lineage.)

(II) A Survey of the Dharma in General and Also of This Particular Tradition

Hark! In order to be of maximum benefit to the countless living beings, whose number is as vast as the extent of the skies, one must first gain the state of peerless, complete, perfect buddhahood. It is with this thought in mind that one receives initiation, the root of the Vajrayana path, and then engages in the various Tantric yogas.

Contemplate this theme, and by means of it generate the sublime bodhi-mind as the motivating factor. Also, cultivate the correct attitudes that are to be maintained when listening to the Dharma, as is explained in the many sutras and tantras, and thus listen correctly.

The Buddha, who himself achieved complete enlightenment and who possessed profound skill and great compassion, taught the nectarlike Dharma in accordance with the mental tendencies, capacities, and karmic predispositions of those to be trained.

The doctrines that he taught may be categorized in various ways. An elaborate manner of doing so is to speak of the Nine Vehicles, or *Yanas*. Alternatively, these nine may be abbreviated into two: the Hinayana and the Mahayana, or the Small and the Great Vehicles.

In turn, the second of these, the Mahayana, is often subdivided into two: the exoteric Causal Prajnaparamitayana (Transcendent Wisdom Vehicle) and the esoteric Resultant Guhyamantrayana (Secret

Mantra Vehicle). These two have the same basic focus, yet the latter is said to be superior to the former for four specific reasons: it is uncontrived, it has more methods at its disposal, its techniques are easier to accomplish, and it is especially designed for those of highest capacity. These four points are clearly outlined in *A Lamp on the Three Ways*,[175] wherein we read, "The Resultant Vajrayana is superior for four reasons. . . ."

As for the Resultant Secret Mantra Vehicle, it can be subdivided into two levels of practice: the External Vajrayana of three outer classes of tantras—Kriya, Charya, and Yoga; and the Internal Vajrayana, which refers to the Anuttarayoga, or "Highest Yoga," tantras. The transmission to be dealt with in this treatise belongs to this second category.

Furthermore, the Secret Mantra Vehicle lineages found in Tibet are of two distinct types: those transmitted through the Old School, or Nyingma, and those transmitted through the New Schools, or Sarma. The Old School lineages of the Hayagriva Tantra are superior to those found in the New Schools.

Within the Old School, there are three different lines of transmission of this tradition: the "Distant lineage" of the original instructions (i.e., *The Root Tantra*[176]) and two "Close lineages": the "discovered treasure texts" and the "profound pure vision texts."

The system that is the subject of this treatise is from the pure visionary experiences of the White Lotus Holder Gongpa Zilnon Zhepa Tsal, the Fifth Dalai Lama.

The outer, inner, and secret biographies of the great lamas of the past speak of three types of pure visionary experiences: those received in dreams, those received in meditation, and direct mystical communications. This particular tradition belongs to the last of these, for Gongpa Zilnon Zhepa Tsal was continually absorbed in the wisdom dance that experiences all appearances as pure vision, and was in constant communion with the oceanic deeds of the great aryas who are purified in spirit. Thus all his visionary experiences were pure direct cognitions.

He later transmitted the tantric lineages that he received in this way to those of his more advanced disciples who possessed conducive karmic predispositions. However, so that those not sufficiently mature would be unable to misuse these mystical teachings, he marked them with the seal of secrecy in the same way that the great guru Dharmodgata had sealed the Prajnaparamita teachings seven times.

Therefore the tradition has come to be known far and wide as *Zab-cho Gyachen,* or "The Profound Dharmas of the Sealed Transmission."

There are numerous scriptures in this "sealed" genre that were written by Gongpa Zilnon Zhepa Tsal. That to be dealt with here belongs to those marked by the seal of the mystic knot. It should not be given to those practitioners who are dominated by indecisiveness or by negative preconceptions.


(III) The Story of the Mystical Origins of This Profound Transmission

It was the eleventh day of the twelfth month of the Water Ox Year (late 1673 or early 1674). The Fifth Dalai Lama was performing various mystical rituals with the Nyingma yogi Jangter Dakpo Rikzin Chenpo Tulku. The fundamental structure of the procedures was based on the occult lineages of Guru Tsokyey Dorjey Kusum Rikdu, with *torma* rites to remove hindrances in accordance with the Lama Gongdu tradition, and also longevity rites accomplished by means of sheep-shaped effigies.

During the ritual, the Fifth Dalai Lama experienced the following vision.

In the space before him appeared Guru Tsokyey Dorjey, seated at the center of a vast sun disc and locked in sexual union with his consort. To his left appeared the yogi Chogyal Tashi Tobgyal, seated on a thick cushion, dressed in white clothing, pressing down on the earth with his right hand, and holding his left at his heart in the mudra of supreme generosity.

To his (Guru Tsokyey Dorjey's) right, sitting slightly lower, appeared the yogi Chogyal Rikzin Ngagi Wangpo. He was seated on a moon disc, was dressed in a mystical hat and occult shawl, and was wearing the robes of a monk. His right hand was at his heart, and his left, poised above his lap in the mudra of meditation, held a longevity vase. During the phase of the ritual when the life energies of the five buddha families are visualized as being summoned, light rays suddenly burst forth from the heart of Guru Tsokyey Dorjey. The tips of the rays bore the five buddhas and five dakinis, each in the color of the respective direction of the light ray. The dakinis were carrying longevity arrows with auspicious threads hanging from the tips, and as they waved them the Fifth Dalai Lama actually felt the threads caress the crown of his head.

When the ritual arrived at the phase when the *tormas* and sheep-shaped effigies are carried outside and discarded, Chogyal Wangpo Dey rose from his seat and, brandishing a mystic dagger, performed a wrathful tantric dance. His appearance was extremely forceful, and all hindrances and obstructing elements were immediately expelled. At that point the life energies of the collection of the three buddha kayas were drawn forth. The lama dressed in white then reached out. In his hand was a longevity arrow draped in threads, with which he made a summoning gesture.

The names of two lamas, Yolmo Tulku and Zurchen Choying Rangdrol, resounded from the sky, and the Fifth Dalai Lama's attention moved over to Lama Wangpo Dey. Instantly Yolmo Tulku appeared to his (Lama Wangpo Dey's) right. He was standing in the royal posture and was dressed in white. His long hair was tied back in a braid, and with his right hand he was turning a rosary made of *raksha* beads. To Wangpo Dey's left, sitting on a slightly lower cushion, appeared Lama Zurchen Choying Rangdrol. He was dressed in the red robes of a monk, wore the pointed hat of a pandit, and was seated in the meditation posture.

Suddenly Lama Zurchen stood up, folded his hands together at his heart, and spoke the following words: "*Kye hoh*! Pay heed. The longevity deities of the mandala of the three buddha kayas. . . ." and so forth, thus transmitting the oral instructions of this unique lineage.

When he had finished speaking, a stream of nectars flowed forth from the longevity vase in Guru Tsokyey Dorjey's hand. They came to the crown of the Fifth Dalai Lama's head and entered his body, completely filling it. He had the sensation that his central energy channel became as firm as an iron arrow, and had red half-vajras at the top and bottom. He later commented that this sensation continued for almost the entire day.

At the conclusion of the vision, the entire assembly of gurus, including Guru Tsokyey Dorjey, dissolved into Lama Wangpo Dey. Wangpo Dey then placed his hand on the Fifth Dalai Lama's heart and said, "Do not forget the instructions that have been transmitted to you." He then transformed into a ball of light and dissolved into the Fifth Dalai Lama. The Fifth experienced a strong sense of bliss and void in union.

That then is the story of the origins of this unusual tantric legacy, a tradition born from auspicious conditions and the unfolding of a great mass of virtue, a wondrous and sacred transmission having the powerful blessings of the revealed "Close lineage" of the omniscient Dorjey Tokmey Tsal (i.e., another of the Fifth Dalai Lama's tantric names).

As for the procedures of performing the longevity initiation that is the central pillar of this tradition, these involve two topics: the activities to be performed by the guru alone and the activities that involve the disciples.

## (IV) The Activities to Be Performed by the Guru

The preliminary activities to be performed by the guru have been explained above: taking refuge, generating the bodhi-mind, performing the self-initiation ritual, making the *tsok* offering, and so forth. Beyond that, his functions involve the participation of the disciples and therefore will be explained below.

## (V) The Activities That Involve the Disciples

The initiating master begins by instructing the disciples:

> In order to receive the blessings of the mandala divinities, who are to be seen as inseparable from the guru, you should first make the offering symbolic of the universe (i.e., the mandala offering).

The disciples do so. The master continues,

> You have performed the symbolic offering well. Now you should request the initiation. But in order to do so you should first generate the following mental image.
>
> This house that we are in is not to be regarded as an ordinary dwelling. Rather, see it as a mystical tantric mansion standing in the legendary pure land of Ngayab Ling.
>
> The guru is sitting at the center of this tantric mansion. Although in nature he is your personal guru, visualize him as having the form of Guru Tsokyey Dorjey, the Lotus-Born Guru, embodiment of all the buddhas of the past,

present, and future. Generate undivided conviction and make the following request:

Kye!!! O guru, embodiment of the three kayas,
Grant us the holy initiation.
Grant us protection from the dangers
Of sudden, premature death.

When this has been repeated three times, the guru admonishes the disciples to create the following visualization, and to take heartfelt refuge and to generate the bodhi-mind aspiration to highest enlightenment:

In the space before you appears the guru inseparable from the principal deity of the mandala. He is surrounded by myriads of buddhas, gurus, meditational deities, dakas, dakinis, and Dharma protectors.

Generate the firm determination to practice in accordance with their instructions and not to transgress their words. Fixing your mind single-pointedly on this image, repeat the following verses after me three times:

Dharmakaya Amitabha, lord of life energies,
Sambhogakaya Avalokiteshvara, the Bodhisattva of
    Compassion,
And Nirmanakaya Padmasambhava, subduer of living
    beings:
I take refuge in these three supreme beings.

In order to be of maximum benefit to the living beings
Whose number is as vast as the extent of space,
I will practice according to the ways

Established by these three sublime beings,
Embodiments of the three kayas.

I will free all living beings
From the dangers of premature death,
And will lead them to the stage
Of supreme, peerless enlightenment.

When this has been said three times, generate the confidence that refuge and the bodhi-mind have been made firm. Then create the visualization of the field of merit:

Guru, meditational divinities, dakas, and dakinis,
I summon you to come forth now
And sit before me on these thrones,
Each of which is made from
A sun, a moon, and a lotus flower.

I bow to you with body, speech, and mind,
Make outer, inner, and secret offerings,
Confess every weakness, negativity, and obscuration,
And rejoice in the practice of the Secret Mantra Vehicle.

Pray, turn the Dharma wheel of the Secret Mantra Vehicle
That so matures and frees the mind.
Do not pass away into parinirvana,
But remain for the benefit of living beings.

And all my merits of body, speech, and mind
I myself will dedicate with purity
For the benefit of the world.
May insight into the pure vajra knowledge arise.

Each of the disciples now must develop the vision of himself/herself as a mandala divinity. This is done by means of the following liturgy:

> From the sphere of the Dharmadhatu,
> In the nature of great compassion,
> My mind appears as the syllable *HRIH*.
> This transforms into a pure realm
> For both vessel and contents,
> The legendary Sindhu Lake, at the center of which
> Is a throne made from lotus, sun, and moon.
>
> There I sit as Guru Tsokyey Dorjey,
> Having one face and two hands.
> My appearance is that of a sixteen-year-old,
> And my face is white tinged with red.
> Above the top of my crown protrusion
> Is a tiny green horse's head,
> And above that, in nature Amitabha Buddha,
> Is a small ball of radiant light.
>
> My right hand holds a vajra,
> My left a longevity vase,
> And I sit in sexual union with the consort
> Chandali, who is white tinged with red.
> She holds a longevity arrow and vase,
> And her arms are wrapped around me.
> Both of us are draped in ornaments
> Of jewels and human bone,
> We wear silks and flower garlands, and
> Are sitting amidst a halo of five hues.

The three syllables *OM, AH,* and *HUM*
Stand at the male's crown, throat, and heart,
And at the heart of the consort
Is a sun and moon disc surrounded
By the syllables of the life mantra.

Above the male's crown is a moon disc, and on it
Sits the Sambhogakaya form of Avalokiteshvara.
At his heart, on a sun and moon disc,
Is the Nirmanakaya emanation Padmasambhava.
Surrounding the male and the consort
Are countless dakas and dakinis.

The master then picks up the longevity arrow and calls forth for the
blessings of the field of merit:

*HUM! HRIH!* Guru Tsokyey Dorjey,
He complete with the three buddha kayas,
Please empower this secret mandala.
Cause these substances which produce longevity
To glow with a special power.
Bestow the powerful initiations
And release the exalted *siddhis.*
*OM AH HUM HRIH VAJRA GURU AYUR JNANA SIDDHI PHAL
ABHESHAYA AH AH.*

The master then touches the statue to the head of each of the disciples while saying,

*HUM! HRIH!* Guru Tsokyey Dorjey,
Embodiment of the three buddha kayas,
Bestow the powerful blessings

Of the physical marks and signs of perfection
Upon these trainees of good fortune.
May they gain the life power
Of the immortal vajra body.
*OM AH HUM HRIH VAJRA GURU AYUR JNANA SIDDHI*
*PHAL RENRA BHUM HUM JAKA AH AH.*

The master should recite this mantra three times, with the disciples repeating it after him. He then touches the rosary to the throat of each disciple while saying,

*HUM! HRIH!* Guru Tsokyey Dorjey,
Embodiment of the three buddha kayas,
Bestow the powerful blessings of divine speech
Upon these trainees of good fortune.
May they gain the life power
Of pure, faultless speech.
*OM AH HUM HRIH VAJRA GURU AYUR JNANA SIDDHI*
*PHAL HUM VAMKHA ABHISHICCHA AH.*

The mirror, symbol of the vajra mind, is touched to the heart of each of the disciples:

*HUM! HRIH!* Guru Tsokyey Dorjey,
Embodiment of the three buddha kayas,
Bestow the powerful blessings
Of the mind of bliss and void united
Upon these trainees of good fortune.
May they gain the life power
Of an undistorted mind.
*OM AH HUM HRIH VAJRA GURU AYUR JNANA SIDDHI*
*PHAL HUM CHITTA ABHISHICCHA HUM.*

The initiation vase is touched to the crown of the head of each disciple:

*OM!* This vase is the tantric mansion.
From it flow forth ambrosial nectars
Of the deities of the three buddha kayas
Which wash away the stains of delusion
And of grasping at the appearance of duality
From within trainees of good fortune.
May they gain the life power
Of the immortal vajra wisdom.
*OM AH HUM HRIH VAJRA GURU AYUR JNANA SIDDHI PHAL*
*HUM KALASHA ABHISHICCHA OM AH HUM HRIH.*

Thus by the power of the longevity initiation the ambrosial nectars of immortality flow forth. They fill the body of each of the disciples and overflow from the crown aperture. The overflow crystallizes above the crown of each disciple and forms into the shape of a horse's head, green in color and releasing neighing sounds. Above this is red Hayagriva, holding a club in his right hand and showing the threatening mudra with his left. Tiny vajras and sparks of flame emanate from Hayagriva's body, forming a ring of protection around the body of each of the disciples.

The master now places the longevity arrow in the hand of each of the disciples and says,

*HRIH!* Now you have a special body
Ablaze with vajra wisdom
Emitting sparks of flame as hot
As the fire at the end of time.
Thus you have gained protection
From the evil forces and hindrances
That lie in wait for the chance to harm.

Thus is complete the steps of the method for attaining the blessings and initiations that produce longevity by relying upon the Hayagriva lineages of Guru Tsokyey Dorjey as clarified and enhanced by the pure visionary experiences of Gongpa Zilnon Zhepa Tsal, the Fifth Dalai Lama.

## PART TWO: A RITE OF MEDICINAL CONSECRATION

Herein follow a healing initiation and medicinal empowerment in accordance with the tradition of the nine-deity mandala of Tamdin Padma Wangchen, "The Powerful Lotus Lord Hayagriva."

### (I) Making the Request and Establishing the Appropriate Motivation

The initiating master begins the rite by giving the disciples the following instructions:

> If you wish to participate in the healing initiation and medicinal empowerment related to the mandala of the nine wrathful deities of the glorious, powerful Most Secret Lotus Lord Hayagriva, then repeat this request after me three times:
>
>> O Vajraraja, bestow blessings and initiation
>> Of the highest *siddhis* of body, speech, and mind
>> Upon this supreme, secret mandala.
>> Manifest now from the sphere of Samantabhadra.

The master continues,

Ah! In order to be of full benefit to all living beings you should try to attain in this very lifetime the enlightenment state symbolized by glorious Hayagriva. This should be your motivation in participating in this healing initiation and medicinal empowerment related to the tantric cycle of practice connected with the nine-deity mandala of Most Secret Lotus Lord Hayagriva. Then, by means of using the mystical substances, one will be able to accomplish vast benefits for oneself and others.

This should be your fundamental motivation when listening to this profound Dharma.

## (II) A General Survey of the Dharma and of This Particular Lineage

As for the Dharma that is to be transmitted, the original source is of course the Buddha himself. This wonderful friend of all living beings, who showed partiality to none, out of profound skill and great compassion taught the eighty-four thousand branches of the doctrine. All of these were but methods to cultivate the minds of the various types of trainees.

These eighty-four thousand branches of the doctrine all collect into the twofold division of sutras and tantras, or the Causal Sutrayana and Resultant Vajrayana. Of these two, the Resultant Vajrayana is the superior.

The Vajrayana itself is spoken of in various ways. One such way is to speak of the four classes of tantras. Of these, the fourth and supreme is the Anuttarayoga class, or "Highest Yoga tantras." It is to this tantric division that the mandala of the Most Secret Lotus Lord Hayagriva belongs.

Guru Padmasambhava, who was like a second Buddha, once wrote,

> The buddhas, fully understanding
> The different stages of the mind,
> Taught the Secret Mantra Vehicle.
> Of all the various doctrines,
> This vehicle is supreme;
> For it contains all the essential points
> Of all levels of training,
> And produces quick enlightenment.

Also, *The Subsequent Tantra of Mystical Emanation*[177] states,

> Because it is free from karma and delusion,
> Its powers of mantra, mudra, and samadhi
> Purify and bless the five impure substances
> And transform them into the five nectars.
> The mystical syllables *YA*, *HAM*, *NA*, *BAM*, and *WA*
> Transform the five meats into five luminosities.
>
> By arising in the form of a tantric deity
> And applying the methods of purification,
> Then merely by eating the consecrated substances
> Powerful *siddhis* are achieved
> And the yogini attainments are gained.
> There is no method more powerful than this.

And *The Directly Imparted Tantra of Glorious Heruka*[178] states,

> Honey, vermilion, and camphor
> Are mixed with red sandalwood powder.
> This is placed in with the *tsok* offering.

The vajra is then taken up,
And the mudra is shown.
The yogi then proceeds with awareness
And tastes the substances.
The mere contact produces *siddhi*.
The five filths become five pure substances
And produce every powerful attainment.

Moreover, it is said that all accomplishments arise from ingesting the mystical substances. Even the immortal vajra body itself can be attained in this way. When one's own vision is pure, the entire universe is seen as a divine mandala and everything in the three worlds is seen as ambrosial nectar.

*The Eight Volumes on Ambrosia*[179] states,

Ultimately speaking, the three worlds
Are in nature constructed from the five nectars,
And all living beings by nature are perfect buddhas.
The three times, three worlds,
And the body, speech, and mind
Ultimately are only ambrosial nectars.
This truth is pronounced from the highest sphere.

Thus, as said above, the basis of everything in existence ultimately is only ambrosial nectar, and all living beings share in the nature of perfect enlightenment. But because of the distortions to perception caused by the impure prejudiced mind, we see the world as impure. However, if we should come to be cared for and guided by a qualified tantric guru and should we practice correctly in accordance with his instructions, then by the power of being shown the central points of the path of the Secret Mantra Vehicle we come to directly perceive for ourselves the essential, pure nature of that which had previously appeared to us as impure. This is how being shown the conventional level of truth leads to an understanding of the ultimate. Thus it is important that we clearly understand the main points of how an appreciation of the conventional directs the mind to a higher knowledge of the nectarlike ultimate.

The *Compendium Sutra*[180] states,

> Countless buddhas of the past
> Made these their main trainings.
> Because they held them as supreme *samayas,*
> They are famed as "classical disciplines."

Also, *The Tantra on Excellent Nectar*[181] states,

> Mainly there are five supreme nectars.
> Eight root and a thousand branch ingredients
> Are combined to make the ambrosial medicines
> Which become *samaya* substances.
> The syllables *KA, SA, YA,* and *NA*
> Transform these into great medicines;
> And then by eating these substances
> The common and supreme *siddhis* are achieved.

As for the authoritative scriptural sources on which this tantric tradition of achieving *siddhi* by means of relying upon mystical substances is based, these are as follows.

Here we will follow the structure of *An Essential Sun Benefiting Others by Bringing Joy to the Three Worlds,*[182] a ritual manual composed by the illustrious yogi Lama Padma Zhepai Dorjey, a holder of many secret traditions. In structuring his text this excellent master extracted the essence of all the earlier scriptures, both great and small, that were related to medicinal consecration, rearranging the materials for easy practice. I have used his manual as my fundamental guide, and on top of that have brought in various themes from the special teachings on the Hayagriva tradition that are concerned with medicinal empowerment, structuring these to suit my purposes.

Moreover, *The Root Tantra of Most Secret Hayagriva*[183] has numerous sections that deal directly with producing mystical nectarlike substances, and I have consulted these throughout.

I should perhaps also say something about the historical background of this particular tradition. Originally taught by the Buddha himself, in the beginning the lineage was transmitted through an occult line of Dharmakaya, Sambhogakaya, and Nirmanakaya emanations, until it came down to the bodhisattva Vajrapani. After this it was passed through the five *dama* knowledge holders (Tib. *Gra-ma-rig-'dzin-lnga*) and descended through the centuries as the undegenerated "Profound Instruction of the Seven Lineages." Eventually the tradition was acquired by the great acharya and vidyadhara Padmakara (i.e., Padmasambhava). From Padmakara come two lineages: that of the original instructions (Tib. *bKa'-ma*) and the tradition of treasure texts (Tib. *gTer-ma*). The former was transmitted through a successive lineage of gurus, such as Vairochana the Translator, King Trisong Deutsen, Gyalwa Choyang, and so forth.

As for the tradition of treasure texts, these were written out by Padmakara himself and then hidden in a cave at Yerpa to the north of Tibet's Vajra Abode (i.e., Lhasa). There they remained until the times had ripened sufficiently for their general propagation. They then were discovered and propagated by the three treasure revealers: Wangchen Gyaltsen, Drey Sherab Lama, and Kyangpo Drakpa Wangchuk.

Thus the sacred and profound instructions uniting both the distant scriptural tradition with the Close lineage of discovered treasure texts has come to Tibet and has become renowned here as "The Combined Scriptural and Treasure Text Tradition of Profound Instruction of the Mandala of Nine Wrathful Divinities of the Cycle of Supreme Hayagriva, the Most Secret Lotus Lord."

### (III) The Actual Rite

Hark! The method of practicing the consecration of nectarlike ambrosial medicines compounded from the eight root and one thousand branch ingredients by relying upon this exalted meditational mandala is as follows.

Begin the ritual as described in the standard manuals: taking refuge, generating the bodhi-mind, etc. Perform the self-generation and generation-in-front, creating the two mandalas as one.

Then visualize the various transformations, such as those of the one hundred supreme families, the five buddha families, the one most secret family, and so forth. Consecrate the medicines in this way.

Then generate the seven levels of the mandala, beginning with the level of physical bone until the level of the immortal vajra mandala, together with the Mystic Dagger (Vajrakilaya) methods of medicinal consecration.

Concentrate on this mandala of seven levels, constructed according to an oral tradition procedure received from holy gurus of the lineage. Above this (mandala) are the substances to be consecrated and transformed into ambrosial medicines.

Then summon forth the essence of all refuge objects, the forms of all good things in both samsara and nirvana, and the quintessence of all nonsamsaric nectars. These come and transform into the great palace of medicines that bestow instant liberation merely upon being tasted and that are the basis for the request for the profound initiations.

The method for requesting the initiations is as follows. The master says,

In the sky before you visualize the kind root guru inseparable in nature from the meditational deity Powerful Lotus
Lord Hayagriva. He is surrounded by great clouds of gurus
of the seven lineages, the eight great classes of practitioners, the various mandala divinities, and also countless buddhas, bodhisattvas, dakas, dakinis, Dharma protectors,
guardians, and so forth.

Single-pointedly request the initiations from them by means of the
verses having six lines beginning with the words "the time has come"
and the verses having four lines beginning with the word "Bhagavan."
(Note: These verses appear in the following pages.)

After the request has been made in this way, the master takes the
longevity arrow in his vajra hand and makes the summoning gesture.
The music of symbols, horns, and drums is offered in order to invoke
the lineage blessings. In brief, the manifesting powers of the mystical
substances, mantras, the laws of interdependent origination, and the
strength of samadhi are applied in order to invoke the compassionate blessings of the divine beings in the visualized field of assembly.

From their bodies there then flow forth nectars and lights of five
colors. Especially, from the body of Powerful Lotus Lord Hayagriva
there emanate forth countless replicas of himself, some large and
some small. These fall like rain upon the world and its inhabitants.
They also fall upon and melt into your body, speech, and mind. The
blessings of the body, speech, and mind of the Mandala Lord become
of one taste with your own three doors. All negativities and obscurations caused by body, speech, and mind, together with all weakened
*samaya*, become cleansed and purified. The forces of your karma and
awareness become blessed with the strength of longevity and wisdom. In brief, all things in the world, including the earth, the mandala substances, all living beings, etc., gain the powerful blessings of
the Lotus Lord Hayagriva and shine with a special radiance.

Especially, the medicine mandala achieves the power to induce all *siddhis*, both common and supreme, merely upon being seen, heard of, thought about, or touched. Fix your mind upon this thought and do not mentally wander from it. Then make the following request:

> O supreme Aryas, grant me your attention.
> The time has come to show your compassion.
> The time has come to show your unique nature.
> The time has come to use your powers.
> The time has come to bestow *siddhi*.
> The time has come to free (us from) enemies and hindrances.
> The time has come to restore weakened *samaya*.
>
> Bhagavan, give of your great powers.
> Bhagavan, bestow the great initiations.
> Bhagavan, please release your great blessings.
> O Bhagavan, fulfill these requests,
> And for all of us here
> Ripen the fruit of our karma.
> *HRIH! VAJRA KRODHA HAYAGRIVA HULU HULU HUM PHAT.*
> *KAYA VAKKA CHITTA VAJRA JNANA ABHESHAYA AH AH.*

This mantra is recited three times, together with an offering of forceful music. The master then says:

As is stated in *The Tantra of the Secret Cycle:*[184]

> Each of the disciples should
> Touch his/her head to the mandala.
> Then with the appropriate procedures
> The initiation should be performed.

When this has been heard, you (the disciples) should focus your attention on the ambrosial medicine mandala and should develop a firm aspiration to receive the initiation.

The blessings of the body, speech, and mind of the Tathagatas flow forth. Their nature is that of vajras but their form is that of brilliantly white, red, and blue nectars. These dissolve into your body, speech, and mind, purifying and cleansing you of all negativities and obscurations collected by means of body, speech, and mind. The wisdom of the threefold vajra (i.e., of vajra body, speech, and mind) is attained, and the supreme *siddhi* of mahamudra is achieved.

Imagine that these are gained even as you sit on your meditation cushion.

> Dharmadhatu, ultimately unborn and pure,
> Free from concepts of pure and impure, and a form
> That never fails to manifest in any of the three times
> With a style blazing with the vibrance of all *siddhis*:
> Whoever wants the initiation of this mandala, prepare to
>     receive it now.

> Like the sun rising from behind the clouds,
> It eliminates the spiritual darkness
> Generated over an aeon of lifetimes.
> By receiving this initiation of kingly nectars,
> May the stages of a kingly vidyadhara be obtained.
> *OM AH HUM SARVA PANJA AMRITA MAHA SHRI HERUKA*
> *PADMA NATA KHRID MAHA KRODHI SHVARI STVAM SAMAYA*
> *ABHESHAYA AH AH.*

> By the great initiation of a Wisdom Krodharaja
> All *siddhis* of body, speech, and mind
> Become of one nature with the stream

Of the body, speech, and mind of the yogi/yogini.
*KAYA SIDDHI OM. VAKKA SIDDHI AH. CHITTA SIDDHI HUM.*

(IV) Enunciating the Benefits

Hark! Hear now the inconceivable benefits that arise from having received this profound healing initiation. A scripture states,

> One gains the eight qualities:
> Lifespan, meritorious energy, and
> Charisma are increased;
> All hindrances are dispelled; and so forth.

Lobpon Rinpochey himself (i.e., Guru Padmasambhava) said,

> Ambrosial medicines to be offered to the Sugatas,
> Nectars which delight the gurus and meditational deities:
> These are like the heart drops of the dakinis.
> When they are ingested, the benefits are inconceivable.
> One gains the qualities of a buddha's five kayas.
> Externally, all diseases and physical obstacles are destroyed;
> Internally, the psychic poisons of five delusions are purified
> And weaknesses in *samaya* are overcome;
> And secretly one gains the self-born wisdom.
>
> Even a shravaka arhat or pratyekabuddha
> Who tastes this ambrosial medicine
> Is transported to the tenth Mahayana *bhumi*
> And becomes a bodhisattva mahasattva.
>
> If one offers this medicine to the guru,
> Great blessings are achieved.

If one offers it to the meditational deities,
Powerful *siddhis* are attained.
If one offers it to the Sugatas,
Their compassion is invoked.
And if one offers it to the dakas and dakinis,
They will deliver a prophecy.

Should a yogi or anyone at all even taste it,
The negative influences and obscurations
Of physical illness and obstacles are purified.
The internal quality of the samadhis
Of generation and completion stage yogas
Becomes firm and clear.
Secretly, self-awareness becomes Dharmakaya,
And all shortcomings and excesses are made right.

Merely by holding this medicine
The dangers of premature death are eliminated
And the strongest poison is counteracted.
By massaging it onto one's body
All sicknesses and obstacles are dispelled.
If one burns it as incense,
Harmful spirits and hindering agents are chased away.

The place where this rite is performed
Becomes equal to the mystical Cooling-Wood Cemetery.
The area gains the blessings
Of countless dakas and dakinis.
Rains will be consistent and crops abundant.
Anyone who later uses the place for retreat
Will easily gain samadhi.

> Should anyone who is about to die
> Ingest a portion of this sacred medicine,
> He/she will gain the state of a vidyadhara
> Regardless of what kind of life was led.
> Indeed, it is a supreme substance.

Also, *The Eight Volumes on Ambrosia* states,

> O Manjushri, should a person work for the benefit of living beings for a thousand aeons, the merits produced are not as great as those generated by this nectarlike medicine. For this medicinal substance even has the ability to lead beings from the eighteen great hells to the path of final liberation.

These and many other nonfallacious scriptural sources speak in detail on the wondrous benefits of the nectarlike medicines produced by this mystical ritual.

In brief, whoever relies upon this ambrosial nectar gains power over every *siddhi* of both samsara and beyond. It effortlessly fulfills the good of both oneself and others. Therefore do not doubt its efficacy.

## Part Three: The Conclusion

This concludes the summary of two traditions of Hayagriva: the first being a longevity initiation in accordance with the lineage of transmission of Guru Tsokyey Dorjey, embodiment of the three buddha kayas, as clarified by the pure visionary experiences of Kunkyen Tokmey Tsal (i.e., the Fifth Dalai Lama), a legacy known far and wide as "The Sealed Transmission of Most Secret Hayagriva"; and the second being the healing empowerment, together with the rites for consecrating the *samaya* substances that become ambrosial medicines, in accordance with the nine-deity mandala of the Heruka Hayagriva Pema Wangchen, the Most Secret Powerful Lotus Lord.

At the end of the ceremony, the disciple should repeat the pledge to maintain all the vows and practice commitments taken during the initiation in the visualized presence of the buddhas and bodhisattvas:

> O masters, I vow to accomplish
> All that you have instructed me to do.

This is to be repeated three times. The vajra master and disciples then perform a *tsok* offering together, and offer prayers associated with the initiation tradition of Hayagriva. The disciples offer the mandala symbolic of the universe in order to express their gratitude at having received the initiations. The standard concluding procedures are then performed: sending out the excess *tsok* to the local spirits, offering prayers to the Doctrine protectors, making the thanksgiving offering, and sending forth prayers and auspicious verses.

The Colophon: In the Earth Bird Year of the Fifteenth Sexagenary (i.e., 1909), the Thirteenth White Lotus Holder (i.e., the Thirteenth Dalai Lama) was on his way back to Lhasa after having visited the Manchu Empress in Beijing. The Tibetans were celebrating his return to the Land of Dharma, and were filled with joy.

While passing through Nagchu he stopped at Zhabgon Droden Dekyiling Monastery. This monastery maintains a tradition of annually performing a vast tantric ritual for the consecration of ambrosial medicines as a method of contributing to the happiness of all beings. The monastery was engaged in this ritual event when the Great Thirteenth arrived, presided over by the great master Drubkhang Tulku, whose mindstream had been ripened by study and practice of the hundreds of sutras and tantras over many previous lifetimes. Drubkhang and the other practitioners requested the Great Thirteenth to stay for some time and lead them in their meditations and rites, and to lead the empowering ceremonies of Hayagriva coming from the Great Fifth Dalai Lama. The Thirteenth consented. The two above texts were edited from notes prepared from that occasion.

# CHAPTER EIGHT:

## The Second Dalai Lama's

### *The Two Yogic Stages of the Vajrabhairava Tantra*[185]

GYALWA GENDUN GYATSO (1475-1542)
*With a commentary by Lama Lobzang Chinpa*

YAMANTAKA

# Translator's Preamble

EVEN THOUGH all schools of Tibetan Buddhism hold one form or another of the Vajrabhairava Tantra, it is probably the most popular *maha anuttara yoga* (or "great highest yoga") system practiced in the Gelukpa School of Tibetan Buddhism. Almost all Gelukpa practitioners meditate on the mandala and recite the mantras on a daily basis, and most Gelukpas have completed one of the three forms of the retreat: short, which takes approximately three weeks; medium, which takes three months; and extensive, which requires three to four years to complete. All Dalai and Panchen Lamas have received initiation into the Vajrabhairava mandala, and most of those who lived to adulthood have done the extensive meditation retreat (three to four years) with it as the focus. Moreover, most Dalai and Panchen Lamas have also written various treatises on the system. The Seventh Dalai Lama's commentary on the initiation and self-initiation ceremonies is still very popular with the lama intelligentsia, as is the Thirteenth Dalai Lama's commentary on the daily sadhana, or meditation practice.

The name "Vajrabhairava" literally means "The Diamond Terror." The implication is that the practice terrifies the obstrucions to enlightenment, bringing quick and easy realization. The principal deity of the Vajrabhairava mandala is also known as Yamantaka, or "The Opponent of Death." The commentaries explain that this is because practice of the yogas eliminates the three forms of death:

outer, which refers to premature death caused by outer forces such as illness, accidents, etc.; inner, which refers to the delusions, such as anger, jealousy, attachment, ignorance, etc.; and secret, which refers to blockages in the the subtle energy system of the body-mind complex, i.e., the chakras and *nadis*.

As the Thirteenth Dalai Lama points out in *A Brief Guide to the Buddhist Tantras*, "Three basic forms of the mandala are presented in these various texts: red, black, and extremely fierce. Of these, the last is the most important in general practice."

He goes on to say, "The Vajrabhairava generation stage yogas usually consist of cultivating the three samadhis on one of the mandalas associated with this last form of Bhairava: the forty-nine-deity mandala, the seventeen-deity mandala, the thirteen-deity mandala, the mandala of eight *vitali* deities, and the mandala of the Solitary Hero."

As for these three forms, referred to above by the names "black, red, and extremely fierce," the black form of the mandala is strongest in the Nyingma (or Old) School, and the red form is still held by the Sakya School. The extremely fierce is the form practiced in the Geluk. The Kagyupas also hold a lineage of the extremely fierce, but show greater attention to the Chakrasamvara systems and the Vajrayogini / Vajravarahi mandalas emanating from them.

The Thirteenth Dalai Lama made his three-year retreat in connection with the yogas associated with the extremely fierce form of the Vajrabhairava mandala. In fact he had undertaken this retreat twice. The first began in 1902, when he was a young man in his midtwenties. Unfortunately, a Japanese spy working for the British managed to make his way to Lhasa at the time, and sent back false information suggesting that the Russian Czar was about to take over Tibet. This led the British Viceroy Lord Curzon to send in an expedition headed by the British officer Lt. Col. Francis Younghusband. The Tibetan government invoked the Nechung Oracle, who from the depths of his induced trance state recommended that the Thirteenth

Dalai Lama be taken out of his retreat and transported to Mongolia for safety. What was intended as a brief interlude ended up being a five-year teaching tour. (In the previous chapter we have included the Thirteenth's reading of a Fifth Dalai Lama tantric manual created during this period on the road.) The Thirteenth returned to his three-year retreat again in 1916, and this time successfully completed it without interruption.

Above the Thirteenth Dalai Lama mentions various forms of mandala used as the basis of the generation stage or mandala meditation of the extremely fierce Vajrabhairava. He lists these as the forty-nine-deity mandala, the seventeen-deity mandala, the thirteen-deity mandala, the mandala of eight *vitali* deities, and the mandala of the Solitary Hero. The Second Dalai Lama's poem, which is translated in this chapter together with the commentary of Lama Chinpa, is in accord with the practice of the thirteen-deity mandala.

One of my lamas commented that today the mandala of the Solitary Hero Vajrabhairava, known in Tibetan as *Pawo Chikpa*, is the most popular for individual practice, whereas the thirteen-deity mandala is most popular as a monastic or communal practice. As the name suggests, in the meditation of the Solitary Hero one visualizes oneself in the form of the solitary lord Vajrabhairava, standing alone and without a sexual consort. Similarly, in the meditation on the thirteen-deity form one visualizes a mandala with thirteen deities. Here Vajrabhairava stands at the center of this mandala, locked in passionate sexual embrace with his consort.

In *A Brief Guide to the Buddhist Tantras*, the Thirteenth Dalai Lama also addresses the topic of the completion stage yogas, the methods of energy control. Here he writes, "As for the completion stage yogas, the Vajrabhairava system arranges these into four categories. Here the phases of body isolation and speech isolation combine as Mantra Yoga. Mind isolation becomes Commitment Yoga. Both impure and pure phases of the illusory body trainings combine as Form Yoga. Finally, semblant and actual clear light phases become the Wisdom Yoga."

Readers will recognize most of these terms from their appearance in earlier chapters of this book, especially the Second Dalai Lama's commentary on the Six Yogas of Niguma, the Seventh Dalai Lama's long poem on Chakrasamvara practice, and the First Dalai Lama's notes on the Kalachakra completion stage yogas, as well as numerous appearances of them in the Thirteenth Dalai Lama's *A Brief Guide to the Buddhist Tantras.*

In particular, however, here the Thirteenth is pointing out how the four completion stage yogas of the Vajrabhairava system contain all of the famous five completion stage yogas of the Guhyasamaja Tantra. The Thirteenth had given a brief description of each of these five Guhyasamaja stages earlier in his *Guide,* and thus the reference to them here in his summary of the Vajrabhairava system is a natural and fluid extension of his discussion.

It could also be pointed out that all core elements of systems such as the Six Yogas of Naropa and Six Yogas of Niguma are contained within the four completion stage yogas of Vajrabhairava. But of course every Anuttarayoga Tantra system has its own forms of these famous six.

The Second Dalai Lama's poem on the practice of the Vajrabhairava Tantra is succinct, as is the commentary to it by Lama Chinpa. It nonetheless has remained very popular with Gelukpa monasteries over the generations, for it touches upon all key elements in both the generation and completion stage meditations. It is commonly used as a teaching tool, partially because its brevity allows for a wide range of approaches in how the master unpacks the meanings embodied in it. An introductory level of meaning can be revealed to novice initiates, whereas a far deeper level of application can be given to those with years of daily practice and retreat under their belts.

I translated this text with my good friend Michael Perrott in accordance with a commentary from Ven. Tubten Tulku.

# The Second Dalai Lama's Text[186]

HEREIN is explained in simple terms the principal points of the Second Dalai Lama's prayer for realization of the two yogic stages of the Vajrabhairava Tantra, or the Tantra of the Diamond Destroyer of Death. It is a treasury of blessings, having been penned by the Second Dalai Lama himself, an embodiment of the compassion of all the buddhas of the ten directions and three times.

The prayer is brief, but its meaning covers the entire path of the Highest Yoga Tantra system. In my concise commentary I shall quote the twenty-two verses of the prayer itself, giving a brief explanation of each verse both in meaning and how the words relate to the actual stages of the yogas of the Vajrabhairava Tantra.

1/ On the surface of the crystal moon of pure mind
The mandala of the Diamond Destroyer manifests like a
    rainbow
Created by the brush of meditative concentration.
Through meditation upon this mandala and recitation of
    the mantras
A force of goodness is generated, brilliantly white
As moonlight, a conch shell, and a *kunda* flower.[187]

This verse reveals the substance to be dedicated. Through practice of the Tantric path a tremendous amount of positive energy is generated. This should be dedicated to the accomplishment of the various levels of the path in order to be able to quickly accomplish enlightenment for the benefit of all living beings. However, in order to progress in the various yogas one must rely upon a competent teacher. The next verse is therefore dedicated to maintaining contact with a qualified guru until enlightenment is won:

> 2/ Until enlightenment is won may I
> Be upheld by a teacher of the Great Way,
> A fully qualified spiritual guide,
> The root of all mystical attainment.

The doorway to every spiritual practice opens for us through cultivating a correct relationship with a spiritual guide. In particular, to practice the Great Way our master must have had Mahayana training. The Highest Yoga tantras, including the Tantra of the Diamond Destroyer of Death, are all a branch of the Mahayana.

But in order to enter into the Tantric path we must first have gained maturity in the practices of the Sutrayana Vehicle, the foundations upon which the higher tantric methods may be built. These are known as "the common practices," being common to both the Sutrayana and Vajrayana. The next verse is dedicated to the accomplishment of these foundation practices:

> 3/ May I see the eight worldly concerns
> As nothing but a childish game,
> And the pleasures and comforts of samsara
> To be a nest of poisonous snakes.
> May I give birth to the spirit of enlightenment
> And dwell constantly in the six perfections.

The eight concerns of this life—caring for gain or loss, praise or blame, pleasure or pain, etc.—are all without an essence. To build a lifestyle upon them is like taking a childish game seriously.

Moreover, even worldly success is self-defeating, like harboring a nest of poisonous snakes. One should replace worldly interest with an interest in the three higher trainings—higher discipline, meditative concentration, and wisdom—which are the essence of the Hinayana; and also an interest in cultivating the spirit of enlightenment, the bodhi-mind. Here "bodhi-mind" means both the wishing aspect of the enlightenment spirit, the altruistic wish for enlightenment based on love and compassion; and the actual bodhi-mind practices of the six perfections and the four ways of benefiting trainees,[188] which are the general Mahayana methods for accomplishing enlightenment.

The above verse also reveals the three levels of motivation—initial, medium, and great—through which one's mind must evolve in order to enter into the Vajrayana path.

As the practitioner of initial scope one must attempt to eliminate attachment to gross worldly activities such as the eight worldly concerns. The practitioner of medium scope eliminates grasping at high samsaric status, pleasure, and meditational ecstasy. Finally, the great practitioner is moved by love and compassion for all that lives and, based on this, eliminates grasping for personal nirvana and instead seeks full buddhahood as a more effective means of benefiting the world. This is the wishing bodhi-mind. To fulfill this aspiration the great practitioner determines to engage in the six perfections and the four ways of benefiting trainees.

Once stability in the above meditations has been achieved one may enter into the esoteric Vajrayana, the path of secret mantras. The gateway to the Vajrayana is initiation, and to maintain the strength of the initiation one must guard one's commitments well:

4/ Having received the four mystic initiations
That wash away all stains of the three doors
And plant the seeds of the four buddha kayas,
May I remain a pure vessel
For the two stages of Highest Yoga Tantra
By guarding the pledges and commitments of initiation
As dearly as the pupils of my eyes.

To enter the Vajrayana path of Highest Yoga Tantra one must receive the four levels of initiation: Vase, Secret, Wisdom, and Highest Word.

The first of these purifies stains of the body, plants the seeds of the Emanation Body of a buddha, and empowers one to practice the generation stage yogas.

The second initiation purifies stains of speech, plants the seeds of the Beatific Body of a buddha, and empowers one to practice the illusory body yogas of the completion stage.

The third initiation purifies the stains of the mind, plants the seed of the Wisdom Truth Body of a buddha, and empowers one to practice the clear light yogas.

Finally, the fourth initiation purifies the three doors simultaneously, plants the seeds of the Natural Truth Body, and empowers one to practice the great union yogas.

On the basis of these initiations one may enter into the yogas of the Highest Yoga Tantra. However, as the root of all mystical attainment in the Tantric path is the guarding of the tantric vows and commitments taken at the time of initiation, one should protect these as carefully as one would one's eyes. Only then does one become a vessel capable of receiving the two types of *siddhi*.

The next section of the prayer deals with the aspiration to accomplish the various meditations and yogic levels of the two stages of Highest Yoga Tantra: the generation and completion stages.

The first of these two stages is the generation stage. The verse that follows explains the general nature and function of these yogas. The nine subsequent verses deal with the various phases of the generation stage meditation.

> 5/ By meditating in four daily sessions
> Upon the profound generation stage yogas
> That open the net of the hundreds of lights
> And totally dispel the darkness of birth,
> Death, and the in-between state,
> May I ripen my stream of being
> And plant the seeds for the accomplishment
> Of the powerful completion stage yogas.

The two main practices in the generation stage yogas are clear visualization and the cultivation of divine pride. By applying these to the various phases of the generation stage meditation, one becomes familiar with the meditations of taking death as a path of Dharmakaya, taking the in-between state as the Sambhogakaya, and taking rebirth as the Nirmanakaya.

Firstly one accomplishes coarse clear visualization by meditating on the entire mandala. Then one visualizes the mandala in the mystic seed, which is drawn into the lotus of the consort. This is subtle clear visualization.

Meditating upon the mandala in this way strengthens the seeds of the three buddha kayas and thus opens a net of light to dispel darkness from death, the bardo, and the rebirth process.

Through meditating in this way upon the generation stage yogas in four daily sessions—predawn, late morning, afternoon, and evening—one quickly lays the foundations upon which the completion stage yogas can be engaged and the state of enlightenment quickly won.

This is the general nature and function of the generation stage methods. Now follows a more elaborate presentation of the individual phases of the process.

This involves three subjects: the preparatory absorption, the absorption of the supremely-triumphant mandala, and the supremely-victorious activities.

The first of these, the preparatory absorption, involves four phases of visualization: purifying death by generating wisdom and goodness; purifying the bardo by generating the Inconceivable Mansion and then arising as the Causal Vajra Holder; purifying rebirth by arising as the Resultant Vajra Holder; and, lastly, uniting with a Knowledge Lady.

The first of these has three subphases: generating goodness, generating wisdom, and generating the Wheel of Protection:

> 6/ May the offerings with which I fill the sky
> Before the host of mandala deities
> While meditating on the noninherent nature
> Of the offering, the act, and the recipient
> Cause my mindstream to mature in goodness.

The meditation begins by oneself arising in the simple form of the Diamond Destroyer of Death. Visualize that lights from one's heart invite one's tantric master, together with the full mandala of deities. They come into the space before you. Visualize filling the skies with offerings to this mystic assembly while meditating on the empty nature of the gift, giver, and act of giving. This purifies death by planting a store of positive karmic seeds.

Next is the meditation of purifying death by means of the accumulation of wisdom. One recites the two mantras that point to the meaning of emptiness—*OM SVABHAVA SHUDDHO SARVADHARMA SVABHAVA SHUDDHOH HAM* and *OM SHUNYATA VAJRA ATMAKHO*

*HAM*—while maintaining awareness of their meaning: that all things in samsara and nirvana from the beginning abide in the natural purity of emptiness.

To symbolize this, the entire mandala and host of deities dissolve into clear light. The object, or emptiness, and the subject, one's own mind, unite in the one-tasteness of blissful wisdom.

Through relying upon this accumulation of wisdom one purifies ordinary death and ripens the root of virtue within one's mindstream by which one is later able to meditate upon the semblant and actual clear lights.

Therefore the Second Dalai Lama writes,

> 7/ The sphere of primordial purity, the great bliss,
> And one's own mind become of one taste
> Through recitation of the two preliminary mantras.
> May I understand the meaning of these mantras
> And thus complete the accumulation of wisdom,
> Abandon the pitfalls of uncontrolled death,
> And attain the Dharmakaya wisdom
> Through the path of clear light.

Having dissolved the mandala into emptiness and absorbed the mind in clear light meditation, one must generate the common and exclusive protection wheels. The former of these includes the mandalas of the vajra elements and so forth. The latter refers to the Lord Sumbharaja and Consort, together with the Ten Wrathful Ones.

Sumbharaja and Consort stand in sexual union at the center of the hub. The Ten Wrathful Ones stand in union with their consorts. Eight take their positions near the rim of the Wheel of Protection, one couple in each of the eight directions. The remaining two couples stand above and below at the zenith and nadir points.

These ten and their consorts afford protection from the friends of darkness, which refers to the inner forces such as afflicted emotions, the external forces such as hindering and negative conditions, and so forth. All obstructions to the fulfillment of the two paths are instantly dispelled:

8/ May I accomplish the meditative absorptions
Of Sumbharaja and the Ten Wrathful Protectors,
And thus destroy the very roots of darkness,
Such as Mara and his army of hindrances.

The method of purifying the bardo and taking it as the path of the Sambhogakaya has two phases: generating the vision of the Inconceivable Mansion which is born from self-manifest wisdom, and purifying the bardo by meditating upon oneself as the Causal Vajra Holder:

9/ The Inconceivable Mansion ablaze with jewels
By nature is the pure form of Buddha Vairochana.
Through meditation upon it may I purify the impure
    bardo state
And produce a mansion of pure wisdom.

Here, Sumbharaja melts into light and reappears as Buddha Vairochana, who symbolizes the pure aspect of one's aggregate of form.

Vairochana then transforms into the Inconceivable Mansion having all features. Through meditating upon it one purifies the world, which is a vessel of impurities caused by negative karma and delusion, a world that nonetheless one must learn to live in and utilize. This is the symbolic mansion. Through meditating on it one becomes able to plant the seed for the completion stage yoga of emanating the mansion symbolized.

Inside the Inconceivable Mansion are the thrones for the deities. On the central throne appears a mystical letter. This becomes a wrathful vajra. The wrathful vajra emanates countless replicas of itself that fill the universe and place all beings in enlightenment.

The vajra then dissolves into light and reemerges with oneself as the Causal Vajra Holder, the Wisdom Bodhisattva Manjushri. My body is insubstantial as a rainbow and bright as a saffron mountain struck by a million suns.

The Second Dalai Lama refers to these processes in the following verse:

10/ Through the yoga of a Causal Vajra Holder—
Self-identification as the Bodhisattva of Wisdom,
Manjushri, he brilliant as a saffron mountain—
May I purify myself of the impure bardo,
Become a vessel for the illusory body yoga,
And quickly produce the Sambhogakaya of a Buddha.

Thus through meditation upon oneself as the translucent Manjushri one purifies the seeds of impure bardo and later becomes a vessel for the completion stage practices of the pure and impure illusory body yogas.

One now transforms into the Resultant Vajra Holder. This is symbolically performed by five phases of transformation: moon, sun, seed syllable, mystical implement, and complete body of the deity. These five are like the five stages of enlightenment, or like the unfoldment of the five wisdoms of enlightenment: the mirrorlike wisdom, the wisdom of equality, the distinguishing wisdom, the all-accomplishing wisdom, and the all-encompassing wisdom.

By means of these five wisdoms one is enabled to purify the rebirth experience through practice of the illusory body yoga, which lays instincts for the Nirmanakaya of a buddha:

11/ By the actual purification of the five wisdoms
Through meditation upon the unfoldment of the symbols
Of moon, sun, seed syllable, mystic implement,
And the complete body of a deity
May I accomplish the yoga of a Resultant Vajra Holder
And thus purify myself of imperfect rebirth,
Becoming a vessel of the generation stage yogas
That plant seeds for the Nirmanakaya of a buddha.

Thus one arises in the full form of the mandala lord, the Diamond Destroyer of Death. This is the Symbolic Being.

At one's heart is the Wisdom Being, youthful Manjushri, Bodhisattva of Wisdom, in nature subtle energy radiant as a hundred thousand suns.

At Manjushri's heart is the Absorption Being, the most subtle aspect of one's own mind in the form of the syllable *HUM*, like the flame of a butter lamp, radiantly emanating lights of five colors.

These are the three sheathed beings: Symbolic, Wisdom, and Absorption. By meditating upon them one causes the threefold purification of the basis, path, and result:

12/ By meditating upon myself as a three-sheathed being
Luminous as a hundred thousand suns—
The magnificent Diamond Destroyer of Death;
The Wisdom Being, Manjushri, at the Lord's heart;
And also the Absorption Being, the primordial sound *HUM*—
May the three beings of the basis be purified,
May the three beings of the path be matured,
And may the three beings which are the fruit be accomplished.

The last phase of the preparatory absorption is union with a Knowledge Lady. Here, while maintaining the three recognitions, one meditates upon oneself as the Diamond Destroyer of Death uniting with the Knowledge Lady Vatali. The supported and supporting deities are generated as the resultant play of bliss inseparable from the wisdom of emptiness.

Such is the nature of practice at the time of the generation stage yoga. This plants the seeds later to be ripened by the completion stage yogas of uniting with either a *karmamudra* or *jnanamudra* as a means to give direct birth to great bliss born simultaneously with insight.

This is referred to in the first line of the following verse. The subsequent lines refer to the activities of generating the supremely-triumphant mandala:

13/ May I unite with a mudra of my own capacity,
Fill the three realms with emanations,
Cleanse the world and its inhabitants of stains,
And generate the supported and supporting mandalas,
Thus perfecting altruism and taking to the end
The absorption of the supremely-triumphant mandala.

The thirteen deities of the mandala, together with the skull-cups, are generated in the lotus of the consort and then emanated outward. The three realms of the universe are filled with clouds of emanations of hundreds of millions of mandalas and deities. These purify the insentient and sentient worlds, transforming them into mandalas and deities.

This is the generation stage practice whereby all that appears (i.e., the world and its inhabitants) arises as the mandala and its deities. It plants the seeds later to be ripened by the completion stage yogas of illusory body and great union, wherein one gains the power of actual emanation of the triumphant mandala.

14/ By the power of absorption, offering, and recitation,
And by relying upon the stages of contemplation,
May I gain the power of a supreme activities king
Easily able to accomplish all deeds
Of pacification, increase, power, and wrath.

Through completing the generation stage yogas one plants the seeds whereby the completion stage yogas—such as vajra recitation in the yoga of speech isolation—may be accomplished, and the state of a supreme activities king actualized.

This completes the presentation of the generation stage yogas. Now follow the verses of prayer to accomplish the various stages of the completion stage yogas.

The first verse explains the general nature and function of these yogas. The subsequent verses deal with the individual yogas constituting the completion stage methods.

15/ The five levels of the profound completion stage
Abbreviate into the four yogas.
By practicing these with the three conducts
May the three kayas of a perfect buddha
Be won in this very lifetime.

The five levels of the completion stage yogas are: speech isolation, mind isolation, illusory body, clear light, and great union. These abbreviate into the four tantric yogas: Mantra, Commitment, Form, and Pure Wisdom.

The three levels of conduct are: distorted, undistorted, and utterly pure.

Through practicing the four yogas with the three conducts one is enabled to win full enlightenment in one lifetime.

As for the four yogas, the first two—Mantra and Commitment—

are the means whereby one brings the vital energies into the central channel. The latter two yogas—Form and Pure Wisdom—are yogas performed on the basis of the vital energies having been already brought into the central channel.

The first of the four yogas, or the Mantra Yoga, has two phases: the meditation upon the compression process at the navel and the actual Mantra Yoga.

> 16/ May I absorb the mind in the wheel
> Of emanation in the lustful Lord and Consort,
> And by the compression method direct
> The vital energies of sun and moon into Rahula.
> Then by the downward-showering and upward-holding
>       movements
> May the four tantric joys be experienced.

Here one establishes the pride of being the Symbolic Being, the Diamond Destroyer of Death, together with Consort. One is adorned with all features, the three energy channels running up one's body through the six energy centers.

At one's navel is the chakra "wheel of emanation." It has sixty-four petals (of energy channels). At its hub, inseparable from one's own mind, is a two-armed form of lustful Vajrabhairava locked in sexual union with his Consort. They are white in color and the size of a mere pea.

Upon a sun disc at the heart of this Vajrabhairava is the Absorption Being as a white syllable *HUM*, half the size of a mustard seed. Above it there blazes a zig-zag, by nature mystic fire, burning like a tiny flame the size of a tip of hair.

One absorbs the mind single-pointedly on this image. Lights radiate forth from the syllable *HUM* which strike the world and its beings, purifying them of all faults. Thus purified, they are absorbed into the

Symbolic Being through the involution compression process. This causes the energies flowing through the secondary energy channels to be diverted into the central channel.

After the signs of this have arisen, the genetic substances in the energy center at the crown melt and flow down to the tip of the sexual organ, giving rise to the four downward-showering joys. The substances are then drawn back up to the crown, giving rise to the four upward-holding joys.

After these two processes have been mastered, one may engage in the actual Mantra Yoga:

> 17/ May I untie the knots at the heart,
> The knots in the central channel
> At the chakra called "wheel of truth,"
> By means of the supreme Mantra Yoga
> In conjunction with the vase-breathing
> And vajra-recitation techniques,
> Thus experiencing the mystical intoxication
> Of the innate great bliss.

As before, one generates the pride of being the Diamond Destroyer of Death, together with Consort. The three energy channels and six chakras are visualized clearly.

At one's heart is the chakra called "the wheel of truth." It has eight petals of connecting channels. Inside the central channel at the center of this chakra is a pea-sized drop, in color white tinged with red. Inside of this is a very small syllable *HUM*, white in color, a tiny zigzag of flame burning above it.

One breathes in slowly through the nostrils and swallows as white life-sustaining energy is brought into the central channel through the white aperture between the eyebrows. It comes to the heart chakra and is forced downward.

Lower energy, yellow in color, is then drawn in through the aperture of the sexual organ. This also enters the central channel.

Both energies, together with the mystic drop and the syllable *HUM*, dissolve and one experiences uncreated ecstasy. One then exhales slowly through the nose, visualizing that the air and energy remain inside one's body. This is the method of vase breathing at the heart.

One then engages in the vajra-recitation technique.

At the center of the heart chakra is the syllable *HUM*, white tinged with red. One brings the energies into the central channel simultaneously from above and below, giving rise to bliss. One recites the syllable *OM*, and the life-sustaining energy enters the zig-zag flame of the letter *HUM* from above, and the lower vowel sign from below. With the sound of *AH* the energies abide, and then with the sound of *HUM* the life-sustaining energies leave the zig-zag from above and the lower energy leaves from below.

One meditates prolongedly in this way, one's mind as the syllable *HUM*, the melodic sound of the three mystic syllables performing the vajra recitation.

Thus are the knots at the heart untied and the energies brought into and dissolved inside the central channel. The signs of this accomplishment manifest, and one experiences the four innate joys and also the innate simultaneously-born joys of bliss and the wisdom of emptiness.

Having in this way released the knots at the heart by means of vajra recitation, one is ready to enter into the Commitment Yoga. For this one must rely upon either a *karmamudra* or *jnanamudra*:

18/ May I engage in the sacred *Samaya* Yoga
And the stages of the involution compression process
To unite skillfully with one of the two mudras
And by absorption be led to ultimate mind isolation.

One visualizes oneself as the Diamond Destroyer of Death, together with Consort. One consecrates the sexual sites of the male and female deities and then with wise and skillful means they enter into union possessed of the three recognitions and four postures. The energies are brought into the central channel, where they abide and dissolve. The signs of dissolution, from the miragelike appearance to the vision of clear light, successively arise.

At the heart at the hub of the chakra called "the wheel of truth" are the male and female drops, the syllable *HUM* between them. Lights emanate from this and purify the world and its inhabitants of stains, transforming them into mandalas and deities. Then everything gradually dissolves into light, beginning from the outside and coming into the tiny zig-zag flame over the syllable *HUM*. This is the training of the involution compression process at the heart. It releases the most subtle knots at the heart and brings the most subtle all-pervading energy, which is extremely difficult to absorb, into the central channel, just as at the time of death. This gives rise to the samadhi that is the final mind isolation. This is produced by the simultaneously-born bliss together with perception of the semblant clear light perceived by general methods of emptiness meditation.

Now follow the prayers to accomplish the methods that depend upon previously having brought the energies into the central channel. The first of these is the Yoga of Form:

> 19/ May I dissolve all vital energies into the heart,
> Just like at the time of death the energies
> Dissolve into clear light.
> And may I perfect the absorption of illusory manifestation
> Of a form having the net of signs of perfection.

Through reliance upon the Commitment Yoga one brought all energies into the central channel and experienced all the stages of energy withdrawal, just like at the time of death. This gave rise to the experience of the semblant clear light and final mind isolation. After this, as though in a dream, the sons and daughters of the great celestial beings come to one and make offerings.

Lights then radiate forth from one's body and attract the attention of the buddhas of the ten directions, who come and bestow the initiations by means of a flood of lights.

One attains the impure illusory body and arises from meditation upon the semblant clear light.

The subtle bodily energies transformed into lights of five colors act as the evolutionary cause, and the clear light of mind acts as the simultaneous cause. Then, through the Yoga of Form, one transforms one's old aggregates and causes them to emerge as the actual body of the deity embellished with the net of major and minor signs of perfection, like a fish drawn out of the depths of a lake.

This is the impure illusory body of nine stages, and its attainment marks the third phase of the completion stage yogas.

Its nature is described by five similes: the body of a dream, a reflection in a mirror, the moon's image in a lake, an illusory person, and a water bubble.

This is the method whereby one produces the rainbow body, the diamond body that is empty of being made of ordinary substances such as flesh and bone.

Although the essential substance of the activity that produces this rainbow body is impure and is still related to one's previous samsaric aggregates, anyone who attains this stage of realization is guaranteed of enlightenment in one lifetime.

At this stage, whatever one wants can be produced magically from nothingness in the moment of a single thought, and one is able to send forth millions of emanations simultaneously, to fulfill the needs of sentient beings.

20/ Then by the Yoga of Pure Wisdom
May that radiant form, immaterial as a rainbow,
Be dissolved like a cloud into space, so that
The actual clear light (which is) reality may be known
And the seeds of grasping
For true existence be extracted.

The meaning of this verse is that the illusory being transforms his previous aggregates into a coarse Emanation Body and unites in meditation with a *karmamudra* as the external condition. Within that sphere he uses the internal condition of dissolving the entire world, including his own body, into clear light by means of the involution compression process. He strives at this, and in the postmeditation period reveals this esoteric Dharma to others.

This meditation is pursued for six to eighteen months while living in the wilds. Eventually one gains the signs of actual clear light realization.

As before, one relies upon a *karmamudra* as an external condition and the experience of the compression process as the inner condition. This causes one's illusory body, which is as clear and vibrant as a rainbow, to melt like a cloud into space.

When this occurs, the dualistic appearance of the illusory body and the clear light subsides. The actual clear light which directly perceives emptiness then brings realization of the Yoga of Pure Wisdom. This pulls out the seed of grasping at true existence, destroying it once and forever from its root.

Now we come to the final phase of the completion stage yogas. This is known as the Yoga of Great Union. The Second Dalai Lama's prayer refers to it as follows:

21/ Then may I accomplish the Yoga of Great Union
By realizing the point of union of a body

Adorned by the marks and signs of perfection
And a mind which is actual clear light realization.

One arises from the simultaneously-born experience of the Yoga of Pure Wisdom. At that time the evolutionary cause—the subtle energy of the body arising as the five lights, which is the vehicle for the simultaneous condition, i.e., the actual clear light of mind—inspires one's aggregates to transform into a fully embellished vajra body adorned by a hundred and twelve signs of perfection. One attains the pure illusory body which has abandoned all objective obscurations, and one's clear light realization becomes fully manifest.

This pure illusory body then enters into the previous coarse Emanation Body, and there arises the union of one-tasteness of the pure illusory body with the pure heart, the wisdom of the actual clear light. This stage is called "the trainee's great union."

The last verse of the prayer refers to the final results of accomplishing the two stages of the path of the Vajrabhairava Tantra. This is the fulfillment of "the master's great union."

When the practitioner on the stage of the "trainee's great union" perceives the signs of being ready to approach the "master's great union," he enters into meditation. As before, one relies upon the external condition of a *karmamudra* and the internal condition of meditation upon emptiness, bringing the energies into the central channel and causing them to abide and dissolve. The first instant of clear light mind following this experience destroys the obscurations to omniscience. In the second instant one directly perceives all objects of knowledge, both conventional and ultimate, as directly as a piece of fruit held in the hand.

22/ May I thus in this life attain
The five kayas which exist for as long as does space
And are possessed of the seven kisses.

In a single moment may I then place
All living beings in that same transcendental state.

The coarse body of the "trainee's great union" becomes the five buddha kayas of the "master's great union" which endure as long as does space. These five are: the Body of Great Union, the Wisdom Truth Body, the Beatific Body, the Emanation Body, and the Body of Innate Wisdom.

Thus does one attain to the state possessed of seven kisses: a complete Beatific Body, union, great bliss, intrinsic realitylessness, fully mature compassion, being of an uninterrupted flow of fulfillment, and being in a state of ceaseless accomplishment.

Having attained this stage, one is now able to fulfill the bodhisattva aspirations and to work fully effectively for the benefit of living beings. This is the fruition of the completion stage yogas, the seeds of which are first cultivated by means of the generation stage yogas.

As stated in the many tantras and in the shastras written by the illustrious mahasiddhas, the teachings of which come to us through our personal gurus, one should strive in every way possible to fulfill the path to enlightenment and thus delight the buddhas and bodhisattvas of the ten directions. It is indeed the most noble of endeavors to apply oneself to taking to perfection the four yogas of the completion stage practice, to fulfill the purpose of guru yoga by residing in a solitary place in order to engage in the four yogas of the completion stage of the Yamantaka Tantra, dwelling in practice as steadily as a river flows.

Thus those wishing to accomplish enlightenment in one lifetime would be wise to learn about and apply themselves to this most wondrous system of yogic endeavor, a Highest Yoga Tantra method.

Colophon (of the Tibetan Commentator): The above commentary to the profound prayer entitled "Opening the Gateway to Immortal Buddhahood's Three Perfect Bodies" is a bit like the mouse (i.e., the author of the commentary, Lobzang Chinpa) playing when the cat (i.e., the Second Dalai Lama) is away. The prayer itself, penned by the unsurpassed tantric yogi Gyalwa Gendun Gyatso, the Second Dalai Lama, is a treasury of profound meanings difficult to fathom. I, Lobzang Chinpa, wrote the commentary while living in the Ganden Choling Hermitage. The composition was requested repeatedly by several of my disciples who were in the Vajrabhairava retreat and practiced the prayer daily.

CHAPTER NINE:

The Second Dalai Lama's
*Living on the Essence of Flowers*[189]

GYALWA GENDUN GYATSO (1475-1542)

PADAMPA SANGYEY

# Translator's Preamble

A NUMBER of extraordinary traditions emerged from within the tantric tradition. The practice of *chu len* is of special interest. The term *chu len* literally means "extracting the essence," and refers to esoteric methods for absorbing universal nutrition and thus being able to live without having to rely upon ordinary food. In all of the *chu len* traditions the yogi or yogini practices mantra and meditation as a means of drawing forth and absorbing universal energy, and then using this energy as a substitute for normal food.

Four main traditions of *chu len* are mentioned in the Dalai Lama literature: extracting essential nutrient from flowers, extracting the essence of stone, taking the sky as food, and living on purified mercury (i.e., quicksilver). In this chapter we have a text by the Second Dalai Lama on the first of these four. We find references to the other three in the writings of the First and Fifth Dalai Lamas.

Although these four practices are maintained as living traditions, the first—extracting the essence of flowers—is by far the most popular today. As we will see later in this chapter, the practitioner makes small pills out of nontoxic flowers, and during the retreat period eats only a few of these each day. The practice is performed both for health and life-extension, and also as a means of rendering the physical body more conducive to tantric training and enlightenment.

As the Second Dalai Lama points out in his commentary, the lineage of the practice was brought to Tibet by the Indian mahasiddha

Padampa in the latter part of the eleventh century, and was passed from him in an unbroken line over the generations. In the early days it was an exclusive teaching within the Shijey and Tsarchod Schools of Tibetan Buddhism, but gradually became absorbed by the other sects.

As we saw in an earlier chapter on the Six Yogas of Niguma, the Second Dalai Lama's father was the head of the Shangpa Kagyu School of Tibetan Buddhism. However, he was also an important figure in the Shijey and Tsarchod Schools, largely through the Second Dalai Lama's grandmother, who was the head of one of the three Shijey subsects. This amazing woman performed a forty-four-year retreat in a remote bricked-in cave, and became one of the great female mystics of her generation. The Second Dalai Lama was very close to her, and this put him in immediate touch with great teachers from this little known but highly esoteric sect. In his youth he received teachings and initiations from many of these nonmainstream masters. The text in this chapter is an example of one such lineage that he received at that time.

During my years in India I met dozens of yogis who regularly made the standard twenty-one-day retreat of "flower essence extraction." Some of them continued the discipline for extended periods of time. Two whom I knew as personal friends achieved the power of the practice, and became able to forsake ordinary food altogether and instead to live exclusively on a few flower pills a day. They did so for years at a time.

One of them was called Geshey Champa Wangdu. He had lived in retreat in the mountains above Dharamsala for many years under the guidance of the great Geshey Rabten, who at the time was considered to be the most accomplished meditator in the Gelukpa tradition. One year Geshey Rabten placed Geshey Champa and a dozen or so other disciples in a *chu len* intensive. The others were only kept in the practice for the standard twenty-one days. Geshey Champa Wangdu, however, was instructed to persevere for as long as he could.

In the first few weeks of the retreat Geshey Champa became quite thin. However, after about three months of perseverance he achieved the full power of the practice, and from that time on began to put on weight. Soon he was his natural somewhat portly self. He even became a bit too fat at one point in the retreat. It turned out that although the pills themselves were small, his mantra practice and visualization were drawing too much universal nutrient into them. He had to go on a diet by cutting down on the amount of universal energy that he visualized being absorbed into the pills. Cutting down his visualized intake in this way, he soon returned to his normal weight.

I originally received the oral transmission and instruction on this lineage from that exalted master.

Geshey Champa passed away a few decades later of old age. As fate would have it, his reincarnation was discovered in a Chinese family in Hong Kong. I happened to be in Nepal at the time, and was visiting with Lama Zopa Rinpoche. Rinpoche told me of the boy in Hong Kong and recommended that I visit him on my way to Tibet. "You were friends with Geshey Champa Wangdu. You will be in Hong Kong next week on your way to Tibet. Check out the boy and tell me if you can see anything of Champa Wangdu in him."

When I arrived in Hong Kong I phoned the parents. "The boy is very reclusive," they told me. "Although he is only eighteen months old, he sits on his bed all day playing with the mantra mala Lama Zopa gave him. He sits there cross-legged, and pretends to recite mantras. Many people have dropped by to see him, but he has refused to come out of his room to greet any of them."

"Anyway, I'll drop by," I replied. "But we won't say anything to him. I'll just sit and talk with you, and we'll see if he responds to the sound of my voice."

A half hour after I arrived the boy's door opened a crack and a pair of tiny eyes peeked out. I looked over, smiled and waved, but kept talking to the mother. The door closed again, but after another fifteen minutes the same thing occurred again. When the door opened for a third time, the child came running out and hopped on my lap.

I used to have a small goatee beard, and the old lama used to love to play with it whenever I visited. Tibetans generally don't have much facial hair, and my goatee always attracted attention. The boy now started to tickle my chin and pull playfully on my beard, just as the old lama had done on so many occasions when I visited him.

The child then suddenly hopped down and ran to the kitchen, coming back with a pot of small ice cream balls. They were almost identical in appearance to the flower essence pills that the old lama had made on so many occasions and had given to me years earlier. The boy then began to pop them into my mouth one by one.

The mother exclaimed in surprise, "This is rather amazing. He never lets anyone touch his little ice cream balls, not even me, his father, or his sister. He has never given any of them away to anyone."

For the next hour the boy continued to sit on my lap playing with my beard and feeding the ice cream pellets to me. When it came time for me to leave and catch the train to China, he ran to the fridge and brought me another pot of the ice cream pellets to take with me. He also insisted on taking my head in his hands and touching his forehead to mine, just as Geshey Wangdu had always done whenever I parted company from him.

The tantric tradition of "extracting the essence" has been used successfully by the great meditators of Central Asia for many centuries now. No doubt it will also prove beneficial to Westerners in the centuries to come.

One of my lamas, the late great Geshey Ngawang Dargyey, commented that he felt the practice was especially relevant to the modern age, when the world has become so filled with toxins, and food has lost much of its natural power because of overproduction, hybridization, and chemical fertilization.

He also jokingly said, "In the old days in our Gelukpa School we never allowed people to do long retreats until they had mastered the powers of *tummo* ("inner fire") and *chu len*. That way we never had to worry about them freezing or starving to death."

Indeed, during my years of training in Dharamsala most of the long-term retreatants had mastered these two powers during short one-month retreats before being allowed to undertake the *nyen chen*, or "great approach," the name given to the three-year retreat.

My translation of this text was aided by the Tibetan doctor Sonam Rabgye.

VAJRAYOGINI

# The Second Dalai Lama's Text

Homage to the exalted Vajrayogini,
Mahamudra in the nature of unchanging bliss,
Glorious one emanating illusive emanations:
Pray, inspire me to gain the state of buddhahood.

For those who see as nothing but enemies
The essenceless obscuring preconceptions of this life
I shall give instruction on Padampa Sangyey's methods
For living on mystical pills
To provide conditions favorable to spiritual practice.

MY TREATISE on the tradition of living on mystical essence pills
will be presented under two headings: the origin of the tradition and the actual body of the instruction.

## THE ORIGIN OF THE TRADITION

This instruction was originally given to Padampa Sangyey by Vajrayogini herself. Padampa Sangyey accomplished the training and by means of it lived for 572 years and achieved full realization. From then until now no breakage of the lineage of instruction has occurred.

Padampa Rinpochey passed the tradition to Minyak Ringyal, and in turn it was passed to Reton Lodro Tsungmey, Lama Tsewang, and eventually to Ngey Nyingpa Chokyi Gyaltsen Rinchen. He passed it to his son, the highly accomplished Delek Rinchen Palzangpo. With pleasure this great guru transmitted the lineage to me.

Therefore the common belief that Minyak Ringyal received the lineage directly in a vision from Vajrayogini seems to be unfounded.

## THE ACTUAL INSTRUCTION

This section has two parts: describing the prerequisite qualities of the trainee who is a proper vessel for this profound instruction and the actual substance of the instruction.

### THE PREREQUISITE QUALITIES OF THE TRAINEE

The disciple who would practice this profound method should have the following qualifications. He/she should have renunciation that sees the entirety of samsara as a pit of fire and considers even the highest pleasures of the world to be as worthless as the dust on the soles of one's shoes.

He/she should have a strong sense of moderation toward sensual indulgence. Those locked in sensual grasping are far from the peerless bliss of spiritual liberation.

To engage in this yoga one should have eliminated the mind that materialistically holds on to the things of this life. Those beings who have eliminated all grasping, and who love the ways of seclusion and the solitary life, are the proper vessels for practice of this method.

Anyone who wishes to receive this instruction because he/she is poor and cannot afford food and clothing is of but mediocre potential; and those who want the method because of health reasons are of the lowest acceptable level of attitude.

This teaching should not be imparted to those who wish to possess it solely in order to save up their material wealth, nor to the foolish meditators who wish to engage in exotic austerities merely to achieve fame and the material benefits that come with it; nor to the miserly people who are unable to spend their wealth. These types of practitioners are doing little but turning themselves into greedy ghosts. No matter how great they may seem to be, their training does not really pass beyond the scope of the Tirthika ascetic practices.

## THE ACTUAL SUBSTANCE OF THE INSTRUCTION

This will be explained under three headings: the preliminaries of gathering the substances to be used in the preparation of the pills and so forth; the method of consecrating and taking the pills, together with related activities; and the conclusion, or benefits of the practice and the methods of concluding the retreat.

### THE PRELIMINARIES

The method of undertaking the practice is as follows. Begin at an astrologically-appropriate time, such as the day of the half moon, in a month when the flowers are in bloom. The practice may be done either alone or else in a small group. Those engaging in the method should take a bath, put on a fresh set of clothing, and prepare to commence the meditations.

Begin by generating the vision of oneself as Arya Avalokiteshvara and reciting the six-syllable mantra OM MANI PADME HUM. Then go to a flower field and, still visualizing yourself as Avalokiteshvara and reciting the mantra, begin to collect the requisite flowers.

If one has no physical disabilities one merely collects all the various kinds of flowers that are nonpoisonous, plucking these from their necks and then drying them out by spreading them on a cloth and placing them in a shady place; or by whatever other methods of drying are effective. The flowers themselves should be free from dust, dirt, bristles, etc. The purpose of the drying process, of course, is to prevent decay.

Should one have a specific illness, the flowers to be used should be altered in accordance with the advice of one's doctor. For example, if you suffer from phlegm problems, use an extra quantity of the *balu* flower; if you have bile problems, add extra *trangdzin* flowers, etc. Similarly, for diseases of the ears, eyes, etc. the flower ingredients should be varied or supplemented as advised by one's doctor. When the practitioner is in good health, all types of nontoxic flowers can be used.

After all the flowers have been well dried they should be ground into a fine powder. Then add these to about half their weight of roasted barley flour (or other whole grain). Mix in three large spoonfuls of yellow *arura*[190] or, if this is unavailable, *arura shachen.* Also, add half this quantity of *wanglak* and one large spoonful of *duti.* All of these are indispensible.

If available, also add a small quantity of the six excellent substances and a pinch of *agaru.*

As said above, if one is unwell one should add an extra quantity of whatever is appropriate to the specific affliction. This should be supplemented with an equivalent amount of *arura* or, in some instances, half a spoon of *arura.* These should be mixed in well with the basic ingredients.

Next one makes the substance into a thick dough by adding either honey or molasses (or both). From this one then makes small pills the size of a sheep dropping.

Finally, place the pills in a clean skull-cup and put the vessel in a high place where it won't be stepped over or otherwise contaminated.

These are the preliminary practices whereby one prepares the mystic essence flower pills to be used in the training. The process is described in numerous manuals on the tradition. The source of the teaching is none other than Buddha Vajradhara himself. My own guru proclaimed this to be the case.[191]

## CONSECRATING AND TAKING THE PILLS

Clean the retreat place, arrange an altar, and, before it, place the general offerings. In front of the altar arrange a meditation seat on which to perform the practice.

Begin the meditation by taking refuge in the Three Jewels and the Three Roots of Attainment, not merely by reciting a refuge formula but by actually taking refuge within one's heart. Then generate the bodhisattva attitude of wanting to engage in the practice solely as a means of accomplishing full enlightenment in order to benefit all sentient beings. Meditate on the four immeasurable attitudes of love, compassion, joy, and equanimity.

Now purify the sphere of meditation in emptiness by means of reciting the *Svabhava* mantra and recollecting the mantra's meaning.

The visualization then proceeds as follows.

"From within the sphere of emptiness I arise as White Vajrayogini, having one face and two arms. My right hand holds a curved knife and my left a skull-cup filled with nectar.

"A *khatvanga* staff rests on my left shoulder. I am bedecked in the ornaments of bone and jewels and am adorned by the five mudras. I stand upon the corpse (of ego), my right leg stretched forward.

"Visualizing myself in this way, I cast a glance at the sky. This summons forth the lineage and root gurus, who come as though in a cloud, surrounded by countless buddhas and bodhisattvas."

At this point the practice is done from two different perspectives: as a means of accomplishing the two purposes and as a means of accomplishing longevity. These processes may be learned in detail from the standard manuals.

In general, what is involved is the consecration of the pills; imbuing them with the essence of the five great elements—earth, water, fire, air, and space; and empowering them with the life energy, merits, and power of all the living beings, the brilliance of everything in the three realms, and the glory and perfection of everything that exists. This is all summoned forth by light rays in the form of hooks that emanate forth and pull back these qualities into the skull-cup. One should visualize that the pills transform into nonsamsaric wisdom ambrosia.

From within the sphere of this meditation recite the following mantra a thousand times: *OM SARVA BUDDHA DAKINI HARINISA AMRITA SIDDHI HUM*. As the mantra is recited one blows on the pills, imagining that thus they become transformed and empowered.

As for this mantra, some versions of it do not include the syllables *HARINISA*. But according to my own guru this is not correct, and the syllables should be included.

This is the method of consecrating the pills that previously were prepared from medicinal ingredients.

Now follows the method of actually taking the pills.

One generally makes the retreat for a period of three weeks. At least in the beginning of the training, one limits oneself to this length of time. The pills are taken either twice or three times a day. One performs the sadhana of arising in the form of White Vajrayogini[192] as before. Then recite the mantra twenty-one times while blowing on the pills that are to be taken.

Advanced practitioners take the pills solely with hot water. Intermediate practitioners do so with light black tea. As for the beginners, or weak practitioners, they may take the pills with black tea and also once a week may have a bowl of light porridge made from roasted barley flour (or some other grain). However, during the last week of the retreat they should take the pills only with tea.

While swallowing the pills, one visualizes that one's body becomes filled with wisdom nectars, and that this gives rise to the samadhi of bliss and emptiness awareness that takes as its object nonsamsaric ecstasy focused on voidness.

As said above, the basic length of the retreat is twenty-one days, although after proficiency is attained this can be extended almost indefinitely. By making the retreat for three weeks great benefits arise.

In the first week one overcomes addiction to the sensation of hunger and one's digestive system is purified. In the second week diseases are eliminated. Then in the third week one regains bodily vitality (lost to illness). These are merely the healing effects that arise when someone suffering from illness makes the retreat.

While engaging in the above methods one should also apply supportive activities. Untiringly make prostrations to the objects of refuge, circumambulate temples and stupas, recite scriptures, meditate on the tantric deity for which you are initiated, and recite the mantras. Strive to eliminate the hindrances of mental stress. Do not overly exert yourself, for this could generate fluid problems in the body and cause various physical disturbances.

Avoid all coarse food. At the most, take a little honey or molasses in black tea. It may also be useful to engage in physical yogic exercises, such as those described in the system of the Six Yogas of Naropa.

### THE CONCLUSION: BENEFITS OF THE PRACTICE AND HOW TO END THE RETREAT

This practice has a wide range of beneficial effects. It heals every type of disease, extends lifespan, and increases bodily vigor. It restores youth and causes signs of age, such as wrinkles and white hair, to disappear. It provides immunity to illness and causes insects and infections to leave and stay away from one's body. These are the physical benefits.

The spiritual benefits are just as pervasive. This practice increases wisdom, generates a clearer intellect, and, by freeing one from negative means of livelihood, makes it easy for profound insight and realization to be accomplished and the spiritual path traversed. One will become loved by people, guided by the divinities, and will achieve every joy and happiness.

These are the beneficial effects of the practice of living on mystical essence flower pills.

In closing, something should be said about how to behave at the end of the retreat.

Here the most important point is to be careful in readapting to ordinary foods. For the first week following the retreat one should take only one bowlful of light, diluted porridge each day. In the beginning avoid rich foods like meat and butter. In the first days after the retreat the food should be modest both in quantity and quality. The amount and strength of the foods can be slightly increased each day until a normal diet is again achieved. To go from retreat directly to a rich diet is dangerous both to the digestive system and possibly even to one's life. Therefore begin with a simple grain porridge and gradually build up the diet over the period of a week or two until the body is again accustomed to ordinary foods.

> O hark! Thus is complete my treatise
> On the profound method of living on flower essence
> As a condition to accomplishing the spiritual path.
> It is written for those who would turn their minds
> From the essenceless pursuits of worldly life
> And live in the glory of solitary meditation.
>
> It is not intended for the blind fools
> Who are seized by the ghost of material grasping,
> Bound in the ropes of miserliness,
> Or deluded by the rosary of falsity.

Colophon: The above treatise on the method of living on pills made from the essence of flowers was written out by the meditator Gyalwa Gendun Gyatso with the hope of benefiting others interested in the spiritual path.

# Chapter Ten:

## A Tantric Prayer by the Eighth Dalai Lama[193]

### Gyalwa Jampal Gyatso (1758-11804)

Vajradhara

# Translator's Preamble

TIBETANS LOVE to chant. They do so as a preliminary to every meditation sitting and afterwards as a concluding adornment. One of their favorite genres of texts for chanting is known as *mon lam*, or "path of aspirations," a term generally translated as "prayer."

The Tibetans adopted this style of liturgy from the early Indian Buddhist masters, including the Buddha himself. Probably the most famous of all Buddhist prayers is the *Zangcho Monlam*, or "Aspiration of Sublime Ways," a liturgy extracted from the *Avatamsakasutra*. This small text is also known as *Mahayanapranidanaraja*, "The King of Mahayana Prayers." Half a dozen commentaries to it were written in ancient India and are preserved in translation in the Tibetan *Tengyur*, or "Canon of Translated Shastras."

Many of the early Indian masters wrote liturgical texts of this nature. The second-century sage Nagarjuna is perhaps the most popular with Tibetans, and his "The Staircase Aspiration" is known by heart to most monks and nuns. Another Indian writer of almost equal popularity is the seventh-century master Shantideva, and the tenth chapter of his *A Guide to the Bodhisattva Ways* is similarly revered by all Tibetans.

The collected works of most Tibetan lamas contain several dozen *mon lam*. Tibetans like to bring important themes from the path that combine the Buddhist Sutra and Tantra traditions into their writings, and this became an important element of their *mon lam* genre of literature. Some Dalai Lamas, such as the Fifth and Seventh, wrote hundreds of liturgies of this nature.

The Eighth Dalai Lama was a more modest yet no less powerful writer. Perhaps because of the prolific character of his predecessors, he did not feel the need to write as much as did they. Nonetheless his *Collected Works* contain several dozen compositions, most of which elucidate topics and lineages not touched upon by them.

His *Jangchub Monlam*, or "Prayer of the Enlightenment Path," is a simple yet powerful work, elegant in expression yet earthy in meaning. Just like Tibetans love to chant a liturgy of this nature as a decoration on the end of every meditation session, the Eighth's liturgy provides us with a wonderfully appropriate jewel with which to decorate the conclusion of this volume.

I was assisted in the translation of this prayer by Ven. Lhading Rinpochey of Drepung Loseling.

# The Eighth Dalai Lama's Prayer

Namo guru.
Homage to the spiritual master,
Male and female energies in harmony,
Manifestation of Avalokiteshvara, the compassion of all buddhas,
Emanating in accord with the needs of trainees.

Driven by karma and delusion since time immemorial,
I have wandered the three worlds and known great pain.
And even now I am caught in attachment to the world.
Show compassion to me, who is sinking
To rebirth in the lowest of hells.

May I firmly establish the root of accomplishment
By relying upon a supreme spiritual master who reveals
The key points of the paths leading to enlightenment—
The complete and unmistaken way of the sutras and tantras—
And make the offering of practicing just as instructed.

This precious human body is an ornament with every beauty.
May I live in awareness of its precious nature—
How it is hard to obtain and is easily lost—
And, never distracted by the superficial things of this life,
Always strive to extract its inner essence.

Body, possessions, and even cherished friends and dear ones
Are illusory, like the objects of a dream.
May I maintain awareness of how they are impermanent
   and illusory,
And always live as though at the threshold of death.

May I arouse the mind that is apprehensive of the sufferings
Of the three lower realms of rebirth most difficult to bear,
And be inspired to train in the ways of karmic law,
And thus gain freedom from lower rebirth forever.

No matter where one wanders in the three worlds—
From the highest heaven to the lowest of hells—
One finds only all-pervading dissatisfaction.
May I transcend it all and find
That firm ground of liberation and spiritual joy.

All the living beings that one encounters
Have been kind fathers and mothers to me in some past life.
Therefore may I cultivate the ways of the great bodhisattva
And place them on the path of liberation and enlightenment.

The spiritual master qualified by great compassion
Has placed me in the doorway of the peerless Tantric path.
May I therefore cherish more than even my life
The commitments and the precepts of the Tantric trainings,
The very root of every spiritual growth.

The dawn of the Tantric yogas of bringing
The three enlightenment qualities into everyday experience
Eradicates the darkness of birth, death, and the bardo.

May I accomplish this mandala adorned with the marks
   and signs of perfection,
Which is free from the stains of the conventional mind.

Vajra recitation at the chakra at the heart
Arrests the fluctuations caused by sun and moon,
Intensifying the four descending and the four ascending joys.
May I accomplish this sublime Tantric yoga in this very lifetime
And bring the experience of integration to fruition.

In brief, in this and in all my future lives
May I be constantly cared for by the gurus and mandala deities;
And may I single-pointedly cultivate the essence
Of the sublime path praised by all enlightenment masters.

In all my lives may I never be parted
From the guiding presence of qualified masters.
May I always have access to the glory of the Dharma,
That I may complete the realizations of the stages and paths,
And quickly gain the state of a Buddha Vajradhara.

# Notes

1 I first published this translation in *The Second Dalai Lama: His Life and Teachings* (Ithaca, N.Y.: Snow Lion Publications, 2005), 190.
2 Ibid.
3 I first published this text in *Path of the Bodhisattva Warrior: The Life and Teachings of the Thirteenth Dalai Lama* (Ithaca, N.Y.: Snow Lion Publications, 1988). That title has been out of print for a number of years.
4 Tsongkhapa's autobiographical poem was originally translated by Alex Berzin and Jon Landaw, with the title "Destiny Fulfilled," and was included in the anthology *The Life and Teachings of Tsong Khapa*, edited by Robert A. F. Thurman (Dharamsala: Library of Tibetan Works and Archives, 1982). I do not quote their translation here, but instead retranslate those verses used by the Thirteenth Dalai Lama so as to maintain a consistency in style and language with the other materials in this book.
5 *Dam-tshig-gsum-bkod-kyi-rgyud*
6 *sMan-mdo-brgyad-rgya-pa*
7 *Nor-bu-rgyas-pa'i-zhal-med-khang*
8 *Byang-chub-rgyan-'bum*
9 *gSang-ba-ring-bsrel*
10 *Rigs-gsum-dbang-gi-rnam-gshag*
11 *gSang-ba-spyi-rgyud*
12 *Legs-grub-kyi-rgyud*
13 *dPung-bzang-gis-zhus-pa'i-rgyud*
14 *rDo-rje-gtsug-gtor-gi-rgyud*
15 *bSam-gtan-phyi-ma'i-rgyud*
16 *bSam-gtan-phyi-mai-'grel-pa*
17 *Pung-bzang-gi-rgyud-kyi-don-bsdus*
18 *rNam-snang-mngon-byang-gi-rgyud*
19 *De'i-rgyud-phyi-ma*
20 *Phyag-rdor-dbang-bskur-gyi-rgyud*
21 *mNgon-byang-bsdus-'grel*
22 *dPal-ldan-de-nyid-bsdus-pa*
23 *bDag-nyid-can*
24 *De'i-rgyud-phyi-ma*
25 *Phyi-ma'i-phyi-ma-rgyud*
26 *bShad-rgyud-rdo-rje-rtse-mo*
27 *dPal-mchog-dang-po*
28 *'Jig-rten-gsum-rgyal*
29 *Ngan-song-sbyong-rgyud*

30 *rTags-pa-dang-po*
31 *rTags-pa-phyogs-gcig-pa*
32 *'Grel-chen-a-wa-ta-ra-na*
33 *'Grel-chen*
34 *Ko-sa-li'i-rgyan*
35 *rTsa-rgyud/De bzhin gshegs pa thams cad kyi sku gsung thugs kyi gsang chen gsang ba 'dus pa zhes bya ba brtag pa'i rgyal po chen po*
36 *bShad-rgyud-chen-po-drug*
37 *rGyud-phyi-ma*
38 *rGyud-rdo-rje-phreng-ba*
39 *dGongs-pa-lung-ston*
40 *Ye-shes-rdo-rje-kun-btus*
41 *Lha'i-dbang-pos-zhus-pa*
42 *Lha-mo-zhis-zhus-pa*
43 *mDor-byas*
44 *mDo-bsres*
45 *Rim-lnga*
46 *Byang-chub-sems-'grel*
47 *sGyu-lus-bdag-byin-brlab-kyi-rim-pa*
48 *sPyod-bsdus*
49 *sKyed-rim-rnam-bzhag-rim-pa*
50 *dKyil-chog-nyi-bcu-pa*
51 *rDzog-rim-las-mtha'-rnam-'byed* `
52 *Rim-pa-gnyis-pa'i-kha-skong*
53 *bsKyed-rim-rdor-sems-sgrub-thabs*
54 *rDzogs-rim-sbyor-drug*
55 *rGyud-'grel-sgron-gsal*
56 *dKyil-chog-byed-bcas-bzhi-brgya-pa*
57 *bsKyed-rim-sgrub-thabs-kun-bzang*
58 *rDzog-rim-sgrol-thig*
59 *'Jam-dpal-zhal-lung*
60 *'Jigs-byed-rtsa-rgyud*
61 *rTog-pa-sum-brgya-pa*
62 *rTog-bdun*
63 *rTog-bzhi*
64 *rTog-gsum*
65 *Las-mkhan-teu-lo-pa'i-rtog-pa*
66 *dGra-nag-gi-rgyud*
67 *gShed-dmar-gyi-rgyud*
68 *rDo-rje-a-ra-gyi-rgyud*
69 *bLa-med-sgyu-dra*
70 *rDo-rje-snying-po-rgyan*
71 *bDe-mchog-nyung-ngu'i-rgyud*
72 *mNgon-brjod-bla-ma*
73 *sDom-'byung*
74 *rDo-rje-mkha-'gro'i-rgyud*

75  *rTsa-rgyud*
76  *brTag-gnyis*
77  *bShad-rgyud*
78  *rDo-rje-gur*
79  *De'i-phyi-ma*
80  *Phyag-chen-thig-le*
81  *De-yang-phyi-ma*
82  *Ye-shes-snying-po*
83  *rTsa-rgyud/mChog-gi-dang-po'i-sang-rgyas-las-byung-ba-rgyud-kyi-rgyal-po-dpal-dus-kyi-'khor-lo*
84  *bsDus-rgyud*
85  *dBang-mdor-bstan-pa*
86  *bsDus-rgyud*
87  *bsDus-rgyud-snying-po*
88  *bsDus-rgyud-kyi-'grel-pa*
89  *Sems-'grel-skor-gsum*
90  *rDo-rje-snying-'grel*
91  *brTag-gnyis*
92  *Phyag-rdor-stod-'grel*
93  *bDe-mchog-rtsa-rgyud*
94  *bSang-'dus-pa'i-phyi-ma*
95  *Phreng-skor-gsum*
96  *rDo-rje-phreng-ba*
97  *rNal-'byor-rdzogs-phreng*
98  *'Od-kyi-nyi-ma*
99  *Kri-ya-kun-bsdus*
100  *dPal-mcog-dang-po*
101  *bLa-ma-lnga-bcu-pa*
102  *Yang-dag-'byor-ba*
103  I first published this work in *Songs of Spiritual Change* (Ithaca, N.Y.: Snow Lion Publications, 1982). This book was later republished by them as *Selected Works of the Dalai Lama VII: Songs of Spiritual Change* (1983). Snow Lion later brought out a third edition, much revised and with essays placing each of the songs and poems in historical and spiritual context, with the title *Meditations to Transform the Mind* (1999).
104  This treatise by the Second Dalai Lama, Gyalwa Gendun Gyatso, was first published in *Selected Works of the Dalai Lama II: The Tantric Yogas of Sister Niguma* (Ithaca, N.Y.: Snow Lion Publications, 1985).
105  *rDo-rje-tshig-rkang*
106  *rGyu-ma-lam-rim*
107  *brTag-gnyis-gyi-rgyud*
108  *rDo-rje-gur*
109  *Yang-dag-par-sbyor-ba-shes-bya'i-rgyud-chen-po*
110  *rDo-rje-mkha'-'gro-gi-rtsa-rgyud*
111  *Lam-rim-chen-mo*
112  *Lam-rim-'bring*

113 *Phyag-chen-thig-le*
114 *sDom-'byung-gi-rgyud*
115 *bDe-mchog-rtsa-rgyud*
116 *mNyam-sbyor*
117 *Them-yig*
118 *Shes-phyin-stong-phrag-brgya-pa*
119 *Shes-phyin-stong-phrag-nyi-shu-lnga-pa*
120 *Shes-phyin-brgyad-stong-pa*
121 *Shes-phyin-sdud-pa-tshigs-su-bcad-pa*
122 *'Jam-dpal-mtshan-brjod*
123 *Zab-lam-na-ro'i-chos-drug-gi-sgo-nas-'khrid-pa'i-rim-pa-yid-ches-gsum-ldan*
124 *Rim-lnga-bsdus-pa-gsal-ba*
125 *bShad-rgyud*
126 *Bar-do-skor-gsum*
127 *rDo-rje-rol-pa'i-rgyud*
128 *'Phags-pa-gnyis-med-rgyal-po'i-rgyud*
129 *rDo-rje-rin-chen-'phreng-ba*
130 *Rim-pa-lnga*
131 *bSre-ba-gsum-gyi-gdams-ngag*
132 *Ye-shes-rgya-mtsho*
133 *gDan-bzhi-rtsa-rgyud*
134 *'Jam-dpal-zhal-lung*
135 *'Pho-ba-rnam-bshad*
136 *Kha-sbyor*
137 *Zab-lam-na-ro'i-chos-drug-gi-sgo-nas-'khrid-pa'i-rim-pa-yid-ches-gsum-ldan*
138 I first published this text in *Essence of Refined Gold* (Ithaca, N.Y.: Snow Lion Publications, 1983).
139 The Dalai Lama originally wrote this small introduction to Kalachakra for the initiation he had been asked to give in Deer Park, Madison, Wisconsin, in 1983. I translated it with Ven. Doboom Tulku, and it was published by Deer Park for free distribution at that event. It was later republished as a pamphlet for free distribution at the Dalai Lama's Kalachakra initiation in Switzerland in 1985. I included it in *The Practice of Kalachakra* (Ithaca, N.Y.: Snow Lion Publications, 1991), a collection of eight Tibetan works related to Kalachakra .
140 The temple in Dharamsala has a Kalachakra mandala painting, with all fourteen Dalai Lamas depicted in the upper corners. All fourteen are shown in the yellow hat, even though the ninth through twelfth died young and therefore never became mahapanditas. Moreover, the Fourth and Sixth incarnations also decided against pursuing this academic degree: the Fourth because his Mongolian guardian felt he should master Tantric Buddhism's shamanic ritual practices rather than the intellectualism of Indian Buddhist philosophy; and the Sixth because he preferred wine, women, and song to the dry indulgences of monastic academia. He disrobed in his mid-teens and exchanged monastic studies for a more colorful night life. Legend claims that he made love to over ten thousand women in the remaining years of his life.

The old Buddhist monastery of Erdene Zuu in Karakorum, Mongolia, has two

complete sets of Dalai Lama incarnation paintings. Both show all of the incarnations in the yellow mahapandita hat, even the ones who did not qualify to wear
it. Erdene Zuu is one of the few Buddhist temples not to be completely destroyed
by the Soviet Communists in the late 1930s. Fifty-eight of its sixty-two temple
complexes were burned down, but four remain. These are now used as a museum
by the Mongolian government.

141 *sNgags-rim-chen-mo.*

142 *The Kalachakra Six-Session Yoga* (Dharamsala: Tushita Books, 1974).

143 Ithaca, N.Y.: Snow Lion Publications, 1991.

144 *rTags-gnyis-gyi-rgyud*

145 The Thirteenth Dalai Lama touches upon this topic earlier in this book in his
essay *A Brief Guide to the Buddhist Tantras.* As the Fourteenth Dalai Lama points
out here, the principal difference between them is in how the fourth initiation is
given.

146 Although karmic predispositions make a big difference in the effectiveness of a
practice on the completion stage, this does not seem to be such an important factor on the generation stage. For this reason the Tibetans often practice the generation stage of one tantric system, such as Yamantaka, and the completion stage
of another, such as Kalachakra.

147 *dPal-dus-'khor-rtsa-rgyud-dang-po'i-sangs-rgyas*

148 *dPal-dus-'khor-bsdus-rgyud*

149 *'Grel-chen-dri-med-'od*

150 It seems that by the tenth and eleventh centuries the Tibetans had become very
influential in the monastic hierarchies of India. Several of these monasteries,
including Nalanda and Vikramashila, even had special departments just for
Tibetans, their numbers were so large. Nalanda also at the time had a department
for Indonesians, and it seems that these were the two largest groups of foreign-
ers in India at the time.

151 As mentioned in the Preamble to this chapter, Khangsar Dorjechang's text was
distributed to the 350,000 people who attended the Dalai Lama's Kalachakra initiation in Bodh Gaya during January of 1974. It is designed as a short liturgy for
daily recitation by initiates, and usually is chanted three times in the morning
and three in the evening.

152 Recitation of the name mantra of one's teacher is a common practice with
Tibetan Buddhists. Each school has a general way to present the name mantras
of its masters; there are perhaps a dozen or so forms in vogue at the moment.

One popular mantric format is that given here for the Dalai Lama's name
mantra. The first four words—*OM AH GURU VAJRADHARA*—are part of the standard mantra, as are the last four words—*SARVA SIDDHI HUM HUM.* The five words
that are in the middle of the mantra as given here—*VAGINDRA SUMATI SHASANAD-
HARA SAMUDRA SHRIBHADRA*—are the personal ordination (monastic) names of
His Holiness—Ngawang Lobzang Tenzin Gyatso, meaning "Eloquent, Wise Doc-
trine-Holder, He of Sublime Glory"—translated into Sanskrit. These, by the way,
are not flowery titles of the Dalai Lama; they are standard Buddhist monastic
names, no more grandiose than those received by the humblest novice at the time
of ordination.

The name mantra is thus tailored to each specific teacher, by substituting the central part of the mantra with the Sanskrit equivalents of the names of one's personal teacher. For example, the way I personally use the mantra sees the central section with the syllables *VAGINDRA MAITRI*. The first four and last four words of the mantra remain the same.

153 In *A Lexicon of Kalachakra Terms according to the Views of Lama Tsongkhapa*, Longdol Lama comments as follows:

As for this mantra, known as "Possessor of Ten Powers," it can be explained either in terms of the form of (the syllables of) the mantra, or else in terms of the sound of the mantra.

In the former case, the explanation can be given in terms of the external world (i.e., Outer Kalachakra), the internal world (i.e., Inner Kalackakra), the generation stage yogas, or the completion stage yogas (these last two being Alternative Kalachakra). . . .

In the latter case, when the mantra is explained in terms of sound, it is said that whenever there is sound there is energy, and whenever there is energy there is sound. The strength (or character) of that energy is one of three types. Male energy, which is aggressive, resounds with the resonance of *OM;* female energy, which is delicate, resounds with the resonance of *AH;* and neutral energy, which is between these two in character, resounds with the resonance of *HUM.* Thus all subtle energies collect into these three mantric sounds. Moreover, the most subtle aspects of both energy and consciousness collect together into the resonance of these three mantric syllables, and therefore they are said to be the root of both samsara and nirvana.

This is the meaning of the mantric syllables *E-VAM,* which most quintessentially carry the sense of the mantra "Possessor of Ten Powers."

The manner in which the most subtle aspects of consciousness and the energies abide together is such that they cannot be differentiated from one another. For example, we can conventionally speak about the difference between the color, light, and shape of the flame of a butterlamp; but other than giving them different names we cannot separate them as actual entities. In the same way, the subtle consciousness and the subtle energies upon which this consciousness rides can be spoken of with different words, but in fact they are inseparable. Recitation of this mantra places us in communion with these subtle levels of energy and mind. . . .

Thus the mantra can be used to explain everything in the external world (Outer Kalachakra), everything in the internal world (Inner Kalachakra), and all the yogic practices of both the generation and completion stages (Alternative Kalachakra). In this way (the mantra) reveals the complete meaning of the entire Kalachakra doctrine.

As His Holiness the Dalai Lama explained at the Kalachakra initiation in Varanasi in January, 1991, the name "Possessor of Ten Powers" is given in reference to the syllables at the middle of this mantra, i.e., *HAMKSHAHMALAVARAYA,* which is the actual body of the mantra, and is composed of seven individual mantric syllables: *HAM KSHAH MALA VA RA YA.* These seven become eight because the vowel sound of *a* pervades each of them. They become ten by counting the *visarga* of the syllable KSHAH (represented by a moon sliver) and the *anusvara* of the syllable HAM (depicted as a solar sphere). Sometimes to this is added an eleventh "power," symbolized by the *nada*, or zig-zag line that stands above the entire mantric composite.

There are various ways to link these ten (or eleven) mantric components to the Outer, Inner, and Alternative Kalachakras. The subject is too complex to outline here; it is perhaps best to content ourselves with the above comment of Longdol Lama, ". . . (the mantra) reveals the complete meaning of the entire Kalachakra doctrine."

154 My translation of this Kalachakra text first appeared in *Bridging the Sutras and Tantras* (Dharamsala: Tushita Books, 1981), which a year later was reprinted by Snow Lion with the title *Selected Works of the Dalai Lama I: Bridging the Sutras and Tantras* (Ithaca, N.Y.: Snow Lion Publications, 1982). This was the first time any major Kalachakra work had been translated into English, or into any Western language. Later Snow Lion brought it out, along with seven other texts that I translated on the subject, as part of a study of the Kalachakra tradition with the title *The Practice of Kalachakra* (Ithaca, N.Y.: Snow Lion Publications, 1991).

155 *bSang-ba'i-'dus-pa'i-rtsa-rgyud-gi-rgyal-po*

156 *dKyil-chog-rdo-rje'i-phreng-ba*

157 *dBang-dor-bstan-pa*

158 *dBang-dor-bstan-pa'i-grel-pa*

159 During this phase of the initiation the disciples imagine that they come in turn before each of the four doors of the Kalachakra mandala mansion. At each door they see a different face of Kalachakra. They request and are given the according initiations. Here Lati Rinpochey commented,

Why is it necessary to receive initiation in order to practice the Tantric path? Just as someone who wishes to undertake an important building project must first acquire the permission of the appropriate building authorities, the spiritual aspirant wishing to undertake the great task of the Vajrayana yoga must first gain the blessings of a qualified lineage master. Moreover, at the time of initiation the master plants the seeds of tantric attainment within the mind of the disciple, and without these seeds our practice of the two tantric stages will be unable to produce the tree, branches, and fruit of enlightenment.

160 *dPal-dus-'khor-bsdus-rgyud*

161 *rTsa-ltung-rnam-gzhag*

162 As we can see, the description of the chakras in the Kalachakra system differs considerably from that given in systems such as Guhyasamaja, Yamantaka, and Heruka Chakrasamvara.

163 *rGyud-rdo-rje'i-phreng-ba*

164 *dPal-dus-'khor-rtsa-rgyud-dang-po'i-sangs-rgyas*

165 *Byang-chub-sems-dpa'i-'grel-skor-gsum*

166 *'Grel-chen-dri-med-'od*

167 *rDo-rje'i-snying-'grel*

168 *Phyag-na-rdo-rje'i-stod-pa'i-'grel-pa*

169 *sByor-ba-yan-lag-drug-pa*
170 *rNal-'byor-yan-lag-drug-gi-brjed-byang-yon-tan-gyis-'gengs-pa*
171 *rNal-'byor-yan-lag-drug-pa*
172 *'Brel-pa-gcod-pa*
173 *bDe-mchog-gi-bstod-pa'i-'grel-pa*
174 I originally published this translation in *Path of the Bodhisattva Warrior: The Life and Teachings of the Thirteenth Dalai Lama* (Ithaca, N.Y.: Snow Lion Publications, 1988).
175 *Tshul-gsum-sgron-me*
176 *rTsa-rgyud*
177 *sGyu-'phrul-gyi-rgyud-phyi-ma*
178 *dPal-he-ru-gah-mngon-pham-'byung-ba'i-rgyud*
179 *bDud-rtsi-bam-brgyad*
180 *'Dus-pa-mdo*
181 *bDud-rtsi-mchog-gi-rgyud*
182 *Kham-gsum-bde-byed-gzhan-phan-nyi-ma'i-snying-po*
183 *Yang-gsang-rtsa-rgyud*
184 *gSang-ba-'khor-rgyud*
185 My translation of this text first appeared in *Selected Works of the Dalai Lama II: The Tantric Yogas of Sister Niguma* (Ithaca, N.Y.: Snow Lion Publications, 1985).
186 The Dalai Lama's verse text is indented while Lama Chinpa's prose commentary is set flush left.
187 Probably the white lily.
188 These are discussed in detail in my book *Essence of Refined Gold* (Ithaca, N.Y.: Snow Lion Publications, 1985).
189 I originally published this translation in *Selected Works of the Dalai Lama II: The Tantric Yogas of Sister Niguma.*
190 Yellow arura: *Terminalia chebula.*
191 That is, Delek Rinchen Palzangpo, from whom Gyalwa Gendun Gyatso received it.
192 The Second Dalai Lama himself wrote a sadhana focusing on White Vajrayogini to be used in conjunction with this method. I have not included it here, however, as it is outside the scope of what I had in mind in compiling this volume.
193 I first published the translation of this tantric prayer in *The Fourteen Dalai Lamas: A Sacred Legacy of Reincarnation* (Santa Fe, N.M.: Clear Light Publishers, 2001).

# Suggested Reading

## Dalai Lamas

Bell, Charles. *Portrait of a Dalai Lama: The Life and Times of the Great Thirteenth.* London: Wisdom Publications, 1987.

Brauen, Martin, ed. *The Dalai Lamas: A Visual History.* Chicago: Serindia Publications, 2005.

Karmay, Samten Gyaltsen. *Secret Visions of the Fifth Dala Lama: The Gold Manuscript in the Fournier Collection.* London: Serindia Publications, 1988. [A paperback edition, omitting the Tibetan texts, appeared from the same publisher in 1998.]

Mullin, Glenn H. *The Fourteen Dalai Lamas: A Sacred Legacy of Reincarnation.* Santa Fe, N.M.: Clear Light Publishers, 2001.

## Tantra

Cozort, Daniel. *Highest Yoga Tantra: An Introduction to the Esoteric Buddhism of Tibet.* Ithaca, N.Y.: Snow Lion Publications, 2005.

Dalai Lama, Tsong-ka-pa, and Jeffrey Hopkins. *Tantra in Tibet.* Ithaca, N.Y.: Snow Lion Publications, 1987.

Dalai Lama, Tsong-ka-pa, and Jeffrey Hopkins. *Deity Yoga in Action and Performance Tantra.* Ithaca, N.Y.: Snow Lion Publications, 1987.

Dalai Lama, Dzong-ka-ba, and Jeffrey Hopkins. *Yoga Tantra: Paths to Magical Feats.* Ithaca, N.Y.: Snow Lion Publications, 2005.

Jamgön Kongtrul Lodrö Tayé. *The Treasury of Knowledge, Book Six, Part Four: Systems of Buddhist Tantra.* Trans. by the Kalu Rinpoché Translation Group. Ithaca, N.Y.: Snow Lion Publications, 2005.

Kelsang Gyatso, Geshe. *Tantric Grounds and Paths: How to Begin, Progress on, and Complete the Vajrayana Path.* London: Tharpa Publications, 1994.

Lessing, F.D., and Alex Wayman, trans. *Introduction to the Buddhist Tantric Systems.* Delhi: Motilal Banarsidass, 1993.

Panchen Sonam Dragpa. *Overview of Buddhist Tantra: General Presentation of the Classes of Tantra, Captivating the Minds of the Fortunate Ones.* Dharamsala: Library of Tibetan Works and Archives, 1996.

Thubten Yeshe, Lama. *Introduction to Tantra: The Transformation of Desire.* Boston: Wisdom Publications, 2001.

White, David Gordon, ed. *Tantra in Practice.* Princeton: Princeton University Press, 2000.

Yarnall, Thomas F. "The Emptiness That is Form: Developing the Body of Buddhahood in Indo-Tibetan Buddhist Tantra." Ph.D. diss., Columbia University, 2003. [Revised book version forthcoming in 2007]

Yarnall, Thomas F., trans. *The Stages of Mantra: Unexcelled Yoga Tantra (sngags rim chen mo, by Tsong Khapa).* 3 vols. Treasury of the Buddhist Sciences series. New York: American Institute of Buddhist Studies, forthcoming.

## TANTRAS

### AVALOKITESHVARA

Thubten Chodron. *Cultivating a Compassionate Heart: The Yoga Method of Chenrezig.* Ithaca, N.Y.: Snow Lion Publications, 2005.

Thubten Yeshe, Lama. *Becoming the Compassion Buddha: Tantric Mahamudra for Everyday Life.* Boston: Wisdom Publications, 2003.

### CHAKRASAMVARA

Gray, David B., trans. *The Cakrasamvara Tantra (The Discourse of Śrī Heruka): A Study and Annotated Translation.* Treasury of the Buddhist Sciences series. New York: American Institute of Buddhist Studies, 2006.

### GUHYASAMAJA

Thurman, Robert A. F., trans. *The Extremely Brilliant Lamp of the Five Stages (rim lnga gsal sgron, by Tsong Khapa): An Instruction in the King of Tantras, Śrī Guhyasamāja.* Treasury of the Buddhist Sciences series. New York: American Institute of Buddhist Studies, forthcoming.

Wedemeyer, Christian K., trans. and ed. *Āryadeva's Lamp That Integrates the Practices (Caryā-melāpaka-pradīpa): The Gradual Path of Vajrayāna Buddhism According to the Esoteric Community Noble Tradition.* Treasury of the Buddhist Sciences series. New York: American Institute of Buddhist Studies, 2006.

### HEVAJRA

Farrow, G. W., and I. Menon. *The Concealed Essence of the Hevajra Tantra.* Delhi: Motilal Banarsidass, 1992.

Snellgrove, D. L. *The Hevajra Tantra: A Critical Study.* London: Oxford University Press, 1959.

## KALACHAKRA

Berzin, Alexander. *Taking the Kalachakra Initiation.* Ithaca, N.Y.: Snow Lion Publications, 1997.

Bryant, Barry. *The Wheel of Time Sand Mandala: Visual Scripture of Tibetan Buddhism.* Ithaca, N.Y.: Snow Lion Publications, 2003.

Dalai Lama and Jeffrey Hopkins. *Kālachakra Tantra: Rite of Initiation for the Stage of Generation.* Boston: Wisdom Publications, 1999.

Henning, Edward. *Kālacakra and the Tibetan Calendar.* Treasury of the Buddhist Sciences series. New York: American Institute of Buddhist Studies, 2007.

Lamrimpa, Gen. *Transcending Time: An Explanation of the Kalachakra Six-Session Guru Yoga.* Boston: Wisdom Publications, 1999.

Lhundub Sopa, Geshe, Roger Jackson, and John Newman. *The Wheel of Time: The Kalachakra in Context.* Ithaca, N.Y.: Snow Lion Publications, 1991.

Mullin, Glenn H. *The Practice of Kalachakra.* Ithaca, N.Y.: Snow Lion Publications, 1991.

Norsang Gyatso, Khedrup. *Ornament of Stainless Light: An Exposition of the Kālacakra Tantra.* Trans. Gavin Kilty. The Library of Tibetan Classics, vol. 14. Boston: Wisdom Publications, 2004.

Wallace, Vesna A. *The Inner Kālacakratantra: A Buddhist Tantric View of the Individual.* New York: Oxford University Press, 2001.

Wallace, Vesna A., trans. *The Kālacakratantra: The Chapter on the Individual together with the* Vimalaprabhā. Treasury of the Buddhist Sciences series. New York: American Institute of Buddhist Studies, 2004.

Wallace, Vesna A., trans. *The Kālacakratantra: The Sādhana Chapter with the* Vimalaprabhā *Commentary.* Treasury of the Buddhist Sciences series. New York: American Institute of Buddhist Studies, 2007.

## SIX YOGAS OF NAROPA

Loden, Geshe Acharya Thubten. *Great Treasure of the Six Yogas of Naropa.* Melbourne: Tushita Publications, 2006.

Mullin, Glenn H. *The Six Yogas of Naropa.* Ithaca, N.Y.: Snow Lion Publications, 2005.

Mullin, Glenn H. *The Practice of the Six Yogas of Naropa.* Ithaca, N.Y.: Snow Lion Publications, 2006.

## VAJRASATTVA

Thubten Yeshe, Lama. *Becoming Vajrasattva: The Tantric Path of Purification.* Boston: Wisdom Publications, 2004.

## VAJRAYOGINI

Dhargyey, Geshe Ngawang. *Vajrayogini Sadhana and Commentary.* Dharamsala: Library of Tibetan Works and Archives, 1992.

English, Elizabeth. *Vajrayogini: Her Visualizations, Rituals, and Forms.* Boston: Wisdom Publications, 2002.

Loden, Geshe Acharya Thubten. *Path to the Union of Clear Light and Illusory Body.* Melbourne: Tushita Publications, 2002.

Tharchin, Sermey Khensur Lobsang. *Sublime Path to Kechara Paradise.* Howell, N.J.: Mahayana Sutra and Tantra Press, 1997.

## YAMANTAKA/VAJRABHAIRAVA

Loden, Geshe Acharya Thubten. *Ocean of Indivisible Method and Wisdom.* Melbourne: Tushita Publications, 1999.

Phabongkha Dechen Nyingpo, Kyabje. *Meditation on Vajrabhairava.* Trans. by Sharpa Tulku and Richard Guard. Dharamsala: Library of Tibetan Works and Archives, 1990.

Phabongkha Rinpoche, Kyabje. *Self-Initiation of Vajrabhairava.* Trans. by Sharpa Tulku and Richard Guard. Dharamsala: Library of Tibetan Works and Archives, 1991.